W0080058

Hauke Heier

Change Paradigms in the Setting
of Knowledge Management Systems

Leiden University Management Research Series

Editors:
Prof. Dr. Hans P. Borgman
Prof. Dr. Hans G. Kuijl RA

Hauke Heier

Change Paradigms in the Setting of Knowledge Management Systems

Deutscher Universitäts-Verlag

Bibliografische Information Der Deutschen Bibliothek
Die Deutsche Bibliothek verzeichnet diese Publikation in der Deutschen Nationalbibliografie;
detaillierte bibliografische Daten sind im Internet über <http://dnb.ddb.de> abrufbar.

Dissertation Universiteit Leiden, 2004

1. Auflage Mai 2004

Alle Rechte vorbehalten
© Deutscher Universitäts-Verlag/GWV Fachverlage GmbH, Wiesbaden 2004

Lektorat: Ute Wrasmann

Der Deutsche Universitäts-Verlag ist ein Unternehmen von Springer Science+Business Media.
www.duv.de

Umschlaggestaltung: Regine Zimmer, Dipl.-Designerin, Frankfurt/Main

Gedruckt auf säurefreiem und chlorfrei gebleichtem Papier

ISBN-13:978-3-8244-0769-9   e-ISBN-13:978-3-322-81150-9
DOI: 10.1007/978-3-322-81150-9

Acknowledgements

The dissertation is the result of work conducted at Leiden University, European Business School, and Siemens Information and Communication Networks. It examines how technology-facilitated knowledge management initiatives can establish supportive knowledge-intensive cultures. A case study approach has been chosen to investigate the explanatory power of two complementary change management frameworks in the new setting of knowledge management systems. Though the research questions, approaches, and findings presented in this thesis reflect my personal research style and understanding, I have been fortunate to receive support from many persons who I would like to acknowledge here.

At Leiden University, I am grateful to the staff and faculty at Leiden University School of Management (LUSM) and the Leiden Institute of Advanced Computer Science (LIACS) for introducing me to the stimulating spirit of a university with a long tradition. My trips to Leiden have always been something to look forward to.

The time spent at European Business School - first as a student, later as a research associate - allowed me to get to know Stefan Baldi and Anett Mehler-Bicher. Thank you for providing the vital conversational context for developing and shaping ideas for the content of this thesis. European Business School has been my professional home for most of the last seven years, though interrupted several times by extended stays at James Madison University and Leiden University. Anett and Stefan, I wish you all the best in your new jobs.

At Siemens Information and Communication Networks I thank my dear colleagues Alfons Kuhn and Andreas Manuth for two summers of fruitful research and for sharing their office with me - a tremendous opportunity for asking lots of curious questions. I really enjoyed our many nice brainstormings - at lunch in the famous Siemens canteen, at dinner in Munich's fancy restaurants. I gratefully acknowledge Siemens Information and Communication Networks' financial sponsorship that made the publication of this thesis possible.

Finally and very importantly, my research has also been stimulated enormously by my family and friends. My parents' unconditional friendship, love, and support made me the person I am. Thank you, mum and dad. Among the many friends who encouraged me during the highs and lows of the past years and to whom I am very grateful, I would like to expressly thank Corvin W. Jonigk and Sascha Krusch for many happy and adventurous days ashore and offshore. As the progress of my thesis has (too) often been the subject of conversation, I suppose some of my friends will be even more relieved than I that it has finally been completed. Thank you so much for keeping me company.

Content

1.   Introduction 1
1.1   Research Problem and Relevance.. 1
1.2   Key Concepts and Significant Prior Research 6
1.2.1   Definitions and Basic Concepts in Knowledge Management 6
1.2.2   Refining the Research Question 9
1.3   Research Objectives and Expected Contributions 13
1.4   General Research Approach... 18
1.4.1   Research Design.. 18
1.4.2   Site Selection.. 21
1.4.3   Unit of Analysis.. 23
1.4.4   Data Collection, Analysis, and Exposition 25

2.   Conceptual Foundations 29
2.1   Change Paradigms Guiding KMS Implementations 29
2.2   Linear, Staged Change... 30
2.2.1   Lewin-Schein's Conceptualization of Change........................... 30
2.2.2   Unfreezing 32
2.2.3   Cognitive Restructuring.. 38
2.2.4   Refreezing 40
2.3   Circular, Continuous Change... 42
2.3.1   Sathe's Conceptualization of Change 42
2.3.2   Behavior 44
2.3.3   Justifications of Behavior 47
2.3.4   Cultural Communications 48
2.3.5   Hiring, Socializing, and Replacing Employees 51

3.   Case Study: Siemens ShareNet... 53
3.1   Project Prologue 53
3.2   Definition and Prototyping 54
3.3   Setup and Piloting 63
3.4   Global Rollout.. 66
3.5   Operation, Expansion, and Further Development....................... 71
3.6   Shifting to a Multi-Community Concept 76

4.   Case Discussion: Change Paradigms Revisited...................... 81
4.1   A Linear, Staged Perspective to Explain Success and Failure........... 81

4.1.1   Revealing Critical Success Factors for Unfreezing 81
4.1.2   Revealing Critical Success Factors for Cognitive Restructuring 89
4.1.3   Revealing Critical Success Factors for Refreezing 92
4.1.4   Findings Related to a Sequential Implementation Perspective 96
4.2   A Circular, Continuous Perspective to Explain Success and
        Failure 97
4.2.1   Unveiling Critical Success Factors for Behavior Change 97
4.2.2   Unveiling Critical Success Factors for Behavior Justifications 99
4.2.3   Unveiling Critical Success Factors for Cultural Communications 101
4.2.4   Unveiling Critical Success Factors for Socialization and Removal... 103
4.2.5   Findings Related to a Cyclical Implementation Perspective 106

5.   Conclusions and Implications for Further Research 109
5.1   Motivators Fitting Knowledge Management Systems 109
5.2   Knowledge Management Systems as Change Drivers 113
5.3   Toward a Culture Change-Based Implementation Framework 119
5.3.1   Combining Conceptualizations of Change 119
5.3.2   Initiation 123
5.3.3   Continuation 126
5.3.4   Termination 129

Appendix 133
Interview Guidelines 133
Interview Synopses 134
Interview with Horst D. Angerer 134
Interview with Felix Baumann 137
Interview with Joachim Döring 140
Interview with Stefan Jenzowsky 142
Interview with Dietmar Krauss 145
Interview with Alfons Kuhn 148
Interview with Andreas Manuth 151
Interview with Rolf Meinert 154
Interview with Dr. Johannes Müller 158
Interview with Barbara Stahl 161
Interview with Ursula Streit 163
Interview with Donald Tsusaki 166
Interview with Gerhard Vogt 169
Interview with Marc Widuch 171

References 175

1. Introduction

The first chapter states the research problem addressed in this study. Before attempting to provide an answer, the issue first requires clarification and delineation. The following paragraphs do so by putting the research question into context, regarding academic and managerial relevance, as well as significant prior research in related areas. Specific research questions and a set of expected (academic and managerial) contributions build on this basis. A section on the research method concludes the opening.

1.1 Research Problem and Relevance

When Deutsche Bank's human resources (HR) division had the project idea for HRbase, an intranet-based knowledge management system (KMS), the future looked bright. The networking tool was designed to enable and facilitate the exchange of information and interaction among staff with two envisaged applications. First, HRbase should serve as a corporate directory for the mapping of internal expertise (yellow pages functionality). The IS would be an easily accessible and searchable repository of HR employees' profiles, containing skills and experiences. All HR people should be able to set up personal home pages and dedicated sub pages for current HR projects. Second, HRbase should foster the creation of knowledge networks. Employees could meet physically and virtually to exchange and amplify knowledge in communities-of-practice (CoPs). Experts in change management and information systems (IS) development staffed the project team. A promising change management strategy was chosen to accompany the applications' rollout. However, two years after the €650,000 project was started, only 14% of the HR employees had ever used HRbase and feedback showed that it was close to failure (Heier & Borgman, 2004). Is this a common fate of many KMS implementation projects?

Academic research and the trade press confirm that the HR division's KMS is no isolated case (Ambrosio, 2000, p. 44; Barth, 2000, p. 37; Fluss, 2002, p. 40; Storey & Barnett, 2000, p. 145). Despite potential usefulness, firms face severe obstacles in bridging knowledge management (KM) strategy and practice: Charles Lucier, Booz-Allen & Hamilton's first knowledge officer, perceives that 84% of all KM initiatives fail; Daniel Morehead, director of organizational research at British Telecommunications, says that 70% of all projects do not reach their stated goals and objectives; other researchers peg failure rates between 50-80%. These findings reveal that - in spite of increasingly sophisticated KM technology and potential huge cost savings - many firms are not yet successfully exploiting knowledge to achieve competitiveness and innovativeness (Hackbarth, 1998, p. 590; Meso & Smith, 2000, p. 226; Nonaka, 1991, pp. 96-97; O'Dell & Grayson, 1998, p. 327; von Krogh, 1998, p. 133).

Numerous authors suggest that lots of first-generation KM initiatives have reached an (insufficient) initial plateau: though technology is no longer a major barrier - all necessary IS solutions already exist, e.g. databases, email, group-ware, and intranets (O'Dell & Grayson, 1998, p. 163) - technology-centric approaches are not sufficient to attain the necessary culture and context which promote organizational learning. Only the simultaneous optimization of cultural, social and technical subsystems ensures the successful carrying out of KM (Bhatt, 2001, p. 68-69; Meso & Smith, 2000, p. 229; Ruggles, 1998, p. 84; Seeley, 2000, p. 24; Spiegler, 2000, p. 12; Stein & Zwass, 1995, p. 96). "In other words, a knowledge management system must be a socio-technical system which has as its objective the management and sharing of knowledge to support achievement of organizational goals. By this socio-technical definition, KMS comprise the knowledge itself, [...] organizational attributes (including intangibles such as culture), policies and procedures, as well as some form of electronic storage and retrieval system" (Damodaran & Olphert, 2000, p. 405).

In their down-to-earth KM research framework, Grover and Davenport (2001, pp. 12-14) postulate that knowledge processes, either deliberate or emergent, exist in duality with a context composed of strategy, structure, people/culture, and technology. This surrounding facilitates and enhances intraorganizational knowledge flows (Alavi & Leidner, 2001, p. 129; Stein & Zwass, 1995, p. 96). For improved second-generation KM initiatives, all context elements illustrated in figure 1 must explicitly be taken into account. Challenging, establishing, and aligning shared context requires change agents to start a critical, honest, and open dialogue with all affected stakeholders. Even for much IS-enabled efforts, complementary non-technological change interventions of behavioral and organizational nature are mandatory (Earl, 2001, p. 229; Fahey & Prusak, 1998, p. 268; Holtshouse, 1998, p. 279). All of these efforts begin to show initial pay-off: some organizations discover the right mix of process, people, and technology attributes; KMS are successfully used as the technical platform for knowledge sharing (Ruggles, 1998, p. 84).

The context element culture is widely acknowledged as a most prominent make-or-break factor of KMS implementation projects, which differ from traditional IS projects due to greater difficulties associated with managing human factors and effectively changing organizational cultures (Alavi & Leidner, 1999, p. 21; Chase, 1997, p. 47; Davenport, De Long, & Beers, 1998, p. 56; Fahey & Prusak, 1998, p. 266; Leidner, 2000, p. 102; O'Dell & Grayson, 1998, pp. 166-168; Ruggles, 1998, p. 56). "[I]nformation is a flow of messages, while knowledge is created by that very flow of information, anchored in the beliefs and commitment of its holder [...] knowledge is essentially related to human action" (Nonaka & Takeuchi, 1995, pp. 58-59). This consequence is confirmed by the IS management literature advocating behavioral and organizational change management as critical success factors for IS implementation projects; the link between culture and technology is an important factor that warrants management control during implementations. Otherwise, employee resistance leads either to failure or to less than the desired organizational change results (Alavi & Joachimsthaler, 1992, pp. 106-107; Cooper, 1994, pp. 18-19).

When managers were polled about the performance of their firms' KM initiatives, academic concerns proved valid: "getting employees to share what they know is no longer a technology challenge - it's a corporate culture challenge" (Hibbard & Carillo, 1998, p. 49). While an international KM survey revealed that only 12% of the respondents believed they did a good job in facilitating knowledge growth through culture and incentives (Chase, 1997, p. 44), an Ernst & Young study of 431 U.S. and European organizations estimated success at 19%; however, the executives by and large deemed it possible to overcome the obstacles by more deliberate management (Ruggles, 1998, pp. 81-82); finally, KPMG's recent European knowledge manager survey (2003, p. 12) identified 65% of firms with current cultures which did not encourage knowledge sharing. Like traditional change management initiatives, KMS implementation projects benefit from a culture aligned with their goals. Though, the knowledge-intensive cultures pursued require more drastic behavior shifts than the majority of other change efforts since they have significant implications for the organizational power structure (Davenport et al., 1998, p. 55; von Krogh, 1998, p. 144).

Figure 1: A Pragmatic Framework for KM Research

	Knowledge Process				Knowledge processes are either the result of deliberate organizational KM initiatives or emergently tied into the work processes themselves. They occur on individual, group, and organization level.
Deliberate	Generation →Codification→	Transfer	→ Realization		
Emergent	Knowledge Process				
	Generation →Codification→	Transfer	→ Realization		
Strategy					
Structure					
People/ Culture					
Technology					

Source: Grover and Davenport (2001, pp. 12-14).

As mentioned earlier, difficulties with KM application rollouts can be explained by aspects of cultural and organizational validity. Particularly Romm et al.'s (1991, pp. 102-103) "risk grid" corrobates KMS' cultural sensitivity. It identifies danger of culture clash along the two dimensions shown in figure 2: predictability of outcome and culture content. The former variable reflects the degree to which system outputs are pre-determined during conceptualization. Given the often fluid ex ante nature of objectives, outcomes, and processes of KMS, as well as difficulties to know a priori what information will be requested, who will request the information, and when and how the information will be used (Hahn & Subramani, 2000, p. 308; Holtshouse, 1998, p. 278), the low outcome predictability increases the likelihood of culture clash.

The latter variable reflects IS' extent of cultural relevance and its visibility in terms of cultural artifacts. Since KMS affect several cultural dimensions, e.g. autonomy in decision-making, cooperation vs. competition, and incentives and rewards, the risk of culture clash is once more increased. Those barriers cannot be effectively diminished or removed by the adoption of firm-wide KMS alone. Profound cultural renovations are often a sine qua non: so far, "organizations have rewarded their professionals and employees based on their individual performance and know how. In many organizations, a major cultural shift would be required to change the employees' attitudes and behavior so that they willingly and consistently share their knowledge and insights" (Alavi & Leidner, 2001, p. 126). The academic and managerial implications are discussed below.

While most academic literature focuses on the source and state of knowledge, further academic research is needed to explore the conditions for KM

Figure 2: The Risk Grid

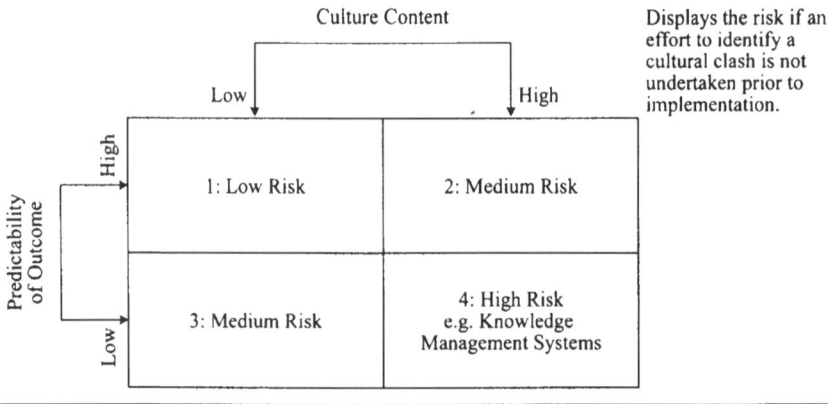

Source: Romm et al. (1991, p. 102).

initiatives, especially for KMS implementation projects. Academic relevance derives from studies which hardly "describe, in anything other than the broadest terms, the people management and organizational processes involved in KM initiatives" (Swan, 1999, p. 5). Up to now, culture has simply been assessed as a critical factor of influence (comp. Davenport & Prusak, 2000; Mertins, Heisig, & Vorbeck, 2001; Stewart et al., 2000). Grant (1996, p. 380) defined it as kind of common knowledge facilitating the knowledge integration within organizations. Only through changes, can a firm gradually modify the pattern of interaction between individuals, techniques, and technologies since core competencies are deeply entrenched into organizational practice (Bhatt, 2001, p. 74). More and more researchers start to recognize the need for a set of change interventions - required to transform organizational cultures and to harness powerful information technology (IT) in the endless pursuit of organizational excellence.

Alavi & Leidner (1999, p. 24) recommend an exploration of KMS-culture fit; their recent work (Alavi & Leidner, 2001, p. 127) posits a linked, specific research question: "[d]o certain organizational cultures foster knowledge creation?" Damodaran and Olphert (2000, p. 406) pity the lacking of guidelines and the insufficient understanding about culture's moderating influence on KMS implementation projects. Grover and Davenport (2001, p. 13) inquire on how to create a culture that values knowledge creation, sharing, and use. O'Dell and Grayson (1998, p. 166) muse what leaders can do to establish and reinforce knowledge-intensive cultures. Stewart et al. (2000, p. 50) are rather concerned about the range of factors which influence the success or failure of KM technology projects. De Long and Seemann (2000, pp. 37-38), Seeley (2000, p. 24), and Storey and Barnett (2000, p. 155) propose to merge change management discipline and practice with the new setting of KMS: "one of the most common mistakes [...] is to leave out the change management perspective, which means failing to anticipate and manage the new organizational and social dynamics associated with changes in how knowledge is created, shared, and used."

While the challenge is now well understood, change agents and managers still lack guidance for taking it on. Managerial relevance is fueled by existing implementation frameworks and guidelines which fall short of overcoming the obstacles. Practitioners perceive them as either too abstract or too nebulous, or might not understand their implications sufficiently; embarking on (culture) change initiatives or only selecting an appropriate mix of change interventions remains trial-and-error learning. In many firms, the use of technology leads to standardized approaches for the collection, structuring and transformation of information into knowledge. Hierarchy-driven, command-and-control cultures - specifying explicitly what employees ought to do - enforce this inclination (Fahey & Prusak, 1998, p. 272). So what can change agents do to institute and maintain a supportive culture (O'Dell & Grayson, 1998, p. 166)?

The pressing managerial need for guidelines is evidenced by many polls and surveys. Already Alavi and Leidner's (1999, pp. 13-14) practitioner survey at a U.S. northeast university pitied little insight and research to guide the successful development and rollout of KMS, as well as to facilitate organizational change for the sake of knowledge sharing. Managers were concerned about their ability to make people proactively share and offer knowledge, their aptitude for cross-departmental and cross-regional knowledge leverage (especially with independent profit responsibilities, and various other change management implications. Damodaran and Olphert (2000, p. 412) criticize lacks of leadership: given the widely held belief that culture is key to achieve (or more characteristic, failure to achieve) the vision of effective KM, often no attempt is made to attain the envisaged supportive knowledge sharing culture. King et al.'s (2002, pp. 93-97) Delphi study of 2,037 KM managers and practitioners identified 20 critical issues for the development of KM initiatives, including guidelines on how to accomplish a knowledge-intensive cultural environment.

My research is an initial attempt to fill a gap in the IS literature - also recognized by Swan (1999, p. 5) - by exploring the interaction effects of the context elements people/culture and technology. Incorporating the above academic and managerial implications, the general research question is derived:

⇨ "How can KMS implementation projects establish knowledge-intensive cultures in order to achieve good fit between the KM context elements technology and people/culture?"

The broad question constitutes the research problem addressed in this study. For refinement and to place them in the context of current knowledge in these areas, the succeeding section focuses on some relevant anchors from significant prior research. This study is situated at the nexus of research on KM in general and KMS in particular, (culture) change management, and IS implementation projects; hence it acknowledges and builds from a variety of different literatures. Given the relative breadth and immaturity of the research issue and the associated diversity of the related areas, the descriptions focus on established theories, i.e. widely accepted and applied to a variety of settings. They are augmented with more restrictive studies representing later advances.

1.2   Key Concepts and Significant Prior Research

1.2.1   Definitions and Basic Concepts in Knowledge Management

Academic research and the managerial practice of KM benefit from a range of definitions and key concepts, some of them imported from related disciplines: the theory of knowledge (epistemology), organizational behavior, and innovation theory (Nonaka & Takeuchi, 1995, p. 18). To refine the research question and to delineate KMS and knowledge-intensive cultures, it is first necessary to obtain an understanding and working definitions of knowledge, knowledge processes, and knowledge management. Particularly the different knowledge perspectives and taxonomies have sound implications for theoretical developments. They inform the formulation of KM strategies, the analysis of IS' role in facilitating KM, and the selection of suitable implementation approaches (comp. Alavi & Leidner, 2001, p. 115; Spiegler, 2000, pp. 1-5).

The "hierarchy" of data, information, and knowledge. Many IS researchers begin the task of defining knowledge by distinguishing between data, information and knowledge. Without knowledge being different from the others, they postulate that there is nothing new or interesting about KM (Fahey & Prusak, 1998, pp. 265-266). Most commonly, data is considered as facts and raw numbers, information as processed data, and knowledge as authenticated information (comp. Bhatt, 2001, pp. 69-70; Davenport & Prusak, 2000, pp. 1-6). However, the presumed hierarchy from data to information to knowledge - each differing along some dimensions, e.g. structure, context, and usefulness - has been challenged by some researchers. Alavi and Leidner (2001, p. 109) claim that information and knowledge are two sides of the same coin: knowledge is "information possessed in the mind of individuals: it is personalized information [...] related to facts, procedures, concepts, interpretations, ideas, observations, and judgments." Tuomi (1999, pp. 3-5) proposes an inverse hierarchy, arguing that knowledge is a prerequisite for the formulation of information and for the measurement of data - which forms information. The steps taken for identification and collection influence each piece of data.

Incorporating the criticism and the works of Huber (1991) and Nonaka (1991), this study posits that information is transformed into knowledge through processing in individual minds; in turn, knowledge becomes information through articulation and presentation in the form of graphics, text, or other symbols. On an individual level, knowledge is a justified belief that increases a person's capacity for effective action. At a higher group or organizational level, it is also embedded in business processes, norms, and routines (Davenport & Prusak, 2000, p. 5). Two implications emerge from the definition: first, IS geared to support organizational KM are not radically different from traditional applications, but instead enable users to attribute meaning to information, to codify personal knowledge in data and information, and to apply it to daily work; second, to make knowledge useful on a large scale, it must be communicated in ways which are accessible and interpretable for other individuals (Alavi & Leidner, 1999, p. 6).

Explicit vs. tacit knowledge. While the philosopher Polanyi (1962; 1967) introduced the underlying concept, the Japanese researcher Nonaka (1991) made its first application to the realm of business administration and knowledge creation. His two categories of knowledge are now widely accepted: explicit knowledge can be expressed in words without difficulty; tacit knowledge cannot be simply articulated since it is embedded in the human body and brain, as well as in products or in the firm-specific processes leading to the product. Some researchers regard it as a part of knowledge which is enmeshed with culture, e.g. self-motivated creativity and learning (Meso & Smith, 2000, p. 225). The tacit dimension of knowledge comprises both cognitive and technical elements. The former relates to individual mental models, i.e. beliefs, mental maps, and paradigms, while the latter refers to crafts, know-how, and skills applicable to a specific work. Tacit knowledge is a double-edged sword: on the one hand, the difficult imitation makes it a critical source of sustainable competitive advantage; on the other hand, individual contributions to teamwork cannot be measured and rewarded accordingly (Osterloh & Frey, 2000, p. 539-545).

While both categories are mutually dependent and reinforcing, i.e. tacit knowledge providing some background and structure for developing and interpreting explicit knowledge, the KM initiatives of most (Western) organizations focus on explicit knowledge. Its simple transformation favors technology-centric codification approaches, with an assembly of software and an associated hardware infrastructure providing the means for explication, storage, and leverage (Meso & Smith, 2000, p. 227; Zack, 1999, p. 125). "Far from being a development of the learning organization with its emphasis on people management, KM is a divergence with its own unique discourse and focus, specifically emphasizing IT and tools driven approaches" (Swan, 1999, p. 4). In contrast, personification approaches rely primarily on interaction among people. Here, the chief purpose of IS is to foster person-to-person communication (Alavi & Leidner, 2001, pp. 110-112; Grover & Davenport, 2001, p. 7; Hansen, Nohria, & Tierney, 1999, p. 107). Particular attention is paid to the human and social factors involved in the generation and transfer of knowledge - both inextricably linked with KMS under a socio-technical perspective (Thomas, Kellogg, & Erickson, 2001, p. 864).

Knowledge management and knowledge processes. Knowledge management is the process of capturing an organization's collective expertise and intelligence and using them to promote innovation through continuous organizational learning (Hahn & Subramani, 2000; Nonaka, 1991; Quinn, Anderson, & Finkelstein, 1996). KM initiatives have been prompted by a range of factors, e.g. employee turnover, rapid firm growth, and cycle time pressure (Leidner, 2000, p. 101). Though the literature shows slight discrepancies in the labeling and number of involved activities, the underlying concepts are comparable (comp. Gold, Malhotra, & Segars, 2001, p. 190). Since knowledge processes are not central to my study but foster an understanding of underlying technologies, I continue with Grover and Davenport's (2001, pp. 7-14) pragmatic KM research framework.

The model outlines four knowledge processes for building and maintaining organizational core competencies: generation, codification, transfer, and realization. All processes are interconnected and intertwined, making KM a complex concept. There also remains the contradiction that knowledge exists in a person's mind while at the same time it has to be captured, stored, and reported (Spiegler, 2000, p. 9).

Knowledge generation refers to the ability of individuals and firms to acquire and develop new useful ideas and skills. Relationships with competitors, customers, and suppliers have considerable potential to produce capabilities which are not yet present in the organization (Inkpen & Dinur, 1998, pp. 465-466; Marakas, 1999, p. 440; Probst, Raub, & Romhardt, 1999, pp. 30-31). Knowledge codification includes the conversion of knowledge into accessible and applicable arrangements of data and information. It literally turns out a code that is explicit, organized and portable (Davenport & Prusak, 2000, p. 68). Knowledge transfer entails sharing and spreading knowledge from the point of origin to the point of application. Transfer occurs at multiple levels: between individuals, from individuals to knowledge repositories, between and across groups, and from groups to the organization (Alavi & Leidner, 2001, p. 119; Probst et al., 1999, p. 32). Knowledge realization means making it more profitable and relevant for the organization in creating values, e.g. through the employment in business processes, products, and services (Bhatt, 2001, pp. 72-73; Lucier & Torsilieri, 1997, pp. 15-16). Without application, all other KM processes remain useless.

1.2.2   Refining the Research Question

This study reports on research into (culture) change management and KMS implementation projects. As outlined in previous sections, several of the fundamental issues underlying this area have been addressed in various research fields. While KM's general and conceptual principles are relatively clear, a major finding of this research, however, is the contingent and hardly explored relationship between the KM context elements technology and people/culture. "Because KMS are just beginning to appear in organizations, little research and insight exist to guide the successful development and implementation of such systems" (Alavi & Leidner, 1999, p. 2). It is very difficult to generalize findings from KMS best practices and failures since there is a general lack of qualitative and quantitative studies outlining the impact of culture and analyzing managerial attempts to promote culture change.

In terms of research method the above mentioned challenges do not only rule out replication studies but also any kind of field or laboratory experiment since the results to date offer no testable hypothesis. This calls for an exploratory approach with a set of relatively open-ended research questions (comp. Borgman, 1994, p. 16). The broad research question put forth earlier might therefore be segmented and restated as:

⇨ "How can a) KMS implementation projects establish b) knowledge-intensive cultures through c) change management in order to achieve d) good fit between the KM context elements technology and people/culture?"

The individual segments will be defined and refined below to provide an initial theoretical foundation for my research.

a) KMS implementation projects comprehend the organizational integration of technology to support knowledge processes. According to Alavi and Leidner (2001, pp. 114-124) KMS "refer to a class of information systems applied to managing organizational knowledge. [They] create an infrastructure and environment that contribute to organizational KM by actualizing, supporting, augmenting, and reinforcing knowledge processes at a deep level through enhancing their underlying dynamics, scope, timing, and overall synergy." Stein and Zwass' (1995, p. 90) raise temporal issues: such systems provide means by which past knowledge is brought to bear on today's activities, resulting in better organizational effectiveness. KMS employ existing technology to expedite and foster intra- and inter-firm KM, e.g. browsers, data warehouses (in connection with data mining techniques), groupware, internet-technologies, intelligent agent software, knowledge repositories, and workflow applications. This study examines intra-organizational KMS since they match organizational cultures' boundaries. They have been chosen to show that failure is often not rooted in technology, but rather in human issues (O'Dell & Grayson, 1998, p. 163-166).

Reviewing the literature illustrating applications of IT to organizational KM initiatives unveils three common KMS categories (comp. Alavi & Leidner, 2001, p. 114-115; Davenport et al., 1998, pp. 45-48; Earl, 2001, pp. 218-229). First, "the coding and sharing of best practices" makes use of knowledge repositories. The typical objective is to take documents with embedded knowledge and store them in a database where they can be easily retrieved. Discussion databases are of a similar, but less structured kind: participants contribute their own experiences and react to comments. Second, "the creation of knowledge directories" (yellow pages functionality) deals with the mapping of internal expertise. Instead of capturing knowledge this application focuses on facilitating its transfer among individuals and providing access. These projects acknowledge and incorporate difficulties with tacit knowledge's codification and transfer. Third, "the creation of knowledge networks" bridges the gap between codification and personalization approaches (Hansen et al., 1999, p. 107). The aim is to bring people together face-to-face and virtually to build and exchange topic-specific knowledge in an interactive, nonroutine, and unstructured way.

Though a European benchmarking study reports that over 60% of the participating organizations believed in good familiarity with infrastructure technologies (Heisig & Vorbeck, 2001, p. 133), many companies still underestimate the complexity of KMS rollouts. According to Myers (1994, p. 52), the term implementation is used in three distinct ways: "implementation as coding" takes the most narrow perspective, it only comprises the realization of systems in hardware and software; "implementation as a step in the systems development life cycle" refers to all activities involved in introducing IT to an organization at a certain stage of development; lastly, "implementation as the successful use of information technology by an organization" equates implementation with the entire systems development process. The rollout "of an information system refers to the process of preparing an organization for a new system and introducing the system in such a way as to assure its successful use" (Tyran & George, 1993, p. 6). Following Lucas (1981, pp. 14-15) and Zmud and Cox (1979, p. 36), my explorative case study adopts the latter broad understanding of KMS implementations that also includes organizational change.

b) Knowledge-intensive cultures comprise one aspect of organizational cultures. The earliest reference to the concept of culture in organizations is attributed to Pettigrew (1979, p. 574), equating a firm's culture to a system of collectively and publicly accepted meanings operating for a select group at a certain time. Despite the topics' growing maturity and popularity, up to now researchers do not agree on a working definition of culture, but only on its functional role, i.e. it should foster the accomplishment of organizations' shared purposes (Robey & Azevedo, 1994, p. 26). Applied to the setting of KMS, culture ought to ensure the effective use of technology for the benefit of individual knowledge workers, groups, and the firm (Brelade & Harman, 2000, p. 28).

Not everybody employs the term in a similar way: some use it to denote the culture of the organization as a whole, others use it to refer to the cultures of all communities within the corporate context (Coombs, Knights, & Willmott, 1992, pp. 59-61; Sathe, 1993, p. 332). Since this study is interested in cultural subsets - the culture of groups using a KMS - it takes the latter position by adopting Schein's (1985, p. 9) widely-accepted definition of culture as "a pattern of shared basic assumptions - invented, discovered, or developed by a given group as it learns to cope with its problems of external adaptation and internal integration - that has worked well enough to be considered valid and, therefore, to be taught to new members as the correct way to perceive, think, and feel in relation to those problems." The notions of culture and organizational cultures are used interchangeably throughout the text.

I define knowledge-intensive cultures broadly as those cultures where employees value learning and show a positive knowledge-orientation. Organization members are free and willing to explore, are proactively seeking and offering knowledge, and their knowledge leverage activities are given credence by managers (Alavi & Leidner, 2001, p. 114; Davenport et al., 1998, pp. 52-53; Meso

& Smith, 2000, p. 232). A culture with knowledge-orientation is likely to exhibit the following attributes: emphasis on external and internal contacts and networking, creativity, fairness, sociability, trust, and sound underlying procedures and systems (Brelade & Harman, 2000, pp. 28-29). As a measure of friendliness among community members, sociability is particularly important for "the creation of knowledge networks" (Jarvenpaa & Staples, 2001, p. 156). Originating from personal and organizational beliefs and values, as well as from behavior related to information processing, knowledge-intensive cultures become an implicit standardization device for handling information. They further include preferences for certain communication channels or media.

If IS are considered artifacts which reflect organizational norms and values (Saffold, 1988, p. 551), open and hierarchy-free cultures are likely to increase the use of collaborative technology (Jarvenpaa & Staples, 2000, pp. 132-134). In contrast, concerns of distrust, power, and rational gain lead employees to hoard and hide information and knowledge, since they are considered sources of power and status. Traditional command and control organizations minimize the interaction between techniques, technology, and people, and thus reduce the opportunities for KM processes (Bhatt, 2001, p. 72). For example, Orlikowski (1992, p. 362) discovered that "in competitive and individualistic organizational cultures - where there were few incentives or norms for cooperating or sharing expertise - groupware did not engender collaboration." Change agents and managers must be aware that KMS alter relationships, as well as patterns of communication and perceived authority, control, and influence which all are interdependent with knowledge-intensive cultures (comp. Keen, 1981, p. 24).

c) Change management is "a set of behavioral science-based theories, values, strategies, and techniques aimed at the planned change of the organizational work setting for the purpose of enhancing individual development and improving organizational performance, through the alteration of organizational members' on-the-job behaviors (Porras & Robertson, 1992, p. 723). In more practical terms, it is the application of management discipline and rigor to change processes (Seeley, 2000, p. 25). In their review of change management research and theory in the 1990s Armenakis and Bedeian (1999, p. 295) distinguish between three change themes: first, "change dealing with content issues", attempting to define factors related to successful and unsuccessful change efforts; second, "change dealing with context issues", focusing on conditions and forces existing in a firm's internal and external environment; third, "change dealing with process issues", addressing the sequencing and timing of actions undertaken during an enactment of intended change. Consistent with process studies of IS implementation research, my exploration below deals with the latter theories which aim for intra-organizational change (comp. Lucas, 1981; Zmud & Cox, 1979).

Congruent with Markus and Benjamin (1997, p. 55) and Orlikowski and Barley (2001, p. 154), I postulate that change initiatives can substantially increase IS implementations' chances of success. Change interventions provide links between classic IS implementation frameworks and the different requirements that KMS place on human factors and organizational cultures (De Long & Seemann, 2000, pp. 37-38). Only by modifying the culture of groups can a firm gradually change the interaction patterns between people, techniques, and technologies demanded by KM (Bhatt, 2001, p. 11). In terms of structure, all process studies of change management outline a set of interventions that change agents have to follow in implementing changes (Armenakis & Bedeian, 1999, pp. 301-302). In terms of content, practitioner advice often includes aims to increase organizational and individual KM commitment, to define and communicate benefits and accountability, to design systems to support the new culture, and to make executives KM champions (Teng, Grover, & Fiedler, 1996, p. 282).

d) Good fit among the context elements people/culture and technology exists when organizational cultures exhibit features and support that correspond with the requirements of voluntary, IT-enabled knowledge processes (comp. Goodhue & Thompson, 1995, pp. 214-218). "[I]t's the culture that helps to bridge the gap between the provision of technology and information and its effective use for the benefit of the organization by individual knowledge workers" (Brelade & Harman, 2000, p. 28). An important influence on KM effectiveness is the interdependent relationship among all context elements. Ideally, the interaction among those elements is compatible, or at least not in opposition. As argued earlier, KMS are related with several cultural dimensions, e.g. cooperation vs. competition, distribution of organizational power, and incentives and rewards (Orlikowski & Hofman, 1997, pp. 18-19).

Any incautious realignments - caused by the introduction of technology - might violate some shared values and meanings, result in a loss of fit, and finally foster culture-based resistance (Cooper, 1994, pp. 18-19; Davenport et al., 1998, pp. 55-56). Though the emphasis of this study is placed on cultural aspects, people aspects cannot be entirely neglected. Organizational cultures are influenced by the actions, emotions, and thoughts of individuals; they can only be changed through personal shifts in attitudes and behavior (Sathe, 1985, pp. 359-363; Schein, 1999, pp. 115-130). For that reason, all change interventions are targeted at the personal level though their ultimate aim is to inflict change at group and/or organizational level.

1.3   Research Objectives and Expected Contributions

As stated earlier, this study should lead to a better understanding and explanation of aspects which influence success and failure of KMS implementation projects. I attempt to show that the failure of KMS implementation projects is often rooted in a neglect of organizational change needs and in inappropriate change interventions. Those have mutual moderating influence both on knowledge-intensive cultures and KMS. To address my refined research question and relying on Damodaran and Olphert's (2000) recent work, I isolated and redrew some relations from Grover and Davenport's (2001, pp. 12-14) pragmatic framework for KM research. The result, outlined in figure 3, is an initial attempt to fill a gap in the IS literature by observing the interaction effects of the KM context elements people/culture and technology (comp. Grover & Davenport, 2001, pp.12-14; Swan, 1999, p. 5). The remaining elements strategy and structure are beyond the scope of this study even though organizations cannot neglect them during KMS implementation projects.

Under the influence of Leavitt's (1965) "diamond model" - which has gained acceptance both in IS (Galliers, 1999; Keen, 1981) and organizational behavior literature (Scott, 1992) - organizations are classified as systems where people, structure, task, and technology are interrelated and mutually adjusting. When change agents modify components separately, the other elements often dampen out the impact of innovation, i.e. homeostatic behavior of firms. While KM researchers generally acknowledge the interdependence of technology, people/culture, and change management (Damodaran & Olphert, 2000, p. 406; Orlikowski & Hofman, 1997, pp. 11-12; Seeley, 2000, p. 29; Thomas et al., 2001, p. 864), so far not much has been done to fill the "black box" with tools. I propose to tackle this gap through the application of (culturally-sensitive) organizational behavior frameworks. While this effort is central to my research, it forms the basis for the two related, more detailed research questions.

Figure 3: Organizational Change Framework for Knowledge Management Systems

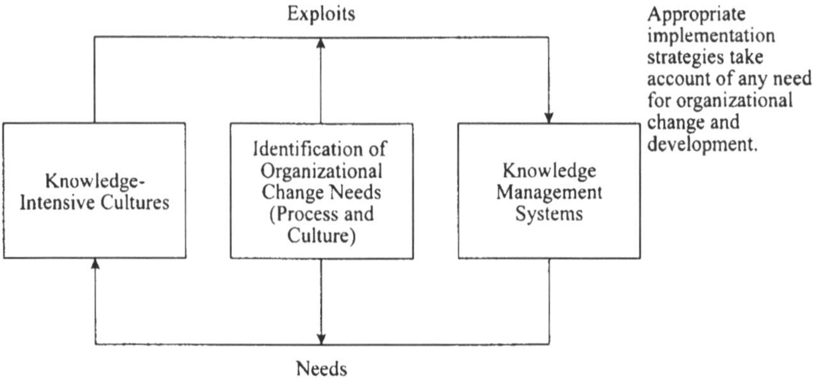

Source: Damodaran and Olphert (2000, p. 406).

Drilling down into the "black box" - and into KM literature - extrinsic and intrinsic motivators emerge as prominent drivers and obstacles for behavior and culture change. Researchers agree that organizations need mechanisms to reward employees for sharing and extracting their expertise (Alavi & Leidner, 1999, pp. 21-22; Sethia & von Glinow, 1985, p. 401; Stewart et al., 2000, p. 48). KPMG Management Consulting's (1998, p. 4) research report and Teleos international survey (Chase, 1997, pp. 46-47) name them among the top ten KM drawbacks. King et al.'s (2002, pp. 93-95) recent Delphi study ranks incentives and rewards among the most effective interventions for increasing KMS usage. The literature acknowledges that motivators must be adapted to different KM approaches: for a codification strategy, people should be motivated to write down their knowledge and contribute it to databases and repositories (Davenport & Klahr, 1998, p. 208); for a personalization strategy, employees ought to be rewarded for direct help and knowledge offered to colleagues (Hansen et al., 1999, p. 113).

Since my research site placed particular emphasis on incentive and reward systems, Alavi and Leidner's (2001, p. 127) research question comprises a significant part of the change interventions' exploration:

⇨ "What types of incentives are effective in inculcating organizational members with valuable knowledge to contribute and share their knowledge?"

I adopt this inquiry as my second research question. The later analysis distinguishes between intrinsic vs. extrinsic, short-term vs. long-term oriented, and individual vs. team-based motivators. Up to now, most firms still base annual reviews and bonuses on individual accomplishments, eventually encouraging knowledge hoarding practices (Ambrosio, 2000, p. 44). I will test academic propositions arguing in favor of team-based intrinsic motivators (O'Dell & Grayson, 1998, pp. 168-170; Sathe, 1985, pp. 386-387), or at least for a well-balanced mix of "hard" and "soft" incentives and rewards (Beer & Nohria, 2000, p. 134-141).

Uncovering the "black box", i.e. delineating change interventions appropriate for KM initiatives, cannot fully answer the broad research question. At which point in time do organizational change needs come into play?

⇨ "Must culture change occur before knowledge management initiatives can be successfully undertaken or can knowledge management initiatives facilitate culture change" (Alavi & Leidner, 2001, p. 126)?

Again, I adopt the research recommendation as my third research question. The literature review reveals heterogeneous academic positions: some authors caution that culture is a fixed variable for short-run IS and KMS rollouts, it even constrains organizational change (Cooper, 1994, p. 27; Romm et al., 1991, p. 101); others argue for prior (culture) change (Seeley, 2000, p. 29); the majority favors a concurrent approach including fundamental changes in processes and systems (Bhatt, 2001, p. 74; Brelade & Harman, 2000, p. 29; Davenport et al.,

1998, p. 53; Macredie & Sandom, 1999, pp. 249-251; Orlikowski & Hofman, 1997, pp. 11-12; Stein & Zwass, 1995, p. 96; Zmud & Cox, 1979, p. 37).

Some researchers and KM practitioners even claim that technology can foster knowledge-intensive cultures: "A new symbiosis is emerging between the human and technological aspects of work: tools [...] can support and maintain a beneficial culture shift, and the culture shift highlights the value of the new tools and promotes their use" (Conklin, 1996, p. 4). Put differently, change and knowledge dynamics are mutually reinforcing. Increasing knowledge enables a series of successful changes and organizations inclined to change adopt KM initiatives more quickly (Lucier & Torsilieri, 1997, p. 23; Thomas et al., 2001, p. 879). For this group of authors, IT enhances the motivation effects of cultural values that support efficiency and innovation. Firms obtain more sophisticated (electronic) means for disseminating and transferring managerial statements and supportive messages, as well as for increasing employee exposure to their colleagues' work (Dewett & Jones, 2001, pp. 332-333). My study's contribution is basically an attempt to answer all three research questions stated earlier. The remaining paragraphs of this section describe the expected academic and managerial contributions in more detail.

For academic contribution, the study's aim is exploratory, building toward constructive guidance for change agents and managers facing large-scale KMS implementation projects in sometimes inhospitable corporate environments. Since my research deals with poorly understood issues in a rich and difficult to control environment, caution ought to be taken in assessing the results. However, taking the exploratory design's restraints into account, several theoretical contributions can be derived. First, my research attempts a better understanding of KMS-culture fit (comp. Alavi & Leidner, 1999, p. 24), i.e. a static view on the interdependent relationship between technology, knowledge-intensive cultures, and organizational change needs. The implementation project's chronological account also provides a dynamic view on culture's moderating influence on IS rollouts (comp. Damodaran & Olphert, 2000, p. 406).

Second, literature research and empirical analysis will determine whether change management recommendations apply to the design of KM incentive and reward systems, whether there are substitute change interventions, and whether motivators suitable for private communities, e.g. expert status and rank, pertain to business-related knowledge exchanges. Do certain infrastructure technologies hold special promises for the remuneration of computer-mediated exchanges (comp. David Constant, Sproull, & Kiesler, 1996, pp. 121-127; Goodman & Darr, 1998, p. 426; Jarvenpaa & Staples, 2000, p. 131)? Third, on a more abstract level Schein's (1992, pp. 318-321) proposition of "unfreezing and change through technological seduction" will be investigated and, if applicable, be concretized for KM research. The exploration focuses on the characteristics and possibilities of concurrent IS rollouts and change initiatives, in particular on KMS' aptness for driving behavior and culture change (Ginzberg, 1978, p. 41; Robey & Azevedo, 1994, p. 28; Romm et al., 1991, p. 101).

Fourth and last, the explanatory power and goodness of fit of two well-known change paradigms from the field of organizational behavior is tested in the new setting of KMS implementation projects (comp. De Long & Seemann, 2000, pp. 37-38; Seeley, 2000, p. 24; Storey & Barnett, 2000, p. 155). I will address most criticism on the two process studies of change. If complementary issues emerge, theory synthesis might result in a tentative implementation framework (comp. Blalock, 1969, p. 2; Kerlinger, 1986, p. 9). Promising directions for further research are presented, especially on the timing and sequencing of change interventions, as well as for quantitative research attempting to transform the discovered relations into causalities. Of course, all hypothetical results require additional substantiation and tests before they can gain general acceptance (Huber, 1990, pp. 64-65).

For managerial contribution, the study's aim goes beyond factor research. In my opinion, the sequencing and timing of interventions has yet been overlooked in KM research. The same issue is raised by Davenport et al. (1998, p. 55), claiming that the "sequence for addressing these factors also matters. There may be a life cycle to building effective knowledge management practices and processes." As wide as the possible applicability of my study is, however, as modest the claim to managerial contribution should be. An exploratory study cannot provide normative prescriptions for real-world situations, regardless of the research's degree of realism (comp. Walsham & Waema, 1994, p. 151). The reason for this is that case studies in principle can only establish the existence of relations but not their direction (Cavaye, 1996, p. 229). Phrased differently, it is only possible to conclude that one variable is related to another variable, but impossible to determine the dependent and independent one. Nonetheless given those constraints, several expected contributions to practice are presented.

First and most important, this study tackles the lack of guidelines for change agents and managers on how to create organizational cultures that value knowledge creation, sharing, and use (comp. Grover & Davenport, 2001, p. 13; O'Dell & Grayson, 1998, p. 166). Up to now, the existing research on KMS generally comprises conceptual and general principles (Alavi & Leidner, 1999; Alavi & Leidner, 2001; Davenport & Prusak, 2000), as well as case descriptions of such IS in a handful of organizations (Alavi, 1997; Heier & Borgman, 2004; Sensiper, 1997); however, there is little insight and research to guide the successful development and rollout. I intend to point out a list of shortcomings encountered with traditional IS implementation approaches. Based on those discoveries, a (hypothetical) implementation framework for managing (culture) change in relation with KMS implementation projects is proposed. It will avoid the shortcomings of traditional approaches, addressing either change dynamics or knowledge dynamics, while utterly omitting their linkage (Lucier & Torsilieri, 1997, p. 23).

Second, a set of hypothetical interventions will be outlined based on the in-depth case study (comp. Damodaran & Olphert, 2000, p. 412; King et al., 2002, pp. 93-97). The interventions try to devise and to implement culture change in a way that gives rise to desired behaviors, instead of commanding them. Otherwise, as the case description will show, it is likely that social systems exposed to that kind of stress fall back to their former natural state. The recommended interventions embrace social systems' natural knowledge dynamics and do not try to supplant them with artificial, managed alternatives (McElroy, 2000, p. 37). Particular emphasis is placed on incentive and reward systems, both on the level of knowledge givers and takers, i.e. users, and on the level of multiplicators, i.e. user champions. Third and finally, I plan to obtain a range of measures for overcoming the major obstacles to IS implementation - lacks of "felt need" and employee resistance (Cooper, 1994, p. 19; Keen, 1981, p. 26; Srinivasan & Davis, 1987, p. 65). While those challenges negatively impact behavior change, they are poison for culture change (comp. Beer, Eisenstat, & Spector, 1990, p. 165; Sathe, 1985, p. 363).

1.4   General Research Approach

1.4.1   Research Design

This section will outline the approach taken to answer the general research question and to reach the research objectives. My thesis responds to the pressing managerial need for establishing knowledge-intensive cultures in order to achieve good fit between KMS and cultural issues. Up to now, most innovation, organizational behavior, and IS implementation studies focus on critical success factors such as top management support, commitment, user involvement, and user training, but do not explicitly acknowledge or incorporate the impact of culture (comp. Finlay & Forghani, 1998, p. 58; Ginzberg, 1981b, pp. 47-55; Hahn & Subramani, 2000, p. 309; Krovi, 1993, p. 334; Stein & Zwass, 1995, p. 106; Storey & Barnett, 2000, p. 154).

For the explorative research effort I propose to apply (culture) change paradigms from the field of organizational behavior to the new setting of KMS implementation projects: the first is a linear, staged approach exemplary for the current change management literature (Lewin, 1947; Schein, 1992, 1999), whereas the second approach favors continuous interventions into culture's self-perpetuating processes, building on its own dynamics (Sathe, 1985, 1993). Goals are to deepen the understanding of rollout success or failure, as well as to explore conditions conducive to the development of knowledge-oriented organizational cultures. Both approaches are influenced by different underlying assumptions and philosophies, but well-recognized and widely-cited in the academic world. They provide different perspectives for examining the same research problem.

Following academic suggestions for combining change management/organizational behavior theories with IS research (Galliers, 1999, p. 229; O'Hara, Watson, & Kavan, 1999, pp. 63-64; Stein & Zwass, 1995, p. 226) - as well as with KM investigations (Seeley, 2000, p. 29; Thomas et al., 2001, p. 864) - both theoretical frameworks' explanatory power is empirically tested in the new setting of a successful KMS implementation project. Orlikowski and Barley (2001, pp. 154-158) contend that IS research profits considerably from the engagement with organization studies, especially in issues of systems implementation and use within particular contexts. Zand and Sorensen (1975, p. 533) made an analogous claim - more than a quarter of a century earlier: "Behavioral scientists, on the other hand, are primarily trained in the social and psychological sciences and have conducted research for many years on the theory and process of change in individuals, groups, and organizations. Since [an IS] project is an attempt to induce organizational change, it seemed desirable to investigate the effective use of management science by using a behavioral theory of change, preferably one which can also organize diverse influences into a small set of variables."

I build on and extend the earlier work of Ginzberg (1981b) and Zmud and Cox (1979), conceptualizing IS implementations as a change process. In their opinion, the key challenge is to create an environment where change is accepted and favored through the assignment of project responsibilities to affected stakeholders, intensive education programs, and the development of a mutual sense of commitment and trust. Though the widely recognized critical success factors surface again, the authors give no recommendation for their combination and sequencing. Both are mandatory to transform factor research into process studies, as claimed in the studies' outlines. Keen et al. (1982) is the only instance where the authors' stated objectives were the exploration and the goodness of fit-testing of process studies, as well as theory-building. Comparable to my research, two change paradigms (the Kolb-Frohman and Lewin-Schein models) and a single case study (with multiple sites) were used for theory testing (comp. Markus, 1989). The two models provided a priori explanations of factors influencing the success and failure of IS implementation efforts.

Relying on those studies and on an analysis of applicable research strategies, I argue that a single, exploratory case study is appropriate for deriving the envisaged academic and managerial contributions and for recommending a culturally-sensitive rollout approach that does no longer ignore the linkage between knowledge and organizational change, but rather builds on it (Lucier & Torsilieri, 1997, p. 23). The "case study is an empirical enquiry that investigates a contemporary phenomenon within its real-life context, especially when the boundaries between phenomenon and context are not clearly evident" (Yin, 1994, p. 13). For examination, it uses multiple methods of data collection to obtain information from one or several entities. Case study research is particularly appropriate for IS research in early, formative stages, as well as for practice-based problems where the actor experiences and the action context are critical. The predominant practical theme in case studies is implementation, i.e. causes of IS failure or success (Benbasat, Goldstein, & Mead, 1987, p. 369-378; Weick & Quinn, 1999, p. 364).

Like all IS research approaches, case studies exhibit strengths and weaknesses. Cavaye (1996, p. 229) summarizes the main issues. In terms of strengths, they allow for the capturing of detail and reality by studying phenomena in their natural setting, as well as for the generation of theories from practice. Different aspects and a large number of variables - which need not to be predetermined - can be explored. Researchers can answer "how" and "why" questions in order to understand the nature and complexity of the processes interdependent with IS implementation projects (Benbasat et al., 1987, p. 370). Moreover, case research is valuable for developing and refining theories for further study. In terms of weaknesses, it precludes the generalization of findings statistically to a population. Researchers have no control over independent variables which might limit the internal validity of conclusions. Even though it establishes relationships between variables, the direction of causation is difficult to infer.

I chose a positivist epistemology, assuming that reality is objectively given and can be described by measurable properties which are independent of the researcher and his or her instruments: positivism "tries to understand a social setting by identifying individual components of a phenomenon and explains the phenomenon in terms of constructs and relationships between constructs. The theoretical constructs describing the phenomenon are considered to be distinct from empirical reality" (Cavaye, 1996, p. 233). Inquiry is considered value free, so that the investigator remains detached, neutral, and objective (Darke, Shanks, & Broadbent, 1998, p. 276). Some authors recommend interpretive research for studying IS implementations and organizational cultures, especially for the deeper levels of values and assumptions (comp. Hatch, 1993, pp. 657-658; Myers, 1994, pp. 45-55; 1997, p. 241). They endeavor to understand phenomena through the meanings that individuals assign to them and do not believe in predefined variables but in the full complexity of human sense-making in emergent situations. However, since my study focuses on observable change interventions/factors - as well as on overt attributes of knowledge-intensive cultures - I believe in positivism's applicability.

Following proponents of the deductive use of case research, e.g. Benbasat et al. (1987), Lee (1989), and Yin (1993; 1994), the second chapter outlines the study's theoretical foundations. In the third chapter, data is gathered on the independent variables indicated by the theoretical frameworks. Chapter four's case discussion then compares the factual conditions and relationships to the theoretical ones. The fifth and final chapter presents and combines the analytical findings, provides preliminary answers to the related research questions, and shows promising directions for further research. My exploratory design allows for guidance from existing literature in thinking about potentially important aspects while remaining open to new insights from the field (Darke et al., 1998, p. 236; Sole & Applegate, 2000, p. 583).

To ensure the quality of the case study design, several tests from the wider area of empirical social research are applied: construct validity, external validity, and reliability. Construct validity is supported by multiple data collection methods which are useful for cross checks (Pettigrew, 1990, p. 277; Yin, 1994, p. 92). This triangulation approach aims at obtaining the best of various data collection methods: my personal interviews provide depth, personal feelings, and subtlety; presentation material and project documentation add facts; direct observations unearth discrepancies between formal statements and actual behavior. Multiple data instances reduce researcher bias, sharpen theoretical constructs, and strengthen case study conclusions (Eisenhardt, 1989, p. 538; Miles & Huberman, 1984, pp. 234-235).

External validity establishes the domain to which the findings of a case study can be generalized. The validity of a generalization from a single case depends not on statistical representativeness, but on the plausibility and cogency of the logical reasoning used to describe the findings from the case study and drawing inferences and conclusions from those findings (Walsham & Waema, 1994, p. 151). Additionally - through theoretical replication - the set of theories tested in the original case study can be applied to a dissimilar set of initial conditions, i.e. embedded units of analysis. Though the resulting different predictions call for different findings, it is still the same theory being tested (Lee, 1989, pp. 40-41). Finally, reliability is ensured through the use of interview protocols and field notes. They make sure that similar procedures are followed in the future, either in multiple cases or with multiple investigators (Yin, 1993, pp. 39-40).

1.4.2   Site Selection

Siemens, a German company ranking among the world leaders in electrical engineering and electronics was chosen as research site. With sales of €84.0 billion and a net income of €2.6 billion in fiscal 2002, it was Europe's industry leader with strong positions in the North American and Asian markets. Approximately 56,000 researchers and developers were employed; research and development

(R&D) investments totaled €5.8 billion. Siemens was a conglomerate of six business segments: Information and Communications, Automation and Control, Power, Transportation, Medical, and Lighting. Siemens' largest business segment Information and Communications comprised three groups. Siemens Business Services (SBS) offered single source IT solutions and services. Information and Communication Mobile (ICM) covered all mobile communication requirements with network technology, terminal devices, and mobile applications. The case study focuses on Information and Communication Networks (ICN) that developed, manufactured, and sold public communication systems, private business communication systems and related software, and provided a variety of consulting, maintenance and other services (Siemens, 2002, p. 3-136).

Each business segment was split into several groups with independent profit responsibility and regional sales organizations (local companies) around the globe. The decentralized matrix structure allowed for entrepreneurial responsibility and the development of close ties to customers. Cross-group and cross-regional cooperation and systematic sharing of best practices enabled the provision of comprehensive and customer-focused solutions. Siemens' managing board confirmed that the "global network of innovation" - 426,000 employees in 190 countries - were the firm's greatest asset. Linked in a global knowledge network, they were key for innovation and finally for offering technologies, tailor-made solutions, and services (Siemens, 2002, pp. 7-20).

Impacted by the telecommunications equipment industry's continuing difficulties, Siemens ICN's sales of €9.6 billion resulted in a negative EBIT of €691 million in fiscal 2002. The 50,600 employees in over 160 countries focused on improving the product base, cost structure, and sales channels (Siemens, 2001, p. 27). It was Siemens ICN's strategy to become a solution provider for other "global networks of innovation". The four business units would provide the physical components of a sales project while the local companies were responsible for customizing and integration into the customer network: Enterprise Networks (EN) offered communications solutions for enterprise customers, Wireline Network Communications (WN) offered circuit-switched, IP-based and converged network solutions for carriers, Access Solutions (AS) supplied end-to-end solutions for copper-, fiber optic-, and radio-based broadband access, and Optical Networks (ON) provided solutions for optical backbones and the edge of carrier and metropolitan networks (Siemens Information and Communication Networks, 2002, p. 5). For the case study, mainly the complementary central functions and the local companies are relevant.

When the market environment is in constant flux, it is indispensable to provide flexible bundles of services and products that can be easily adapted to individual customers. The prerequisite for becoming such a solution provider is an organizational setting that allows for the fast and purposeful identification and exchange of relevant information and knowledge. As a response, ShareNet, a global knowledge sharing network for the sales and marketing community, was considered for the first time in 1999. Both explicit and tacit knowledge were taken into account by the KMS: for explicit knowledge, the aim was to provide structured knowledge objects in the form of project descriptions, functional and technical solutions, customers, competitors, and markets; for tacit knowledge, the global cultivation and support of personal collaboration with urgent requests, discussion forums, news, chats, and advertisements was intended.

1.4.3   Unit of Analysis

My case study's unit of analysis is the implementation of ShareNet with a special focus on the context elements people/culture and technology. It is presented in chronological order to allow for time-series analysis (Yin, 1994, pp. 113-118). I argue that a single case is appropriate: ShareNet represents a critical case with all necessary conditions for theory testing; additionally, Siemens ICN's successful, culturally-sensitive rollout is a polar and unique case. The KMS implementation project combines KM and change initiatives and offers multiple embedded units of analysis, i.e. business units and regional sales organizations. It allows for the isolation and exposition of appropriate change interventions, as well as for the goodness of fit-testing of prescriptive models (comp. Darke et al., 1998, p. 277; Pettigrew, 1990, pp. 275-276). According to Yin (1984, p. 42): "To confirm, challenge or extend a theory, there may exist a single case, meeting all the conditions for testing the theory". Keen at al. (1982) take this reasoning a step further when they attempt theory-building from a single case study, albeit with multiple sites.

The stated goal of this study is to explore how knowledge-intensive cultures can be established in relation with KMS implementation projects. Consequently, a successful rollout was chosen where no knowledge-oriented attitude prevailed in the beginning. A former Siemens employee diagnosed an engineering "do it all yourself" culture - giving up individual power for the benefit of the whole firm had no strong appeal (Gerndt, 2000, p. 10). Building on earlier works from Davenport et al. (1998, pp. 48-49), Finlay and Forghani (1998, p. 54), and Lucas (1981, pp. 11-14), I derived ShareNet's implementation success from several, widely-accepted measures for non-mandatory IS: first, usage and contribution rates, i.e. the number of knowledge repository postings and retrievals or the number of participants for discussion-oriented content; second, user satisfaction, i.e. self-report measures on questionnaires and interviews; third, financial return on investment (ROI) for the KM initiative or for the larger organization, e.g. cost savings and increased turnover; fourth, degree to which the KMS accomplishes its original objectives; fifth and last, external recognition, e.g. academic acknowledgement and awards received.

In terms of all the above measures, ShareNet's implementation has been doing well. Siemens ICN uses a statistical software tool to track usage and contribution patterns with country/regional granularity. It enables the ShareNet operating team to check the level of participation via the number of registered users and actually posted contributions. The initial target of 10,000 registered users was widely exceeded: by the end of September 2002, more than 18,000 employees from more than 80 countries signed up for ShareNet. The KMS held more than 20,000 knowledge objects and some 4,000 urgent requests for help accumulated annually. At the same time, an online survey revealed that user satisfaction was favorable as well. The results from 1,677 responses, presented in table 1, show particular acclaim for ShareNet's availability, for the care and support from the Munich ShareNet team, and for the KMS' usability. Other topics, especially the quality of postings and the benefits for daily work, had some more

Table 1: ShareNet Survey Results (October 2002)

Question	Mean	+3	+2	+1	0	-1	-2	-3	N.R.
Availability of ShareNet	2.01	490	741	347	46	7	4	1	41
Usability (i.e. how you can use and handle the application)	1.18	111	497	682	269	59	10	4	45
Content structure (i.e. range of object types, set of discussion forums, offered categories, etc.)	1.03	64	430	691	348	51	13	5	75
Quality and re-usability of knowledge objects	1.04	69	414	651	312	67	11	5	148
Quality and significance of urgent requests and their responses	1.13	105	416	522	277	51	12	8	286
Quality and significance of usual (i.e. non-urgent) discussion postings	0.87	51	247	629	334	45	11	15	345
Practicality and meaningfulness of online help, online tutorials, and quality guidelines	1.04	67	308	546	265	39	4	10	438
Care and support by the Munich ShareNet team	1.60	224	482	411	104	16	2	9	429
Care and support by your local ShareNet manager and/or your local ShareNet coach	0.96	111	273	365	213	66	14	38	597
Benefit from ShareNet for your daily work	0.73	102	311	500	435	109	21	53	146

potential for improvement.

Estimating ShareNet's ROI is more contentious. The one time implementation and maintenance costs added up to €7.7 million in fiscals 1999 and 2000. Major cost components were personnel, IT, and promotion activities accounting in sum for €6.0 million, i.e. workshops, incentives, and marketing material. In fiscal 2000, ShareNet created a pro forma gross profit, calculated as 5% from €145.9 million in additional revenues obtained through knowledge exchange. One year later, 81% of users reported time savings of at least one hour per month and the ShareNet operating team estimated an additional turnover of €117.6 million. The KMS' business case achieved break-even in the same year. Albeit Siemens ICN's business situation and outlook changed drastically, ShareNet remained profitable in 2002.

Externally, ShareNet was acclaimed as a KM benchmark (MacCormack, 2002, p. 14). After the implementation project's formal conclusion, the American Productivity and Quality Center (APQC) named Siemens one of five global organizations serving as role models for the successful conduct of KM initiatives. The firm presented its best practices along with the other honorees Chevron, Hewlett-Packard, the World Bank, and Xerox at the APQC knowledge transfer session at Houston, Texas in February 2000. Moreover, Siemens was a five-time winner of Teleos' Global Most Admired Knowledge Enterprises (MAKE) research program. A panel of Fortune Global 500 senior executives and KM experts measured the finalists against eight knowledge performance dimensions: e.g. creating a knowledge-oriented culture, delivering knowledge-based products, services, and solutions, and creating an environment for collaborative knowledge sharing. Up to 2002, a group of eleven organizations had appeared in all five studies as Global MAKE winners and formed the select Global MAKE hall of fame.

1.4.4   Data Collection, Analysis, and Exposition

Empirical evidence for this study was collected at different organizational levels and through a variety of methods: semi-structured personal interviews (lasting for two hours on average), reviews of presentation material and project documentation, and direct observations. The triangulation of data collection techniques provides multiple perspectives for the issues under study and allows for a cross-checking of existing and emerging concepts (Eisenhardt, 1989, p. 538; Pettigrew, 1990, p. 277). I interviewed a cross-section of Siemens ICN's KM department, several members of the IT department, the president, vice president and employees of the central function responsible for strategy, as well as user champions and users from the sales and marketing community, i.e. the business units. A three-month field visit in summer 2002 allowed for observations of knowledge processes and interaction effects with and between the context elements people/culture and technology. Ongoing access to corporate documentation provided the means to triangulate interview reports and observed behavior. Of special interest was information about change interventions and a variety of qualitative and quantitative metrics that Siemens ICN regularly employs to assess the KMS' usage.

Case study data analysis depends profoundly on the researcher's integrative power; however, multiple methods of data collection lend greater support to conclusions (Benbasat et al., 1987, p. 374). According to Miles and Huberman (1984, pp. 21-23) data analysis consists of three concurrent activities: first, data reduction is the process of selecting, simplifying, abstracting, and transforming the raw case study data; second, data display happens in the form of charts, graphs, matrices, narratives, and tables; third, conclusion drawing/verification involves drawing meaning from data and building logical chains of evidence, making use of causal networks, clustering diagrams, and various types of matrices. To support these activities - and following the advice of Darke et al. (1998), Myers (1997), and Weitzman and Miles (1995) - I employed a special-purpose software tool for qualitative research, i.e. QSR NVivo. The application is an optional upgrade and partner product to QSR NUD*IST, a widely used software package for non-numerical, unstructured data indexing, searching, and theorizing.

NVivo provides facilities for the storage, coding, retrieval, and analysis of textual data, as well as for theory testing (QSR International, 2002, pp. 10-12). Like a case study, it has the capacity to integrate mixed research methods by bringing quantitative data into qualitative projects (Bazley, 2002, p. 229). I examined corporate documentation, field notes, and interview protocols with the help of the software tool which performed a categorical analysis of the information. Free-form significance/textual units from the transcripts were placed into conceptual categories (nodes in a tree structure), derived from chapter two's theoretical predictions. The tree structure is a simple organizing system that enables more efficient database interrogation and flexible restructurings at any time. Deductively, all categories were hierarchically grouped and mapped to the change paradigms, i.e. time-series analysis and pattern-matching (Yin, 1994, pp. 106-118).

In theory-testing mode - the major part of this study - I looked for goodness of fit and counterexamples. Fellow researchers claim "that (any) use of such software makes analysis more visible, thereby enhancing transparency, and so the quality of evidence and argument might be more easily judged" (Crowley, Harré, & Tagg, 2002, p. 193). In explorative theory-building mode - at the end of this study - I tried to surface events, opinions, and outcomes which required additional explanations (comp. Keen et al., 1982, p. 128). Since the continuous comparison of data and theory revealed significant overlap among factors from both theoretical frameworks, I used inductive theory synthesis to derive a hypothetical implementation framework. The emergent construct was systematically compared with evidence from multiple embedded units of analysis in order to determine the fit with empirical case study data.

Enfolding literature which discussed related findings helped me to tie together phenomena normally not associated with each other. While the result was a theory with higher conceptual level, stronger internal validity, and wider generalizability, true cross-case replication can further enhance the relationships' validity (comp. Eisenhardt, 1989, pp. 541-544). NVivo supported the theory-building approach through assay tables, memos, and visual networks, depicting interrelationships in a hierarchically structured tree of nodes. Its various clustering and dimensionalizing techniques - either based on individual coding or on matrix output - assisted me with construction and evaluation. The final result is a tentative, complex network of categories, sometimes related to each other, that allows for the subsequent (quantitative) testing of coincidences, differences, and discrepancies (Weitzman & Miles, 1995, pp. 238-256).

2. Conceptual Foundations

The second chapter presents the conceptual basis for the case study. It builds a framework for KMS implementation projects, bringing together the literature on culture change, IS implementation, and KMS. The meta study augments two complementary process studies - Lewin-Schein's linear, staged theoretical framework (Lewin, 1947; Schein, 1992, 1999) and Sathe's (1985; 1993) circular, continuous approach - with supportive findings from IS and KMS implementation factor research. To guide a later analysis, conceptual variables/factors are introduced with concrete examples for comparison and clarification.

2.1 Change Paradigms Guiding KMS Implementations

Earlier studies on success factors in IS and KMS implementation projects (e.g. Levasseur, 2001; Seeley, 2000) typically focused on the well-known Lewin-Schein change paradigm and an extension (Kolb & Frohman, 1970). Since Lewin's (1947) theory stimulated research but did not isolate influences, Schein (e.g. 1992; 1999) made it more concrete in empirical studies of coercive persuasion, group dynamics training, and management development. Kolb and Frohman's (1970) model of the consulting process put further emphasis on the relationship between client and consultant and the nature of their joint work. As argued in the first chapter, there are additional reasons for selection: the Lewin-Schein change paradigm places the most emphasis on culture change, serves as a means of integrating material from other process studies (Armenakis & Bedeian, 1999, p. 304), and its application to the new setting of KMS has explicitly been encouraged by a fellow researcher (Seeley, 2000, p. 29). While the theoretical framework presents important cultural insights on an individual, group, and organizational level, some assumptions have attracted criticism.

First, it oversimplifies culture change by considering the normal state of organizations as "frozen" (Macredie & Sandom, 1999, p. 248; Myers, 1994, p. 54). Second, there are specified beginning and ending points for the change paradigm which may have been appropriate for relatively bounded, stable groups and firms. Under today's flexible, turbulent, and uncertain environmental and organizational conditions, such a model might become less applicable (Orlikowski & Hofman, 1997, pp. 11-12). Third, user groups or organization members are to some extent deemed recalcitrant and resistant to culture change; some social force is needed for motivation. Given the increasing acceptance and diffusion of computing skills, the majority of affected stakeholders is not always opposing. The process model's assumed behavioral rigidity may no longer be appropriate (Srinivasan & Davis, 1987, p. 67). Fourth and last, Schein takes a rather stable and deep (less conscious, less tangible, less visible) perspective of culture: it "is so stable and difficult to change because it represents the accumulated learning of the group - the ways of thinking, feeling, and perceiving the world that have made the group successful" (Schein, 1999, p. 21).

Nonaka (1991, p. 97) and others have challenged linear, staged change paradigms in the context of KM where they claim that new knowledge generation requires organizations "to re-create the company and everyone in it in a non-stop process of personal and organizational self-renewal." Many argue that a purely linear A-to-Z transition with a limited number of variables is not favorable when designing change programs. "Feedback could take us to Z and back before we reach our destination, with a myriad of unconsidered interconnected variables influencing our journey" (Stickland, 1998, p. 132). Change is often broken up into small pieces that are then supposed to be managed. But the task is to manage the dynamics and not the pieces, the key to success is not attending to each piece in isolation but it is connecting and balancing all pieces (Duck, 2001, p. 57). "Changes have multiple causes and are to be explained more by loops than lines" (Pettigrew, 1990, p. 270). As opposed to a Newtonian perspective and as an expansion of traditional theories, this group of authors favors nonlinear, continuous change paradigms more congruent with notions of complexity and chaos (Eisenhardt, 2000, p. 703; Hatch, 1993, pp. 660-661; Marshak, 1993, p. 412).

According to Ginzberg (1981b, p. 48), a sequential handling of issues may no longer be valid for present day implementations. Contemporary IS' complexity might necessitate a more dynamic handling of critical success factors; they are rather themes that run across all implementation stages. Consequently, I argue that the understanding of KMS implementation projects may benefit from (also) applying change models based on a continuous-change-process-paradigm (Carroll & Hatakenaka, 2001; Pettigrew, 1990; Weeks & Galunic, 2001). The selected model - proposed by Sathe (1985, 1993) - places as much emphasis on culture change as the Lewin-Schein change paradigm but takes a more dynamic perspective of culture in constant evolution. I consider it most effective to build on two reinforcing dynamics: organizations that are inclined to (culture) change adopt KM initiatives quickly, and advancing knowledge enables successful change initiatives (Greenwood, 2000, p. 11; Storey & Barnett, 2000, p. 154).

2.2   Linear, Staged Change

2.2.1   Lewin-Schein's Conceptualization of Change

The theoretical framework, widely acknowledged both in descriptive studies (e.g. Keen et al., 1982; Zand & Sorensen, 1975) and prescriptive analysis (e.g.

Lucas & Plimpton, 1972; Urban, 1974), views groups and organizations as moving from an old stage of quasi-stationary equilibrium to a new one. Those equilibriums are maintained by driving forces promoting change and resisting forces maintaining the status quo. Changes can be inflicted by adjusting their combination and strength toward a desired state (Macredie & Sandom, 1999, p. 248; Zand & Sorensen, 1975, p. 534). Since the first approach increases resistance with symptoms of higher aggressiveness, lower constructiveness, and higher emotionality, the second approach should be preferred (Lewin, 1947, p. 209). If the change management effort is to succeed, the change paradigm suggests key issues which must be resolved, e.g. reasons for change, likely organizational impacts, and measures for evaluation (Ginzberg, 1981a, p. 463).

The change paradigm has special appeal to implementation researchers since major organizational changes are inflicted by the introduction of IS while consultants and managers have to assume the role of change agents. It allows for a structured, staged conceptualization and management of culture change; "looking before you leap" is an accepted managerial practice. If change is to happen and be permanent, i.e. to achieve good implementation results, midlife or mature organizations have to pass through all three stages depicted in table 2. Those take considerable time to unfold and efforts of bypassing and mistakes in any stage might slow down implementation or even negate hard-won progress (Armenakis & Bedeian, 1999, p. 303). The corresponding sub stages highlight a sequence of critical success factors and prior explanations of success and failure for IS and KMS implementation projects (Keen et al., 1982, p. 128). The model's predictions will be used for later theory testing or time-series analysis, i.e. goodness of fit-testing (Yin, 1994, pp. 113-118).

Table 2: A Model of Transformative Change

Stage One Unfreezing: creating the motivation to change	• Disconfirmation • Creation of survival anxiety or guilt • Creation of psychological safety to overcome learning anxiety
Stage Two Cognitive restructuring: learning new concepts and new meanings for old concepts	• Imitation of and identification with role models • Scanning for solutions and trial-and-error learning
Stage Three Refreezing: internalizing new concepts and meanings	• Incorporation into self-concept and identity • Incorporation into ongoing relationships

Sources: Schein (1992, pp. 298-303; 1999, p. 117).

2.2.2   Unfreezing

In Lewin-Schein's first stage - "unfreezing: creating the motivation to change" - people become aware of the need for culture change and see the necessity to deviate from prior behavior patterns and mind-sets (Srinivasan & Davis, 1987, p. 65). They must continuously refine their organization's knowledge-based core capabilities which would otherwise result in core rigidities or cultural inertia (Leonard, 1998, p. 30; Tushman & O'Reilly, 1996, p. 18). Here, a parallel can be drawn to KMS implementation projects that aim to identify and leverage the organization's knowledge in order to remain competitive and innovative (Hackbarth, 1998, p. 590; Meso & Smith, 2000, p. 226; Nonaka, 1991, pp. 96-97; O'Dell & Grayson, 1998, p. 327; von Krogh, 1998, p. 133). Firms realize the need to refine their intellectual capabilities and resources (Zack, 1999, p. 125). Three intertwined processes, i.e. sub stages, create motivation to change: first, disconfirming data causing serious discomfort and disequilibrium to the organization; second, a connection between disconfirming data and important goals and ideals leading to anxiety and/or guilt; and third, sufficient psychological safety, meaning having enough sense of identity and integrity to explore new opportunities (Schein, 1992, pp. 298-299).

"To break open the shell of complacency and self-righteousness, it is sometimes necessary to bring about deliberately an emotional stir-up" (Lewin, 1947, p. 211). Disconfirming data are mostly symptomatic without revealing the true source of troubles. Disequilibrium is created instead, making the organization members uncomfortable by simply pointing out that something has gone wrong. Some goals are not met or some of the business processes are not accomplishing what they are supposed to: e.g. sales are off, customer complaints are up, or there is high employee turnover (Schein, 1992, p. 299). Employees must deeply experience dissatisfaction with the prevailing status quo leading to a lack of confidence in the organization and themselves.

Dissemination of information - especially those previously restricted to top management - is the most widely used method for spreading disconfirmation (Spector, 1989, p. 30). Beer (1988, pp. 1-2) recommends four approaches suiting change agents. "Top-down creation of competitive awareness" entails the generation of problem discussions among employees through information about the firm's competitive environment, e.g. benchmarking (O'Dell & Grayson, 1998, p. 171). "Bottom-up communication of employee concerns" is a contrasting path. Attitude surveys, i.e. interviews and questionnaires, are powerful tools for shaking up superiors. "Joint diagnosis of business problems" complements the mere presentation of disconfirming data. Managers and employees must arrive at a common understanding and shared explanation of challenges. "Setting high standards and expectations" combines demands for profit performance with guidelines for specific behaviors.

Disconfirmation alone does not produce motivation to change, as long as it is not linked to important objectives and ideals. The same holds true for expensive KMS implementation projects: these get support when they are somehow related to business purposes or competitiveness. Several benefit calculations may be used, e.g. cost savings, product/service innovations, and time to market (Alavi & Leidner, 1999, p. 22; Davenport et al., 1998, p. 50; Wilson, 2000, p. 9). Insufficiently specified business objectives are severe obstacles to KM initiatives (Lucier & Torsilieri, 1997, p. 15; Storey & Barnett, 2000, p. 154). Once the linkage is clear - and disconfirming facts can no longer be denied - the organization members begin to feel survival anxiety or guilt.

My case discussion will explore disconfirmation and business purpose linkage factors (respectively denoted by "DIS" and "BPL" in chapter four) and their application to create survival anxiety. Since KMS use is generally not mandatory (Lucas, 1981, p. 8), both factors create the necessary impetus and motivation for end users. However, learning anxiety will be the consequence as soon as employees realize the need for learning new habits and ways of thinking. They try to preserve the organization's identity - once a sustainable source of success - even though this would cause organizational failure. Continuous adaptations to the environment become impossible (Schein, 1992, p. 300).

The complex change dynamics are created by the interaction of these two anxieties that have to be addressed by change agents. First of all, survival anxiety or guilt should be greater than learning anxiety. Furthermore, learning anxiety should rather be reduced instead of increasing survival anxiety or guilt. Schein (1999, pp. 124-126) advocates psychological safety for reducing learning anxiety, i.e. seeing new ways to work on problems, as well as a direction of learning that was not obvious before, all without fearing a loss of integrity and identity. "Psychological support in unfreezing is an emotional climate that leads one to feel that ineffectiveness is undesirable but can be remedied and that facing up to it is, in the long run, more useful and satisfying than denying it" (Zand & Sorensen, 1975, p. 535). It can be created by simultaneously paying attention to eight factors: a compelling positive vision towards change, formal training, involvement of the learners in designing their own informal methods of learning, informal training that takes into account the group as a whole, practice fields, coaches and feedback, support groups of people experiencing similar difficulties, and consistent systems and structures, e.g. incentive and reward systems.

The innovation, organizational behavior, and IS implementation literature consistently establishes only four matching factors' impact on rollout success or failure: top management support, commitment, user involvement, and user training (e.g. Finlay & Forghani, 1998, p. 58; Ginzberg, 1981b, pp. 47-55; Hahn & Subramani, 2000, p. 309; Krovi, 1993, p. 334; Stein & Zwass, 1995, p. 106; Storey & Barnett, 2000, p. 154). For the purpose of my analysis, top management support incorporates the change vision, coaching, feedback, and the provision of consistent systems and structures. User involvement mandates the participative development of KMS and change process. User training involves formal and informal trainings, practice fields, as well as support groups of people experiencing similar difficulties, e.g. user champions. Finally, commitment is included in my theoretical framework due to its widespread application to IS implementation studies. However, the comparison with other isolated factors indicates that commitment is rather an indicator for change motivation than a true intervention. I posit that this factor is mainly influenced by extrinsic and intrinsic forms of motivation and/or top management support.

Earlier findings on the first critical success factor - top management support - are in congruence with 46% of the respondents to an international KM survey: a lack of executive commitment and support was seen as one of the major "soft" obstacles to the successful introduction of KM (Chase, 1997, p. 46). Large scale rollouts inflict massive change with potential instantaneous shock on organizations: they break open the prevailing status quo and require significant changes of jobs and processes. Top management can support these transformational KM projects through encouragements of systems development efforts and the allocation of non-routine resources. Logistics, money, and personnel give the organizational experiment momentum (Keen et al., 1982, p. 130; Schultz, Slevin, & Pinto, 1987, p. 36; Tyran & George, 1993, p. 7). Support from executives is less essential for smaller change initiatives, e.g. improvements of individual functions or processes.

Employees are wary of (culture) change and will show resistance unless top management sends messages that KM is critical to the company's success, provide funding and resources for an adequate (technology) infrastructure, and clarify what types of knowledge matter most to the company (Davenport & Prusak, 2000, p. 156). In addition, they must manage employees' expectations that KM often requires a long-term change management initiative (De Long & Seemann, 2000, p. 43; King et al., 2002, p. 93). Obviously, top management support for KMS implementation projects and culture are interdependent: management teams committed to KM will likely have influenced some aspects of knowledge-intensive cultures and support changes in performance assessments, key to altering motivation (Davenport et al., 1998, pp. 54-55).

However, few investigations have tried to determine what type of managerial support is likely and/or organizationally appropriate. Jarvenpaa and Ives (1991, p. 206) make a clear distinction between executive participation as "activities or substantive personal interventions in the management of IT" and executive involvement as a psychological state, "reflecting the degree of importance placed on information technology". While their empirical research found only moderate support for the prediction that executive participation is positively associated with an organization's progressive use of IS, strong evidence for executive involvement was found. In contrast, other researchers predicted that it is favorable to "unfreezing" when executives and line managers get personally involved with analysis and solution and revise some of their former assumptions (Teng et al., 1996, p. 278; Zand & Sorensen, 1975, p. 545). The case discussion will consequently carefully explore managerial roles, types of support, and their perceived impact.

Management must make a credible attempt to communicate the nature and impact of proposed changes related to the introduction of new technology, i.e. building and communicating a compelling vision and business case for KM investments (De Long & Seemann, 2000, p. 43; Levasseur, 2001, p. 72). "A clear corporate vision that stresses the organization's goals and values (i.e., valuing knowledge) and the role that knowledge plays in achieving those goals are fundamental parts of a strong knowledge culture" (Gold et al., 2001, p. 195). In addition, change agents must choose an appropriate terminology to avoid misinterpretations and uncertainty (Davenport & Prusak, 2000, p.158).

While providing some guidance, the vision should remain open-ended and allow for a variety of interpretations. Less ambiguity gives the impression of orders and instructions which harm the personal commitment required for the leverage of knowledge (Nonaka, 1991, pp. 103-104). Visionary leadership enables culture change while command-and-control, top-down micromanagement inhibits it; doubters do not feel any longer that they have a say in adopting new ways of working (Levasseur, 2001, p. 73; Spector, 1989, p. 33). Put differently, management should specify a general direction for the culture change without insisting on specific solutions (Beer et al., 1990, p. 159). Since culture change is often short-lived, i.e. employees regularly revert to a previous level of behavior, permanency of the new level for a desired period should be part of the vision (Lewin, 1947, p. 211). The KM initiative should not be perceived as another short-term project demanding precious resources (Rothnie, 2001, p. 188).

The second critical success factor - commitment - is required to create a climate and a contract for change. Close attention and effort for careful acculturation are mandatory: "change must be self-motivated and based on a "felt need" with a contract between user and implementer built on mutual credibility and commitment" (Keen, 1981, p. 26). The psychological contract entails goals and expectations for the planned IS (Jin & Franz, 1986, p. 69; Schultz et al., 1987, p. 36). The findings are in line with Ginzberg's (1981b, pp. 54-55) identification of three critical issues for successful IS implementations, the two with the highest explanatory power pertaining to commitment. "Commitment to change" describes the willingness to accommodate changes in behavior, procedures, etc., which are necessary for IS to work. "Commitment to the project" pertains to a more direct commitment of managers and users. They must ensure a smooth systems requirements assessment at pre-design, followed by a post-implementation check whether the IS meets all specifications (Tyran & George, 1993, p. 7). Successful rollouts require both personal commitment and action from managers and users, as well as organizational commitment; alone neither is sufficient.

Kolb and Frohman's (1970, pp. 54-56) sub stages "scouting" and "entry" also emphasize the change agents' careful attention to "unfreezing", especially the negotiation of a psychological contract. Later implementation efforts may be futile when an organization is not inclined to change from the outset (Zand & Sorensen, 1975, p. 542). During "scouting", the nature of the client's problem is identified. Facts and knowledge about all events leading up to the current (diffi-cult) situation are explored (Jin & Franz, 1986, p. 69). Since client and consult-ant have not yet committed themselves to working with the other, each party is free to seek some preliminary data about the other: while the client is trying to acquire resources and solutions, the consultant is "scouting" his or her interests, priorities, and values to decide whether to take on the assignment. The client system's following characteristics should be considered: major resources and limitations, cultural and social norms and values, relationships among subsys-tems (e.g. departments, divisions, and subsidiaries) and with the environment (e.g. competitors, customers, and suppliers), attitudes toward authority and change, and general inclination to improvement.

Since culture change must make use of recognized power structures, choos-ing a formal entry point in the client system is non-trivial. Resentment and reser-vations by line managers during "unfreezing" can cause major difficulties during later "cognitive restructuring": data are withheld; managers do not become suffi-ciently involved in developing solutions and do not understand alternative inter-ventions and consequences. Results are only a superficial commitment to change, a lack of confidence in the change agent, and a general resistance of the top-down change management initiative (Zand & Sorensen, 1975, p. 542). After the establishment of a formal entry point, client and consultant begin to negotiate a psychological contract, i.e. determining who will champion the KMS imple-mentation project and specifically how the change management initiative will be carried out (Jin & Franz, 1986, p. 69). Emphasis is placed on congruent expecta-tions and perceptions; both parties' potential contributions should be outlined in some form of (contractual) agreement. To establish credibility and influence, Kolb and Frohman (1970, p. 56) recommend to build a collaborative relation-ship between client and consultant, e.g. stakeholder representative task forces and joint planning exercises.

The third critical success factor - user involvement - mandates an active par-ticipation of all affected stakeholders in the intended culture change. A lack of effective communication and involvement creates huge barriers which cannot be scaled in later stages (Levasseur, 2001, p. 72). According to Keen et al. (1982, pp. 139-140), first implementation obstacles can be overcome by measures of "expectation setting" and "technology mobilization". To avoid unrealistic expectations, the project team and sponsors should learn from the experience of other sites, communicate resources, timeframes, and commitments required, make arrangements for consulting, support, and education, and identify the appropriate mechanisms for stakeholder and user involvement, e.g. joint understanding and diagnosis of business problems. Once the organization members develop a common understanding of problems and possible remedies, management can mobilize the initial commitment to trigger the change process (Beer et al., 1990, p. 161).

Reconsidering earlier findings, Ginzberg (1981a, pp. 475-476) no longer proposes user involvement in order to foster a sense of ownership and to increase the assessment of system requirements' quality (Tyran & George, 1993, p. 7). Rather, users should be involved so that they can form realistic expectations about the IS. Building on the first measure, "technology mobilization" involves the nomination of carefully selected user representatives, i.e. internal change agents, coordinators, and educators, particularly in "unfreezing" the firm in order to make it more receptive towards change. It is helpful to promote system use under most opportune circumstances in which the use appears both successful and visible (Curley & Gremillion, 1983, p. 206). Common tasks include championing of the IS, demonstrating executive support and leadership, building a forum for discussions around project plans and schedules, defining concepts and vocabulary mandatory for user involvement, and developing skills (Jin & Franz, 1986, p. 69; Keen et al., 1982, pp. 139-140).

Nevertheless, few researchers actually tried to determine what type of user involvement had the greatest impact on success and failure of KMS implementation projects. Nutt (1986, pp. 246-248) makes a clear distinction between four key variations linked to a decreasing amount of commitment: "comprehensive participation" entails the delegation of all implementation efforts to fully representative stakeholder task forces; "complete participation" also calls for full participation of all affected stakeholders, but requires only a framing rather than a specification of implementation details; "delegated participation" makes merely use of selected stakeholder advocates to specify implementation details; finally, "token participation" involves select stakeholders simply for an initial solution framing.

Of particular use is the provision of the fourth critical success factor - user training - which entails explaining the scope of the IS and its relation to the organization (Krovi, 1993, p. 334). Training can furthermore be used to instill teamwork at all organizational levels: individuals should develop new ways of working on the basis of cooperation and knowledge sharing (Brelade & Harman,

2000, p. 28). A learning plan highlighting learning topics, delivery methods, responsibilities, timing, and feedback mechanisms is often a key deliverable for change agents (Seeley, 2000, p. 28).

Schein's (1992, pp. 318-321) concept of "unfreezing and change through technological seduction" appears applicable within the setting of KMS. Often, KM initiatives are deliberate, managed IS implementations to seduce employees into new behaviors. In turn, those require a reexamination - or even a redefinition - of present values, beliefs, and assumptions, i.e. culture change. As soon as the concept's explanatory power has been examined, it could guide an answer to Alavi and Leidner's (2001, p. 126) prior research question: "[M]ust cultural change occur before knowledge management initiatives can be successfully undertaken or can knowledge management initiatives facilitate cultural change?" Interdependence between KM and change initiatives could then either be established or rejected. My case discussion will pay attention to all means fostering psychological safety: top management support, commitment, user involvement, and user training factors (respectively denoted by "TMS", "COM", "UIN", and "UTR" in chapter four).

2.2.3   Cognitive Restructuring

Lewin-Schein's second stage - "cognitive restructuring: learning new concepts and new meanings for old concepts" - implies moving groups and organizations from an old to a new quasi-stationary equilibrium to better cope with a changing environment. It involves the gathering of new information, adopting new behavior, and experiencing the new behavior's contribution to improved performance (Srinivasan & Davis, 1987, p. 65). At this point, the examination of existing IS and the development of new IS gets underway. Success is dependent on maintaining a sense of teamwork and effective communication with affected stakeholders (Levasseur, 2001, p. 73). A particular course of action is chosen and implemented (Krovi, 1993, p. 328). This can be achieved by changes in attitudes and behavior, organizational shake-ups, or any other move into a positive direction. After sufficient motivation to change has been created, there are two different paths to move on with "cognitive restructuring" (Schein, 1999, pp. 128-129).

On the one hand, "imitation of and identification with role models" works best if the new ways of working and the concepts to be acquired are easy to understand. Academics and practitioners agree that example setting, i.e. individuals, organizational units, and pilot studies can encourage culture change: "they provide a vision of the future, and they can also help spread dissatisfaction with the status quo" (Spector, 1989, p. 32). Once the IS' capabilities and implications are appreciated, it can be deployed to the rest of the organization (Orlikowski, 1992, p. 369). Units which have either been successfully revitalized or have already become accustomed to new practices can serve as role models for the entire company (Beer et al., 1990, p. 165). Their successful application of managerial innovations fosters credibility with line managers and a better understanding of the change process (Beer, 1988, p. 3).

On the other hand, "trial-and-error learning" provides a better fit with the learner's personality and happens by scanning the work environment for possible options. Prototyping the KMS and the change initiative are often effective means for better communication, building commitment, and developing more concrete appreciation from stakeholders (Krovi, 1993, p. 334; Teng et al., 1996, p. 282). The learner has a personal choice about the means but not about the goal. Even though experiments are natural organizational phenomena, few firms make explicit use of them for knowledge purposes. While many organizations disseminate best practices to potential internal users, they forego the benefits of best practices leveraged to other business units (Fahey & Prusak, 1998, p. 272). Both mechanisms entail a cognitive restructuring of some underlying assumptions shifting one's own frame of reference. Such cognitive shifts are feasible provided that the company has created enough psychological safety in the first stage. This goes even further than mere rationalization; in my opinion it can be described as "retooling".

Most change processes call attention to the need for behavior change paving the ground for later cognitive restructuring. In line with McElroy (2000, pp. 35-37), Schein (1992, p. 302) suggests interventions which give rise to desired behaviors instead of commanding them. Due to their greater importance to continuous-change-process-paradigms, incentive and reward systems will be explored in a later section. Unless cognitive restructuring has taken place, it is likely that social systems exposed to that kind of stress fall back to their former natural state. Similar to traditional IS implementations, top management usually provides some directive or mandate while a central project team has the responsibility to carry out the application's rollout and maintenance. Local management retains partial responsibility for implementation and adaptation to local needs. Keen at al. (1982, pp. 132-140) advocate the definition of a clear maintenance strategy and ongoing reviews between central and local teams. Ambiguous authorities and a lack of clear signals from the top can generate negative political stress.

Kolb and Frohman (1970, pp. 56-61) dispense more advise in the consulting process model's corresponding sub stages "diagnosis", "planning", and "action". Diagnostic data should focus on the discrepancy between the client's felt problem and goals as well as on the client's and consultant's resources to improve the situation. To obtain the necessary information, interviews, observations, previous performance data, and questionnaires are most commonly used. Joint gathering of data and empathy help the consultant to appreciate the client system's culture and language, i.e. interpreting events the way the client perceives them.

Again, commitment and readiness to change are mandatory on an individual and organizational level. The consultant should explore internal resources which can be developed and utilized for problem solution. Through their accelerated development, external dependency should be reduced in the long-term.

Change should be planned cooperatively with the client to ensure appropriateness, understanding, and commitment to execution. Successful "cognitive restructuring" seems to be supported by managerial evaluations and reviews of alternatives and consequences, sequential improvements of proposals, and keeping executives informed of progress (Zand & Sorensen, 1975, p. 542). During the first planning step, clear-cut objectives for behavior change are defined in detail. For people/culture change, a mix of formal, explicit interventions and informal, implicit interventions must be selected. Consistent systems and structures, e.g. promotions, incentive and reward systems, and working procedures, belong to the first group, while norms and values of the organization, e.g. handling of conflicts and peer expectations, belong to the latter. The failure of many change initiatives pertains to unanticipated consequences: technical changes, e.g. KMS implementation projects, often do not account and plan for the social changes inflicted, e.g. power shifts (Kolb & Frohman, 1970, p. 60). Change agents might fail to communicate the benefits of the proposed IS and new way of working.

Employee resistance is often treated as a negative and irrational force that needs to be overcome by all available means. Nevertheless, it ensures that the interventions' consequences are carefully considered before implementation. Consequently, Zand and Sorensen (1975, p. 545) identified the change agents' feeling that analysis was concluded too quickly for a thorough analysis of alternatives as a final unfavorable force to "cognitive restructuring". My case discussion will examine the path chosen to implement culture change, i.e. example setting factors vs. trial-and-error factors (respectively denoted by "ESE" and "TAE" in chapter four). Emphasis is placed on the means and quality of cooperation between top management, central project team, consultants, and affected stakeholders. Since the Lewin-Schein change paradigm places less importance on extrinsic and intrinsic motivators, they are discussed in relation with Sathe's model.

2.2.4   Refreezing

Finally in Lewin-Schein's third stage - "refreezing: internalizing new concepts and meanings" - the new distribution of social forces is reinforced to maintain and stabilize the new quasi-stationary equilibrium (Zand & Sorensen, 1975, p. 534). The new behavior and set of underlying assumptions are solidified to bring back the organization to stability (Krovi, 1993, p. 328). The change agents must work actively with the organization members to ensure the new IS' installation, testing, debugging, usage, measuring, and enhancements. Just delivering an executive report and leaving the implementation to the affected stakeholders is not acceptable. Freezing requires strong and determined leadership, as well as commitment to active involvement until new behaviors have replaced those existing prior to the culture change (Levasseur, 2001, p. 73). Unlike simple reorganizations or mechanical fixes, culture change takes time and is hard work. It is easy to "unfreeze" the traditional values and beliefs of an organization and begin to change them but it is a different challenge to "refreeze" the change.

"Refreezing" comprises the following major activities: first, the determination of evidence for behavioral and cultural shifts, i.e. technology's fit with people/culture; second, the IS' organizational integration, i.e. technology's fit with strategy and structure (Grover & Davenport, 2001, pp. 12-13; Jin & Franz, 1986, p. 71); third, the dissemination of confirming data. Employees often revert to their former behavior patterns unless the new behavior is both congruent with the learner's personality and expectations of social and work peers. In this case, new habits and ways of thinking become personally internalized and later group norms and routines (Schein, 1999, p. 129).

Kolb and Frohman's (1970, p. 61) sub stage "evaluation" requires a thorough assessment of behavior change. All parties must give careful attention to testing and devising measures and standards for evaluating results. "Refreezing" is supported by evidence of successful application, user satisfaction with the new IS and ways of working, and positive feedback from change agents to stakeholders (Zand & Sorensen, 1975, p. 542). To reduce long-term dependency on consultants, client self-analysis - based on objective evaluation indices - is encouraged. Depending on whether the planned solution is actually working, change agents must either decide on conclusion, on progress with "cognitive restructuring", or even on return to "unfreezing".

For successful conclusion, the new behavior and set of cognitions have to be reinforced, i.e. to be made a permanent part of an individuals' repertoire (Srinivasan & Davis, 1987, p. 65). Once again confirming data is produced to stop the employees' search and coping processes. When these confirming data are fixed, they will stay like this until disconfirming data set in again (Schein, 1992, p. 303). The central project team faces the problem of institutionalizing and embedding the IS into the organizational context. It is also important to "refreeze" the level of trust and cooperation that evolved between the rollout participants. Change agents should gradually withdraw and users should finally assume ownership and responsibility for the IS' maintenance and evolution (Jin & Franz, 1986, p. 71; Keen, 1981, p. 26). The transformation of the central project team into a service unit with capabilities for consulting and teaching to provide ongoing user assistance is helpful. Everybody should feel free to discuss post-implementation problems and further IS enhancements (Keen et al., 1982, p. 141; Krovi, 1993, p. 334).

Since consultant-client relationships are temporary by definition, the issue of termination should receive considerable attention throughout the change management initiative. Kolb and Frohman's (1970, pp. 61-62) corresponding sub stage "termination" distinguishes withdrawal after success or failure. Two measures establish implementation success: first, a solution of the client's problem with an accomplishment of the respective goals; second, an improvement of the client's ability to tackle similar challenges in the future. Consultants may either leave too early with the initial objectives accomplished but abandoning the helpless client in spite of future turbulences; no attempt is made to reestablish stability. On the opposite, consultants may linger for too long, increasing the client's external dependency in the long term. Failure is even more embarrassing: while the client loses money and time, the consultant's professional reputation is at stake. Mutual face-saving efforts commonly preclude learning from experiences. Common reasons are managers ignoring valuable proposals or solutions incompatible with the needs and resources of the organization (Zand & Sorensen, 1975, p. 545).

Since KMS implementation success is established by the measures outlined in chapter one, my case discussion focuses on moderating organizational integration factors, i.e. responsibility transfer, behavioral and cultural diagnosis factors, and confirmation factors (respectively denoted by "OIN", "BCD", and "CON" in chapter four). I will unearth examples of confirming data to stop employees' adaptation processes.

2.3   Circular, Continuous Change

2.3.1   Sathe's Conceptualization of Change

In contrast to the three-stage Lewin-Schein change paradigm, Sathe's (1985; 1993) model presents the underlying self-perpetuating processes that shape organizational cultures and their manifestations, depicted in figure 4. Again, those processes' recommended intervention factors serve as predictors of success and failure for KMS implementation projects. They will be used for later theory testing or pattern-matching, i.e. goodness of fit-testing (Yin, 1994, pp. 106-110). Change in this context is viewed as an ongoing process rather than as a project that can be completed (Carroll & Hatakenaka, 2001, pp. 77-78). Several dynamic processes have to interact before culture can be modified. Mangers can facilitate culture change following two broad approaches: getting people to buy into new values and beliefs (processes one, two, and three) and socializing and removing members of the organization (processes four and five). If the prevailing culture is to be preserved, managers must focus continually on the well-functioning of the processes in order to ensure that cultural momentum does not slow down and lead to cultural drift.

Whereas the Lewin-Schein change paradigm explains resistance to change with driving and resisting social forces, Sathe's (1985, pp. 381-384) argumentation takes into account the content and/or the strength of the prevailing organizational cultures. On the one hand, changes in culture's content may entail reorderings, modifications, or even removals of existing beliefs and values. Sometimes nonexistent beliefs and values, i.e. those pertaining to knowledge-intensive cultures, have to be integrated. Employees will show greater resistance to change when a larger number of important shared assumptions are affected and a movement toward more alien, i.e. less intrinsically appealing, shared assumptions is desired. On the other hand, there is greater cultural resistance in strong organizational cultures than in weak ones: in the first case, a greater number of organization members must acquire new concepts and ways of working. Generally, culture change will be more difficult and time-consuming the greater the cultural resistance and the number of people affected.

Figure 4: How Culture Tends to Perpetuate Itself

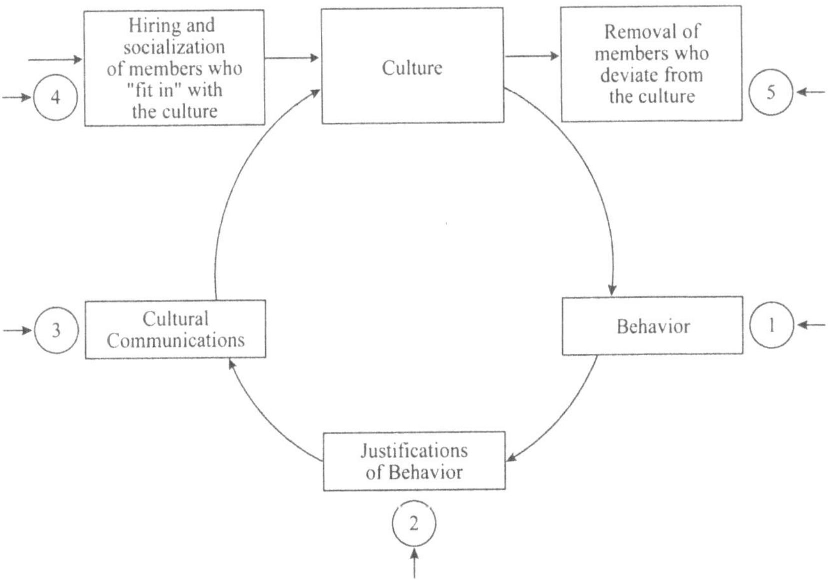

Source: Sathe (1985, p. 385; 1993, p. 337).

2.3.2   Behavior

One of the most effective ways to change people's beliefs and values is an intervention into the first process - "behavior". And IS are basically "a package of ideas about how people should work differently" (Markus & Benjamin, 1997, p. 58). For successful KM initiatives, greater self-discipline and personal responsibility for communications and relationships are mandatory (Drucker, 1988, p. 47). Employees should reach out to peers for knowledge sharing across functional and organizational barriers instead of playing political games, e.g. "not invented here" and knowledge hoarding (Seeley, 2000, p. 25). Before the change management initiative begins, culture has already set the stage for employee behavior: when it values internal competition for resources and individualistic, short-term incentives and rewards, knowledge leverage does not occur. For those firms, the return on KMS investment is likely to be unsatisfactory. In contrast, if employees engage in cooperation and teamwork, knowledge-orientation will be fostered and the KMS implementation project is likely to add significantly to the bottom line (Kydd & Jones, 1989, p. 280).

Since 56% of the participants in an Ernst & Young study named changing people's behavior as the biggest difficulty in knowledge leverage (Ruggles, 1998, p. 86), change agents have to confront inappropriate or ineffective behavior early (Beer, 1988, p. 4). Both Sathe (1985, pp. 360-363; 1993, pp. 335-336) and Schein (1992, p. 302) argue in unison that culture changes can precede, follow, or occur simultaneously with behavior changes. The first occurs when there is persistent and irrefutable evidence that certain new assumptions have greater value and validity than the existing ones. Soon the organization members face the need to acquire new knowledge, competence, and skill in order to behave in accordance with the new assumptions. The second occurs when the existing underlying assumptions cannot be replaced quickly and invalidated with compelling evidence. It often takes time to establish and validate the "superiority" of novel assumptions (Sathe, 1985, p. 384). Finally, both behavior and culture can change concurrently. The resulting permanent change is mutually reinforcing and self-sustaining: employees strongly believe in and value their new habits which is intrinsically motivating and this in turn reinforces the behavior (Sathe, 1985, p. 363).

This learning fosters effectiveness even further and enhances commitment to culture change (Beer et al., 1990, p. 165). The organization members would e.g. benefit from a KMS in a sense that it would increase their responsiveness and innovativeness in spite of an increasingly complex environment, a task no longer possible without IT (Hackbarth, 1998, p. 590). Vice versa, the employees' behavior, i.e. using the KMS, becomes even more internalized. Managers should be aware that behavior changes do not always lead to changes in culture due to countervailing processes. When no culture change is feasible or intended, e.g. in a restricted timeframe or when a transient situation requires only a temporary adaptation of behavior, the employees' behavior must be constantly monitored to ensure compliance. Lacking a constant "payoff" from rewards and punishments, novel behavior quickly dries up (Sathe, 1993, p. 336). Employees require incentives and rewards to leverage knowledge (Hansen et al., 1999, p. 133). Those should be well aligned with the intended group culture: carelessly applied, they can quickly undermine the behavioral shift top management wants to encourage.

To make people change, extrinsic and intrinsic sources of motivation have to change as well: from incentives and rewards promoting reinvention, knowledge hoarding, and individual achievements to those emphasizing reaching out to peer groups, knowledge sharing, and community participation (Gold et al., 2001, p. 189; Seeley, 2000, p. 25). Motivators reflect the realization that such behavior is a desired aspect of employees' work (Stein & Zwass, 1995, p. 108). Stewart et al. (2000, p. 47) agree that "the ability to engage employees in the process and to illicit from them the codification of their expertise in a usable form is typically the real challenge".

Motivation's importance has also been recognized by the international KM study mentioned above: 46% of the respondents consider rewards/recognition as severe obstacles to successful KM initiatives (Chase, 1997, p. 46). Individualistic incentive and reward systems and rapid downsizing will only lead to intense competition between employees; team-based motivators can encourage individuals to share personal knowledge for the sake of the group's and the organization's overall performance (von Krogh, 1998, pp. 142-144). Top management should promote, recognize, and reward people for the adoption of best practices, both individually and for collective improvement (O'Dell & Grayson, 1998, p. 172).

The literature makes a further distinction between extrinsic and intrinsic motivators. On the one hand, extrinsic motivation can coerce behavior changes; employees are not sure about the change's intended benefits but feel they have to comply with new rules and aspirations. While commitment is more desirable to achieve change, Beer (1988, p. 3) suggests that compliance is inevitable for a start. It is gradually transformed into commitment once people engage in new behavior and participate in the change design. On the other hand, intrinsic motivation makes people truly want to learn and adapt new behaviors, i.e. they believe in the need for change. Intrinsic motivation caters well for tacit knowledge transfer that warrants neither direct observation nor a relation between outputs and particular employees. Helping one another reinforces employees' technical competency and consequent feelings of self-esteem. Only the absence of feedback about successful adoptions - likely in many KMS-mediated exchanges - may mitigate this motivation's strength (Goodman & Darr, 1998, p. 421). Moreover, intrinsic motivators cannot be changed and steered as well as extrinsic motivators (Osterloh & Frey, 2000, p. 540; 2001, p. 102).

According to Sathe (1985, pp. 386-387) permanent change can best be achieved if motivation stems from intrinsic driving factors; the heavier the use of extrinsic motivators, the more difficult it is to achieve a corresponding culture change as it denies people to seize the inherent worth of new assumptions. O'Dell and Grayson (1998, pp. 168-170) found only a minority of firms using extrinsic motivators for knowledge sharing. Organizations with successful KM initiatives focused rather on a close tie with their employees' daily work and personnel development systems. Schein (1992, p. 299) argues that the serious discomfort and disequilibrium caused by disconfirming data often provides the necessary intrinsic incentive to learn the new behavior. Change agents should make use of environmental threats, crises, and others disrupting the status quo and leading to deviations from regular organizational routines (Sathe, 1985, pp. 387-388). Then it might be easier to articulate and demonstrate the need for change, to adopt new habits and ways of thinking. Whereas an external crisis is a vehicle for managing change, companies do not necessarily need the precipice for adaptations to new conditions. "Change can be stimulated and managed without a crisis" (Beer, 1988, p. 1).

Generally, incentives and rewards to encourage a behavioral shift should be long-term oriented and tie in with the organization's evaluation and compensation systems (Davenport et al., 1998, p. 54). Within a knowledge environment, a mixture of short-term and long-term motivators might be applicable as well: whereas rewards and incentives (e.g. recognition) can build initial enthusiasm for knowledge transfer, a KMS has to be self-rewarding to the user in the long term, i.e. offering knowledge needed or expert recognition (Brelade & Harman, 2000, p. 27). To increase acceptance, time for leveraging knowledge must be budgeted; if employees feel that they have to set time away from "real" work, it will not happen. Goodman and Darr (1998, p. 420) recognize that for knowledge leverage to occur there must be both a choice to contribute and to adopt. Contributing means that individuals are willing to share solutions with others across space and time. The sharing may happen as a response to a request for help or when the solution is provided to a knowledge repository. Adopting implies that individuals are willing to search for solutions to problems they encounter. If knowledge givers feel not similarly valued, content runs dry quickly (O'Dell & Grayson, 1998, p. 170).

Beer and Nohria (2000, pp. 134-141) advocate an interesting alternative in this context, a synthesis of two archetypical change management frameworks and their corresponding incentive and reward systems: "theory E" emphasizes the maximization of shareholder value and the motivation of employees through extrinsic motivators, "theory O" strives for the development of organizational capabilities and cultures through trust and emotional commitment to the firm. The authors acknowledge that extrinsic motivators can have negative impact on teamwork, commitment, and organizational learning. This crowding-out effect or undermining is particularly true for expected and monetary rewards that the recipients perceive to be controlling (Osterloh & Frey, 2000, pp. 542-543). Consequently, organizations promoting knowledge leverage through knowledge markets and extrinsic motivators might actually encourage competitive actions and hoarding behavior, both detriments to the free flow of organizational knowledge (McLure Wasko & Faraj, 2000, p. 162). Companies should simultaneously pay attention to both theories to thrive in and adapt to environments in flux; essential are motivators that reinforce change instead of driving it.

Change agents should keep in mind that the type of KM initiative determines incentive and reward systems as well (Hansen et al., 1999, p. 113). For a codification approach, change agents need to develop a consistent system that motivates people to write down their knowledge and provide it to a knowledge repository. Real motivators - no small enticements - are mandatory to get employees encouraged. Both quality and quantity of their contributions should be part of annual target agreements: e.g. at McKinsey & Company, number and frequency of use of a management consultant's publications is an important indicator for promotion decisions (Alavi & Leidner, 1999, p. 22). For a personalization approach, people should be rewarded for direct knowledge exchanges with other people and help provided to colleagues.

My case discussion will explicitly "address the issue of what types of incentives are effective in inculcating organization members with valuable knowledge to contribute and share their knowledge" (Alavi & Leidner, 2001, p. 127) making use of KMS (King et al., 2002, p. 96). It can be predicted that a KMS' effectiveness in leveraging knowledge will be reduced if the extrinsic and intrinsic motivation factors (denoted by "EIM" in chapter four) do not promote sharing behavior. However, if the technological attributes and conditions, e.g. user-friendly interfaces and wizards, reduce the psychological costs of sharing - or even create intrinsic motivation - deliberate and emergent organizational KM processes should prosper (Goodman & Darr, 1998, p. 426; Jarvenpaa & Staples, 2000, p. 131).

2.3.3   Justifications of Behavior

One of the reasons change in behavior does not necessarily produce culture change is the second process - "justifications of behavior". Even if employees' behavior changes, they tend to rationalize their actions in terms of the new formal systems, i.e. extrinsic prime motivations for knowledge exchange, and continue to adhere to the prevailing pattern of beliefs and values. In this case, people might say that their behavior can merely be attributed to incentives and rewards, resulting in compliance in lieu of cultural commitment (Sathe, 1993, pp. 337-338). The case study will in detail unearth behavior rationalization assessment factors (denoted by "BRA" in chapter four), i.e. whether the intrinsic motivation of knowledge exchange has already made the KMS' usage self-perpetuating. This factor has significant overlap with Lewin-Schein's behavioral and cultural diagnosis factor but mandates more constant attention. According to Constant et al. (1994, p. 404), the more employees believe that knowledge leverage is "usual, correct, and socially expected workplace behavior" the more willing they should be to contribute.

Further empirical research has recognized personal beliefs in "fairness", "trust" and "organizational ownership" as favorable to culture change: employees in such organizations show more involvement in IS implementations and knowledge leverage since they feel trusted to do a good job and feel valued for their opinions (Harper, 2001, p. 14; Jarvenpaa & Staples, 2001, p. 165). Managers involved in culture change must pay careful attention to "justifications of behavior" and take the necessary steps for altering them. An alternative approach besides relying on intrinsic motivation requires nullifying inappropriate justifications, i.e. giving employees a way out. Those not accepting the new pattern of beliefs and values should be given the option to leave to a different organization; those left behind are more committed, as they made the choice to stay. This alternative might be dangerous in a way that some valued people may decide to leave without giving change a try. Nonetheless, many of those employees are highly marketable and tend to look for new jobs once they feel coerced. Not complying with employees' expectations and not reverting to proven methods for problem solving is another option for change agents to nullify inappropriate justifications (Sathe, 1985, p. 388).

2.3.4   Cultural Communications

Moving on to the third process - "cultural communications" - it is important to utilize a rich and creative mix of explicit and implicit forms to get employee buy-in and help organizations cope with change and adversity. Change agents must consistently and constantly emphasize the necessity to share and leverage knowledge for the sake of the whole organization (O'Dell & Grayson, 1998, p. 173). Especially the interrelationship between knowledge creation, knowledge leverage, and the change management initiative must be realized and understood. Regressions to traditional ways of working based on direct command and low trust happen too easily when challenges arise (Storey & Barnett, 2000, p. 155). Courage, openness and trust must be explicitly stated values by executives and serve as formulated expectations for employees' behavior. Emphasis should be put on the particular components of a culture which recognize the importance of team players, encourage knowledge creation, and foster a free flow of knowledge (von Krogh, 1998, p. 144).

A communications plan outlining change progress, key messages, target audiences, delivery methods, responsibilities, timing, and feedback mechanisms is often a key deliverable for the central project team (Seeley, 2000, p. 27). Culture change objectives, organizational coordination, status and changes have to be understood by every employee. Feedback mechanisms, i.e. dedicated channels or review meetings, allow for corrections and suggestions from stakeholders (Schultz et al., 1987, pp. 36-40). In particular implicit means of communications, such as the use of appropriate cultural language and symbols, story-telling from company history or individual experience foster a continuous internalization of beliefs and values since they are convincing and memorable. Direct and explicit communication often triggers defensiveness as well as defensive countermoves, i.e. is non-sufficient to build mutual trust (Thomas et al., 2001, p. 869). Major obstacles for culture change are poor vertical communication (Beer and Eisenstat, 2000, p. 37) and a communication campaigns' general lack of credibility. Especially if a new pattern of values and beliefs lacks intrinsic appeal, it is often dismissed as mere corporate propaganda.

As a remedy, cultural communications should not only be credible and emphatic but persuasive as well (Sathe, 1985, p. 389; 1993, p. 338). Messages should be consistent, clear, and perpetually repeated before the employees start to believe that the call for change is not a passing fancy (Duck, 2001, pp. 61-62). Particularly KMS, fostering digital conversations and discussions, can enhance persistence by extending formal communication lines across time and space (Alavi & Leidner, 2001, p. 121; Orlikowski, 1992, p. 368; Thomas et al., 2001, p. 872). "The application of e-mail, intranet, bulletin board, and newsgroup can support the distribution of knowledge throughout the organization and allows organization members to debate, discuss, and interpret information through multiple perspectives" (Bhatt, 2001, p. 72).

The promotion of cultural expectations, norms, and values is fostered, too: change agents can communicate more rapidly and with greater precision to targeted groups; information must no longer move sequentially from person to person but can be spread at once (Dewett & Jones, 2001, p. 8; Yazici, 2002, p. 550). Further advantages include greater access to knowledge repositories (especially from remote locations), improved means for testing and challenging prevailing assumptions and routines, and the creation of new knowledge through discourse (Robey, Boudreau, & Rose, 2000, p. 146). Intelligent agent software can develop employee interest profiles in order to identify the organization members interested in point-to-point electronic messages (O'Dell & Grayson, 1998, p. 162). KMS themselves might serve as an argument for change or even represent important change drivers.

The first intervention into "cultural communications" is the credible communication of the new pattern of beliefs and value. Often, user champions "make decisive contributions [...] by actively and enthusiastically promoting [the KMS'] progress through the critical stages of its development and adoption" (Curley & Gremillion, 1983, p.203). It is important to build personal credibility and to rely on formal and informal face-to-face communication, i.e. backing up words with actual deeds (Jin & Franz, 1986, p. 72; Keen, 1981, p. 30; von Krogh, 1998, p. 145). If a change agent failed to do so in the past, in the worst case the organization must find a substitute as lost credibility is irretrievable. Furthermore, managers should not apparently advocate something that is only in their self-interest. Significant personal sacrifice and loss as a result of the proposed change will build trustworthiness. One of the indirect procedures to foster credibility is to rely on informal means of communication. Especially effective are neutral intermediaries who initially were cynical and opposed to new habits and ways of thinking. The intermediaries' role is two-dimensional: first, providing user assistance for IS learning and operating; second, facilitating the internalization of the IS (Ginzberg, 1981b, p. 69).

Other measures are implicit forms of communication that are regarded as more memorable and plausible, e.g. appropriate cultural language and symbols, story-telling from company history, or individual experience (Sathe, 1985, pp. 390-391; 1993, pp. 338-339; Thomas et al., 2001, p. 879). This is underscored by Thomas et al. (2001, pp. 869-871), who emphasize that story-telling caters well to the communication and presentation of knowledge. Whereas readers and listeners of fictional stories for entertainment will buy internally consistent tales, the audience of stories for fostering change must additionally perceive them in congruence with external reality. A recent development - IBM's "story markup language (SML) - helps to collect and provide access to stories. The software does not only capture the story's internal content but its social context in the form of meta-data, e.g. reasons for telling stories, the teller's knowledge of the audience, the role the audience takes in the telling, and the stories' history. Nevertheless, there is danger that the listeners might infer a contrary moral from the story.

The second intervention into the third process is to strive for an internalization of the new pattern of beliefs and values, to achieve culture persuasion especially if it is less intrinsically appealing to the audience. Similar to Schein (1999, pp. 128-129), a feasible approach is personal identification with one or more persons, e.g. "folk heroes" or "opinion leaders" who believably communicate their attachment or adaptation to the pattern in question. Well suited are persons to whom others naturally turn for guidance and information (Curley & Gremillion, 1983, p. 206). Another possible approach is to persuade people to give it a fair chance, i.e. "try it, you will like it". Without reverting to extrinsic forms of motivation and risking external justifications, managers can appeal to their employees' higher values and challenge them in a positive way. Once they made positive experiences, the new pattern of beliefs and values becomes gradually accepted and internalized (Sathe, 1985, pp. 393-394; 1993, pp. 338-339).

Since only few people can effectively learn about new ideas just by reading books, similarly few people can absorb new ways of working just by applying technologies designed to facilitate them. In contrast, many people learn new ideas from discussions with other people "embodying" the new idea. This proposition of "change as a contact sport" (Markus & Benjamin, 1997, p. 59) has been confirmed by empirical research on organizational cultures and successful IS implementation projects: group actions and group decision-making have positive impact on IS acceptance and succeed in bringing more ideas and people into the implementation process; free information flows minimize contradictory interpretations of messages (Harper, 2001, p. 14). My case discussion will focus on all change communication factors (denoted by "CCO" in chapter four) and their relations to the proposed interventions. It is explored whether KMS can facilitate culture change through additional communication channels.

2.3.5   Hiring, Socializing, and Replacing Employees

The second broad approach to facilitate culture change includes "hiring and socialization of members who "fit in" with the culture" - process four - and "removal of members who deviate from the culture" - process five. It has to be noted that a perfect culture-person fit is not desirable; it is only obligatory to avoid irreconcilable mismatches. To increase culture's strength - the cohesion and order of beliefs and values - a consistent HR philosophy is suggested: a stable workforce offers a higher chance to develop a common cognitive and behavioral ground. To alter culture's content - the number and order of essential shared beliefs and values - attentive HR policies and practices are mandatory to alter the "breed" of employees (Sathe, 1985, pp. 394-395; 1993, p. 339). Davenport and Grover (2001, p. 4) voice the same idea: "We must begin to hire workers for their aptitude and motivation around knowledge, design knowledge activities into everyday roles, and create a culture in which every worker views knowledge management as part of his or her job." Organizations routinely attract and hire people who reinforce this orientation (Davenport et al., 1998, p. 52).

From a KM perspective, "filling jobs" is less relevant than filling knowledge gaps, either current or anticipated. Nevertheless, the use of sophisticated selection procedures - especially those based on "cultural fit" - has dangerous implications: it might rule out some creative and innovative individuals to the detriment of effective KM encouraging precisely those attributes (McElroy, 2000, p. 37). Those predictions have partially been supported by empirical research: successful KM initiatives are less concerned with artificial barriers to the transfer of knowledge; rather they protect their intellectual capabilities and resources by hiring and developing committed, intelligent, and loyal employees and supporting them with a culture based on commitment, collaboration, and learning. Competitiveness and innovativeness therefore result from the organization's ability to faster absorb and integrate external knowledge in order to develop insights faster than competitors (Zack, 1999, p. 141).

The socialization process is especially critical in determining how new members learn the important corporate realities, including organizational cultures. Mentoring is often an effective tool for acculturation (Quinn et al., 1996, p. 73). Tenured employees act as role-models and their protégés try to identify with them or even seek to imitate them due to their accomplishments and virtues. As the new employees bit by bit understand culture's full scope, they gradually become more committed to it. Mentoring programs should also motivate seniors to share personal knowledge with newcomers. Since knowledge is often perceived as a source of influence and power, hoarding tactics have been found in unsuccessful KMS implementation projects (Davenport et al., 1998, p. 52).

Management must open up access to corporate expertise by defining two sets of individual responsibilities: the responsibility to acquire personal knowledge and skills, and the responsibility to help those in need as your own expertise grows (von Krogh, 1998, p. 144). KMS and other material artifacts can embody cultural assumptions as well. Saffold (1988, p. 551) has coined the term artificial penetration which occurs "when intangible elements of the cultural paradigm become embedded in visible cultural artifacts". Knowledge repositories might be useful to accelerate the sharing of knowledge with newcomers, traditionally happening through socialization, storytelling, and the general transmission of corporate rituals and routines (Davenport et al., 1998, p. 45).

According to Beer et al. (1990, p. 163), interventions in processes four and five are quite common once employees have acquired familiarity with vision and new organizational requirements. Replacement sometimes becomes the only final option when people do not accept new ways of working, i.e. when participation and performance appraisal fail. Transfer or termination of some employees and the promotion of others, seem to be widespread if change efforts actually take hold. "If no replacements are taking place there is probably no major culture change going on" (Beer, 1988, p. 4). My case discussion will specifically look for the hiring, socialization, and replacement factors (respectively denoted by "HIR", "SOC", and "REP" in chapter four) introduced in this section. Attention will be paid to the role of KMS in newcomers' mentoring processes. Due to the highly exploratory nature of my research, all isolated conceptual variables/factors represent only first ideas about what makes a KMS implementation project successful. Further refinements - and first ideas for theory synthesis - are derived from the chapter four analysis.

3. Case Study: Siemens ShareNet

The third chapter provides a chronological account of ShareNet's development and international rollout. After a short preface to the case study's unit of analysis and setting, the five key project and evolution stages are described in detail: "definition and prototyping", "setup and piloting", "global rollout", "operation, expansion and further development", and "shifting to a multi-community concept". The report pays explicit attention to the change paradigms' conceptual variables/factors introduced in the theoretical foundations of this study.

3.1 Project Prologue

In an increasingly difficult market, characterized by deregulation, increasing complexity of the business, and disintegration of traditional value chains, Siemens ICN's group executive management recognized the importance of international cooperation in combination with competence management and KM early in 1995. The central function culture change (CC) was established to facilitate a shift towards knowledge sharing vs. knowledge hoarding and proactively seeking and offering knowledge (Siemens, 1999, p. 9). Heinrich von Pierer, Siemens president and chief executive officer (CEO), demanded that Siemens exploits its expertise more systematically and intensely than before: "Our first priority - and this will be vital for our future effectiveness - is the electronic networking and management of our internal knowledge, in order to make us even more efficient and to bring our customers greater benefits. Our ultimate goal is to ensure that all of our people can access the company's unequaled pool of knowledge at the right time - and to do this systematically and not just by accident."

Until the 1980s, telecommunications equipment customers around the globe were mostly monopolistic, vertically integrated, and government-owned telephone companies. The range of activities involved in providing wireline analog voice service to the end user in defined regional markets, i.e. the entire value chain, were concentrated in a single entity. The service operators' technical staff planned networks, purchased switches, transport and access equipment from suppliers, installed and maintained the equipment, and ran billing and service operations. Suppliers resembled their few stable customers: they were vertically integrated and less sensitive to costs and time to market.

Times changed. Over the past two decades governments deregulated the telecommunications services markets in order to provide more competitive pricing and services to customers. Moreover, technological advances in electronics and computer science led to an explosion of new products and specialized service offerings. The splitting apart of the monolithic, integrated phone companies of the past, i.e. value chain deconstruction, created disconfirmation in the telecommunications equipment business: few long-term customer relationships were replaced by many, customers competing on cost became sensitive to equipment prices, and customers competing on innovative services demanded new generations of equipment brought to market quickly. The equipment business became more concentrated and competitive (to amortize development overhead and realize scale advantages) and had shorter time horizons.

New business opportunities arose as well. The new entrants were profit-rather than service-oriented, often lean organizations without technical expertise. Thus, customers demanded from a supplier a package of all the services involved in running a telecommunications services business (solutions), including financing, business planning, engineering, and operations. Shifting from "box selling" to a service focus and solutions approach enhanced the complexity and knowledge intensity of Siemens ICN's business (Gerndt, 2000, p. 7). The organization's front lines soon experienced learning anxiety since the novel way of doing business required new mind-sets and skills. Leveraging local knowledge and refining it into global competencies became mandatory.

3.2   Definition and Prototyping

The first key project stage - "definition and prototyping" - lasted from July 1998 to the end of March 1999. Objectives were to establish the ShareNet project team, to create conceptual definitions and refinements, to start prototyping the technical platform, and to ensure early executive and user buy-in. CC was renamed to Business Transformation Partners, later Business Transformation and Coordination (BTP/BTC), headed by Joachim Döring. Making knowledge and competence management one of Siemens ICN's core competencies was an integral part of the mission. To set high standards and expectations, BTP/BTC developed the vision of a structured KM initiative for the sales and marketing community: "ICN ShareNet is the global knowledge sharing network. We leverage our local innovations globally. We are a community committed to increase value for our customers and ICN by creating and re-applying leading-edge solutions."

Change communications emphasized several benefits: costs should be reduced by avoiding expensive mistakes made in the past, or simply by reusing technical and functional components that had already been developed; project delivery times ought to be shortened through reuse, leading to higher project throughput/utilization by the sales force; quality should improve as reusable modules were repetitively sold and improved; lastly, besides representing benefits in their own right, lower costs, shorter delivery times, and improved quality would lead to more successful tenders and consequently higher revenues. Four crucial elements, listed in figure 5, were defined to guide the KMS' conceptual development, prototyping, and later implementation: Sales Value Creation Process, ShareNet Content, ShareNet Community, and ShareNet Systems.

ShareNet's central part - the Sales Value Creation Process - was a sequence of important sales activities and decisions where knowledge ought to be reused. The ShareNet project team, i.e. six BTP/BTC employees plus four consultants from The Boston Consulting Group (BCG), realized early that the KMS' development should be no isolated effort (ivory tower), later parachuted into the local companies. Consequently, the team was augmented by 40 sales representatives from headquarters and 15 local companies. Hiring and socialization were based on good "fit in" and capability to represent regional markets in all development stages (deployment, extension, upgrade, and customization). The stakeholder representatives' involvement served three distinct change management goals: they specified KMS solutions, supported a network of people experiencing similar difficulties, and set examples for the combined KM and change initiative's progress. Siemens ICN's group president, the head of BTP/BTC, and high ranking sales managers formed the steering committee responsible for project supervision and top management support.

The core team was assembled for the first time in October 1998 at the kick-off workshop at Frankfurt airport. Goals were the definition of the KMS' content, objectives, and structure. BTP/BTC and BCG presented first ideas for ShareNet's vision, basic concept, and graphical user interface (GUI) mock-ups for prototyping. Afterwards, the ShareNet core team engaged in a joint diagnosis of business problems in order to make sure that the KMS provided value-add to the sales and marketing community. The concentration on a single process ensured a community of people who shared the same problems and experiences,

Figure 5: ShareNet as an Interplay of Four Crucial Elements

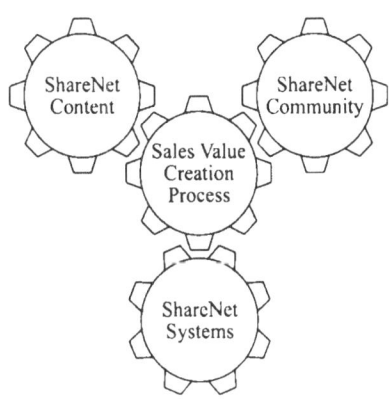

Sales Value Creation Process:
Sequence of important sales activities and decisions where leverage of knowledge is critical

ShareNet Content:
Valuable knowledge and best practice externalized and structured to facilitate knowledge reuse in sales

ShareNet Community:
Global human network of the creators and users of the sales knowledge committed to drive sharing

ShareNet Systems:
Technical and managerial systems enabling and encouraging the leverage of sales knowledge

who had a common language and similar business backgrounds. A map of the solutions-selling process with the required knowledge for each step was jointly developed: business development, pre-acquisition, bid preparation, deployment/implementation, and after sales/operation. Since margins in the product business declined rapidly, the participants decided to focus on the first three phases where more value could be created than after the contract was signed. To maintain user involvement, i.e. to make sales and marketing employees aware that they had a vested interest in the KMS' evolution, two additional German brainstorming workshops were planned.

At the kick-off workshop, participants quickly recognized that knowledge sharing between local project teams in the same country could lead to significant competitive advantage since they focused on the same market and competition, and therefore faced similar problems. However, the benefit of leveraging knowledge globally remained unclear since telecommunications markets were in different stages of development and demand. In brainstorming sessions, regional markets were clustered on a two-dimensional graph according to economic development and telecom landscape development, characterized by degree of deregulation. The four market stages obtained suggested that local companies could reuse some former work. The same solution - slightly customized - might as well be offered to customers at a same market stage.

To foster market development and to help its customers remain competitive, Siemens ICN also leveraged higher stage solutions to lower stages. The Share-Net project team concluded that a single KMS would cater all three types of knowledge sharing: by utilizing a single, globally interoperable IS for knowledge sharing within one country, knowledge transfer between peer countries and market stages would happen automatically (Gibbert, Jenzowsky, Jonczyk, Thiel, & Völpel, 2002, pp. 49-51). The communication flow would change from a broadcast-oriented "enabling" approach, i.e. headquarters to local companies, to a meshed network approach required for fast global learning.

The core team's sales representatives were asked to identify projects, solutions, and practices in their home regions that could be leveraged globally, i.e. early win-showcases. BTP/BTC and BCG employees served as coaches and held informal user trainings all over the world. An intranet site with a preliminary database, discussion and feedback groups, and core team member profiles was soon established. Altogether, the knowledge of 18 sales projects was captured, more than 30 sales tips and tricks identified, and a first concrete sharing of knowledge initiated. Two Malaysian carriers were interested in a global voice-over-IP network based on WN products. Since a rollout of a similar solution for US GlobalLink had already started, the responsible sales representatives from the U.S. and Malaysia were connected. Besides creating strong pull-effects from local companies, i.e. behavior changes through example setting and socialization from peers, this first cross-regional leverage of knowledge created commitment to change.

All content gathered was reviewed in November 1998 at the global exchange workshop in Garmisch. This second workshop had even more participants than the first; "expanding the global network" was well under way. Based on their previous experiences, the ShareNet project team decided early on two categories for ShareNet Content: codified knowledge was structured knowledge about everything needed to create a solution; personalized knowledge supported global cooperation, fostered human networking, and provided quick help. The explicit knowledge derived from different stages of the solutions-selling process fell into distinct categories of ShareNet solution objects (e.g. technical- or functional solution knowledge) and ShareNet environment objects (e.g. customer or market knowledge), depicted in table 3.

Core elements of Siemens ICN's future business were technical and functional solution components. Basically, technical solution components were all technology-related parts of solution packages provided to the customer. Functional solution components were all the non-technical tips and tricks or generic methods offered, e.g. consulting service, financing, etc. Together with other knowledge objects they comprised ShareNet's knowledge library representing generic fields of interest to the sales and marketing community. The purpose was to support Siemens ICN employees in concrete decision making processes with action-oriented, context-related knowledge. The explicit content reflected the diverse views of the different contributors/users and provided a learning opportunity for all members. Useful documents (e.g. customer presentations, spreadsheets) could be linked and references to other content in ShareNet were possible. The linkage was to some extent inherent in the structure, e.g. a sales project naturally contained a pointer to a customer, etc. Additionally, contact persons were named for further help.

The core team proposed a structured way of knowledge capturing and storing for this part of ShareNet to make tacit knowledge explicit, to represent a minimal set of knowledge in a way that others expect, and to make string searching and knowledge-class browsing more powerful. In addition, a defined review process should further increase quality. Quality guidelines mainly focused on the knowledge objects' relevance and level of detail, clear presentation of content, correct linkage of objects, and unambiguous naming and ownership. Every object could be made private, i.e. discontinuing the broadcast of the information unless the owner decided to make it public again. While some relevant knowledge could be stored in a database (explicit knowledge) other knowledge was only available in expert brains (tacit knowledge). ShareNet's tacit content consisted of urgent requests, discussion forums, news, and chats.

The urgent request feature allowed ShareNet members to post an urgent message or question to alert the other ShareNet users. Urgent requests were treated with priority to other requests and discussion forum entries and were generally answered within a few hours. If members of the sales and marketing community needed feedback on general ideas or suggestions to solve low priority issues, discussion forums were rather to be chosen. An arbitrary number of discussion groups for the interchange of information on a range of topics could be created.

Table 3: Overview of Database Object Structure (adapted to Sales Value Creation Process)

Projects (PRJ) Central description of a customer sales project with a specific focus on critical success factors	• Different types of customers have to be served with fundamentally different processes • E.g. new entrants need financing
Functional Solution Components (FSC) Functional solution competencies represent additional non-technical competencies	• Key in delivering solutions • Increasingly determine differentiation • E.g. financing, business case analysis
Technical Solution Components (TSC) Technical solution components represent the technical solution integration competencies	• Increasingly critical as product landscape becomes more complex • E.g. hardware, billing systems
Technologies (TCH) Product-independent technology platforms	• Understanding needs to go significantly beyond in-house offering • E.g. core networks, mobile switching
Markets (MRK) Helps understanding market evolution through deregulation and technological change	• Understand change in spending pattern • E.g. all new entrants keep attacking incumbents similarly
Customers (CUS) In-depth customer understanding helps tailor the solution and selling process	• Mindset: solve customer's problems • E.g. understanding of decision making, strategic intent, partnerships
Competitors (COM) Companies that are active in the same markets as Siemens ICN	• Competitor understanding becomes more important regulatory barriers fall • E.g. what are their offerings and weaknesses
Complementors (CPL) Partner companies which sell products or services complementary to Siemens ICN	• Successful partnerships are key in world where nobody can do everything • E.g. how to interact with partner companies
Contacts (CON) Any valuable contact person for the relevant knowledge objects	• Effective deployment of tacit, i.e. people-bound knowledge • E.g. people to interface legacy networks

Discussion forums provided a sort of virtual meeting place in which individuals could informally exchange ideas with a group. Messages within individual threads were posted in chronological order on the ShareNet workspace. Contributors/users could later read up on the discussion and/or provide comments. The ShareNet project team felt that richness and openness were key communication factors.

ShareNet news was a specific type of forum that served as bulletin board for the ShareNet Community. Contributors/users could post latest and general news about markets, competition, and their daily business environments. Unlike the news section on most websites, interactivity was intended: anybody who had something of relevance to "broadcast" might do so. ShareNet chat was a feature to facilitate the management of personalized knowledge. The global virtual meeting room for the KMS' members combined internet relay chat (IRC) and email functionality. Friends or specialists could be directly invited to join the chat room by an email. The final element in ShareNet's people-to-people section was the ShareNet member directory. Similar to yellow pages, it comprised a directory of all users with contact information and organizational details. Activity statistics provided a link to all contributions made to the knowledge library and the people-to-people section.

The ShareNet Systems included both the technical systems to facilitate low effort global publishing and searching, and the managerial systems to encourage the capturing, sharing, reuse, and global leverage of knowledge and best practices. These comprised - among others - incentives, ownership, methodologies of how to externalize knowledge, and dedicated resources maintaining and evolving the KMS. The core team decided to start with rapid prototyping of the technical platform and to leave the definition of the managerial systems for the final workshop.

ShareNet's technical systems were a corporate web service of the Siemens intranet and had three goals: sharing of sales and marketing knowledge (knowledge library with annotation function for every object), fostering collaboration (e.g. discussion groups, feedback, common language/glossary), and user personalization. Early in the first development stage, Siemens ICN's central function information technology (IT) contracted with the external vendor Bitlab. The basic application logic was programmed and the web-based user interface designed and implemented. However, the working prototype was not well received. The GUI's look and feel was too complex and the performance was too low. The ShareNet project team decided to keep the content as simple as possible; it should not include large downloads and graphics for those accessing the KMS over a low-bandwidth connection. Several changes were made to the programming language, database, and GUI. The core team switched from Microsoft Access to an Oracle database and chose a new technology partner, i.e. ArsDigita, an open-source content management provider that was later acquired by Red Hat (MacCormack, 2002, pp. 5-6).

ShareNet employed three-tier client/server architecture. The first tier was the user interface/personal workspace accessible via regular hyper text markup language (HTML) browsers. It ran on the client, usually a PC. The second tier did most of the processing: a SUN SparcServer served as the designated application and web server for all local companies and business units. It ran a software toolkit based on open internet standards: open source web server (AOLServer) and open source community system (ACS - ArsDigita Community System). The application was flexible for future changes and comprised tried and tested functions for community building and virtual cooperation. ShareNet's dynamic web implementation based on AOLServer Dynamic Pages (ADP), an HTML derivate. Web pages were generated by scripts loading meta data (e.g. object structure and graphical layout) and actual data (e.g. customer description) from the relational database management system (Oracle 8i). It was housed on the same server and comprised the third tier. The add-on module Squid implemented tight security mechanisms: secure socket layer (SSL), user authentication at login, and object-level read/write access control for the knowledge library.

The final workshop in the "definition and prototyping" stage was held at Munich airport in February 1999. Content gathered and reviewed from three regions was posted on the prototype system and set an example for the successful application of managerial innovations. Issues still open were further changes and refinements of the technical platform and the definition of managerial systems. The participants were unsure about incentives, rewards, and culture change: how could they ensure that ShareNet was lived by the whole organization? Döring estimated that 80% of technical changes failed for non-technical reasons: lack of capability to execute, missing readiness or commitment to change, defunct change communications, and poor strategy. All domains of change management had to be addressed simultaneously: strategic change, process change, technological change, and especially organizational and people change.

For the managerial systems, the core team decided on a range of objectives: first, to increase the usage of ShareNet to leverage knowledge and experience and thereby improve value creation in sales; second, to support the capturing of innovation/knowledge created in the sales processes; third, to lay out a path for the transformation of information into best practices and "wisdom" for Siemens ICN, a process meant to happen within "knowledge cells" or smaller communities; fourth and last, to enable ShareNet's further development and growth by adopting a culture that rewards the proactive seeking and offering of knowledge. As the ShareNet project team members' experience in the "definition and prototyping" stage suggested, there was a great need, willingness, and understanding to do so within Siemens ICN. The core team admitted that the third goal had not been realized for two reasons. Contributors/users regarded ShareNet as an informal network; "knowledge cells" were resisted as a formal way to collaborate with an unclear pay-off. Furthermore, a lack of resources forced concentration on other goals.

In order to make ShareNet a fruitful platform for sharing and developing knowledge, the core team members were convinced that every member of the sales and marketing community had to participate, either as giver or taker of knowledge. The ShareNet project team felt that sharing know-how should ideally become incorporated into every employee's self-concept and identity and in the long-term embedded into the majority of Siemens ICN's organizational cultures. Providing knowledge in return for reusing other knowledge, being a part of a community, pride of excellence, and demonstrating expert status should cater for this intrinsic motivation. The KMS should be user-friendly to provide low barriers of entry and reduce the psychological costs of sharing, e.g. with a capturing wizard. In the short term, extrinsic motivation was needed to create awareness, to reach a critical mass of content and reuse, and to succeed in the "battle" for capturing time against other important daily issues. The ShareNet project team members were aware that extrinsic motivation could only inflict short-term behavior change and should not become the prime motivation for knowledge exchange. Otherwise, most employees would tend to rationalize their actions in terms of external justifications while adhering to the prevailing pattern of values and beliefs.

In order to ensure that all ShareNet crucial elements (processes, content, community, and systems) were developed and improved further, the Munich workshop participants proposed a consistent organizational structure. The distinct tasks and roles for the "global rollout" stage are depicted in figure 6. Contributors/users were sales and marketing people worldwide bringing their project experiences, methods, and key learnings into the KMS' knowledge library or using its content. ShareNet managers drove the local ShareNet processes as coaches and role models, devoting 20-50% of their working time. Key responsibilities were implementing and promoting ShareNet in the local companies, facilitating formal training through local ShareNet workshops, and monitoring quality and completeness of inputs. A defined review process made the revision of four knowledge objects per month mandatory. ShareNet consultants supported and coordinated the ShareNet managers in promoting and developing ShareNet in the local companies. They run conferences to set each of them up and interfaced with them once a country was up and running. Furthermore, the ShareNet consultants policed the KMS, i.e. monitored content quality and offered feedback where it was deemed appropriate.

The global editors provided additional support for ShareNet managers: they ensured the global synthesis of knowledge and had the ultimate control over the quality of content. Their role was to check the contributions' clarity and usefulness, to assess their potential for reuse throughout Siemens ICN, and to determine the ease with which submitted solutions could be understood. IT support ensured the technical systems' availability, integrity and flexibility, handled security issues, and integrated ShareNet into the technical environment. The user hotline provided technical and editorial contributor/user support. The ShareNet committee was the highest decision body for ShareNet's strategic development and implementation. It comprised Dr. Roland Koch, group president, two members from BTP/BTC, and eight local company representatives. This composition ensured that local ShareNet contributors/users were actively involved in development and implementation. The committee members should champion Share-Net on top and line management levels, set examples for knowledge-oriented behavior, ensure the allocation of proper resources, and react quickly to stimuli and suggestions from the field.

Top management support mainly relied on explicit means of change communications to bundle organizational resources and individual commitment to the project. Line managers served as neutral intermediaries to spread ShareNet's idea across organizational levels and functional departments. Implicit means of

Figure 6: The ShareNet Organization

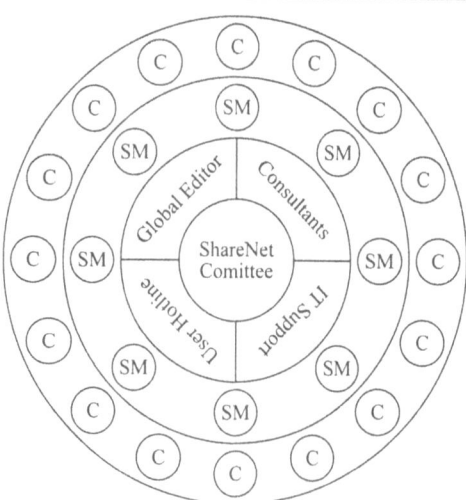

Contributors/Users (C): Sales and marketing people worldwide bring their project experiences, methods, and key learnings into the ShareNet knowledge base

ShareNet Managers (SM): Support contributors in capturing the project experiences and marketing know-how, drive the development of reusable knowledge

ShareNet Consultants: Support ShareNet Managers in local companies promoting and developing ShareNet locally

Global Editor: Supports the ShareNet Managers and ensures the global synthesis of knowledge

ShareNet Commitee: Highest decision body for the future development of ShareNet change communications should ensure appreciation and socialization. Neverthe-less, in the long-term the ShareNet Community should assume responsibility for ShareNet's maintenance and evolution through its input and formulation of re-quirements. The KMS should become institutionalized and embedded into the organizational context. In March 1999, Koch decided to continue the project and to proceed with the next development stage: "This [ICN ShareNet] network will be of key importance for the success of ICN's solutions business, because the company that is able to make use of existing experiences and competencies quickest has a distinct competitive edge over the other players. We need to be among the first to realize this strategic competitive advantage through efficient knowledge management."

3.3   Setup and Piloting

The second key project stage - "setup and piloting" - lasted from April to mid July 1999. Objectives were to test and improve the technical platform, to ensure local company commitment to the project, and to develop a phased implementa-tion approach including training material. BCG's assignment ended with the final workshop in Munich and the remaining ShareNet project team (BTP/BTC and the sales representatives) took over full responsibility. The KMS was rolled out in four pilot countries (Australia, China, Malaysia, and Portugal) chosen for the following reasons: they showed good "fit in" with the core team, represented Siemens' global operations well, and their first cross-regional sharing of experi-ences set examples for the entire company. A pilot project team conducted in-formal trainings for the pilot participants. The workshops were developed by Rolf Meinert, vice president change management, and became the origins of the training program for the international rollout (local company workshop brief-cases). Several site visits ensured congruence between deliverables and original objectives (Rothnie, 2001, p. 189).

The pilot projects were considered critical success factors for the KMS' im-plementation. They would trigger long-lasting behavior change required to bring about a permanent culture change, as intended in the managerial systems' fourth goal. Potential contributors/users had to internalize the desired benefits of the KM initiative over and above their intrinsic motivation, even early in the "setup and piloting" stage. The core team saw the pilots as an important means to rap-idly establish buy-in at headquarters and local companies. BTP/BTC and ShareNet committee members began to meet key executives in local companies (i.e. local ICN heads, local company heads) and at headquarters, first in the pilot countries and later in the countries earmarked for the "global rollout" stage. They tried to make sure that the managers understood the benefits of knowledge-orientation, were committed to the project and informed the core team about local particularities, nominated or supported ShareNet managers, and identified projects for later capturing and reuse.

Besides the training material, the ShareNet project team had no codified/formal change management strategy but a range of measures to overcome most common implementation barriers. Keeping the right balance between challenging and realistic goals avoided most "scope creep". Involving users in developing their own KM solutions helped to build personal networks, to create buy-in and trust with internal customers, and to secure top management support. On the one hand, there were some people who questioned the value of knowledge exchange. The core team reacted by explaining the difficult business situation, providing the right incentives, and addressing the "evangelists" first. On the other hand, the majority of employees generally supported the idea but felt that a lack of time might hinder further implementation. As a response, a give-and-take model of knowledge exchange, high usability, and adaptation to individual goals were pursued. The ShareNet project team continually emphasized that ShareNet was no replacement for existing IS, but was rather a logical and necessary complement to existing applications.

The core team strongly believed in a bottom-up approach for ShareNet manager nominations. Koch sent a personal letter to all local companies to create awareness for the KMS and to request the nomination of one part-time ShareNet manager per country. Many of the 40 sales representatives who attended the three German workshops in the "definition and prototyping" stage volunteered to become committed ShareNet managers: proactively searching and offering knowledge already was part of their self-concept, identity, and ongoing relationships. In addition, Meinert approached potential ShareNet managers all over the world making use of his large personal network. Only in the case where countries without voluntary participants were detected, the local company heads were asked to nominate some of their employees as ShareNet managers. A lack of competence and commitment or a too strong focus on technology was often the result of forced nominations. In very few cases, a removal of ShareNet managers who did not live up to their obligations was necessary.

Technical systems accounted for only 25% of total project costs; the majority was spent on the selection and training of prospective ShareNet managers, communication campaigns, and training material. The core team and the external consultancy Change Factory jointly developed a range of user trainings/workshops (e.g. boot camps, ShareNet manager implementation review conference) and tools to enable "evangelists" for the global rollout. Local company workshop briefcases were a self-explanatory training concept for ShareNet managers to conduct local workshops. Training videos served as a visual guide to the ShareNet philosophy and its basic functionalities. ShareNet joggers were illustrated, easy-to-use pocket references to guide the average user through

ShareNet's most relevant applications and processes. ShareNet marketing material included giveaways and promotion items to raise curiosity: e.g. ShareNet
flyers, caps, posters, postcards, display stickers, business card holders, and pens.

Furthermore, a mission statement concretized ShareNet's vision and explicitly linked it to economic benefits: "ICN ShareNet intends to network all local
sales efforts to facilitate global learning, local reuse of global best practices, and
the creation of global solution competencies. ICN ShareNet shall realize considerable and measurable business impact through time and cost savings and
through the creation of new sales opportunities. ICN ShareNet shall be integrated in the daily work of every sales person. ICN ShareNet is a self-organizing
growing system."

The ShareNet project team decided on two-sectioned local company workshops as a central element of the change management initiative. The first section
- creating necessary know-how for using ShareNet - followed the participants'
working routines. They would learn about ShareNet's philosophy, discover its
benefits for daily work, and get to know the structure and handling of the technical platform. Coaches would provide walk-through examples, live exercises, and
stimulate discussions about the value-add of global knowledge exchange. During
the second section - capturing knowledge with ShareNet - the participants would
start to capture and peer review some sample projects they brought to the workshop.

At the beginning of every workshop, a case study about an almost lost Malaysian sales project created a sense of disconfirmation, i.e. an intervention used
for unfreezing, and clarified the link between knowledge-orientation and business purpose. Stress was further intensified by describing Siemens ICN's shift
from a "box seller" to a solution provider. The participants should reflect their
working routines and arrive at new justifications of behavior: they ought to discover that only the global leverage of knowledge ensured long-term competitiveness. A positive, knowledge-oriented attitude was considered the workshops'
basis for success.

The pilot project team began to test the KMS' database, GUI and usability,
response times, and reliability. Objectives were to have secure and stable technical systems available for the "global rollout" stage, including collaboration functionalities, capturing wizard, string search and knowledge-class browsing functions, and user administration. To ensure smooth integration with Siemens'
intranet, the ShareNet project team took a close look at Siemens ICN's global
technology infrastructure and the level of the local sales representatives' intranet
know-how. All feedback forms/change requests were resolved before the international rollout started. Early on, the core team planned for integration with
other knowledge sources and systems. Much relevant content was available
within Siemens ICN and Siemens-wide, but not in the format needed for Share-

Net. Only arbitrary indirect integration of external knowledge was possible, i.e. if an object owner made a link. The full mapping of all content into the ShareNet data model was never realized since speed of implementation was favored over lengthy coordination with other IS owners.

3.4   Global Rollout

The third key project stage - "global rollout" - lasted from mid July 1999 to mid February 2000. Objectives were to have ShareNet implemented in 30 major countries, to establish the ShareNet organization and managerial processes, and to capture and reuse valuable knowledge. BTP/BTC provided user trainings, controlling to steer the global rollout, and communication material to enable "evangelists" for the KMS' implementation. The core team decided on four phases for the international rollout: buy-in and preparation (partly accomplished in the preceding stage), ShareNet manager handover, ShareNet workshops in local companies, and ShareNet manager review meetings.

Early in the "global rollout" stage, the introduction of the consistent incentive system bonus-on-top put even more emphasis on top management support. Some local executives felt threatened by ShareNet because their employees were bypassing traditional hierarchies in search of solutions. They feared that their influence would diminish once knowledge was made available in a KMS. Up to that point, local management was mainly rewarded according to the achievement of local business goals. A one-time promotion scheme in fiscal 2000 should link knowledge sharing with economic benefits: local ICN heads should now be rewarded for inter-country business generated through substantial international knowledge exchange. "Business generated" was the total order income of projects secured with knowledge from other countries and the revenues from other countries created with knowledge from the ICN head's local company. "Substantial international cooperation" comprised reuse of knowledge via ShareNet and/or a verifiable exchange of human resources which together accounted for more than 10% of the order income generated, and/or more than 10% of total project cost or time savings.

To be eligible for a bonus of approximately 10% of their fixed annual salary, the overall revenue achieved should sum up to at least 5% (up to 30%) of local ICN revenue (Gibbert, Kugler, & Völpel, 2002, p. 273). The local ICN heads had to complete forms which contained all cases of collaboration, i.e. success stories. Several restrictions applied: since a successful knowledge transfer was described, knowledge giver and taker had to work in distinct departments and project groups and the amount of time and money saved or additionally earned turnover had to be stated. For approval, the ShareNet project team required written proof, e.g. invoice, purchase order, or delivery confirmation. The success stories could be checked against each other just like consolidated balance sheets to ensure accuracy. Bonus-on-top yielded remarkable results. The financial outcome is shown in figure 7: during fiscal 2000, Siemens ICN reported additional revenue of €130.9 million resulting from international knowledge exchange, some 50% obtained through ShareNet. In addition, the success stories set examples to foster managerial commitment and clarified the change process.

The ShareNet manager handover took place at the end of July 1999. Participants from some 30 countries were assembled for the first time at a one-week boot camp in Feldafing, Germany. The ShareNet project team selected rollout countries primarily on the basis of annual sales, availability of local ShareNet project team members, advanced market stage, and advanced technology infrastructure. The ShareNet managers received in-depth formal training enabling them to take over the responsibility for the introduction and utilization of ShareNet in local companies. Coaches explained ShareNet's philosophy, processes, organization, and incentives and demonstrated knowledge capturing with the KMS. Moreover, the ShareNet project team intended to build-up committed social networks, first among ShareNet managers, later throughout the sales and marketing community. The hiring and socialization of supporters grew in importance.

To enable and motivate the ShareNet managers, problem solving team building events, e.g. trying to build a raft without tools to cross the Lake Starnberg,

Figure 7: Revenue Through Knowledge Exchange in Fiscal 2000 (€ Thousand)

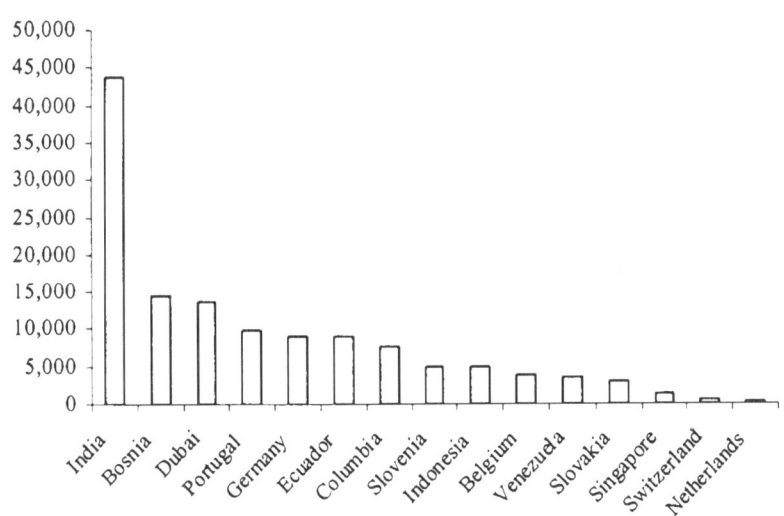

and a friendly and relaxed climate were important change management measures. Döring recalled the team spirit at the boot camp: "All they had to work
with were steel drums, logs, pontoons, and some rope. Another catch: no talking.
The managers, who gathered from offices around the world, could only scribble
messages and diagrams on a flip chart. For the better part of the day, it was
knowledge-sharing at its most basic. Yet the group managed to put together a
small fleet of rafts, which they paddled about triumphantly on the placid waters
of the lake." Soon, the ShareNet managers were seen cooperating on a regional
basis. With the help of coaches from BTP/BTC, Argentine's ShareNet manager
conducted joint rollout workshops in the Andean region for sales representatives
from Venezuela, Peru, Ecuador, and Colombia. ShareNet managers from U.K.
and Lithuania participated in Finnish workshops and Egypt's ShareNet manager
helped out in Greece.

There was low headquarter participation at the first boot camp. Since the
core team believed that it was necessary to embed local companies' project
specific knowledge into a wider marketing and strategic context, 17 ShareNet
managers and promoters from business units and central functions were brought
together at a second Feldafing boot camp in January 2000. Goals were to review
headquarters' rollout, to overcome obstacles, and to define processes for the
integration of headquarters' knowledge structures and content. All business units
agreed to develop rollout roadmaps and to provide top management support, i.e.
showcase usage. Nevertheless, headquarters showed higher implementation
resistance than local companies: business units were afraid to lose sales opportunities for internal services, questioned ShareNet's positioning among other IS
and KM initiatives, and did not fully appreciate value creation in local companies. Since they faced less disconfirmation and pressure from customers, survival anxiety or guilt did not create sufficient commitment to change. In addition, headquarters were afraid of sharing centralized knowledge, i.e. a source of
influence and power.

Whereas more than half of the local companies' employees supported the
KMS and some 20% resisted its implementation, numbers at headquarters were
roughly vice versa. Resistance came in several flavors: inactivity and lack of
implementation support, postponing decisions, preventing employees from posting safeguarded knowledge, denying the right to use ShareNet, and all kinds of
mobbing and politics. The ShareNet project team decided to continue the implementation with central funding and a focus on key impact areas, i.e. the local
companies. The KM initiative should not be perceived as another headquarters'
initiative demanding precious resources (Rothnie, 2001, p. 188). In the long run,
example setting and business impact ought to win over resistance at headquarters
and ensure buy-in.

Soon after the boot camps, the ShareNet managers began with the local roll-outs. On average, each local implementation required project work for two or three months: one week for "selling" ShareNet in the local companies, three weeks for user training/workshops to teach contributors/users the necessary skills to capture knowledge, up to two weeks for the review of captured content, two to three weeks for the support of local staff, and two days for a final review meeting. BTP/BTC coaches and ShareNet committee members visited 18 countries to support the implementation with communication campaigns (e.g. buy-in presentations) and workshops. The coaches delivered feedback forms with change requests, workshop results, and suggestions for improvement.

Alfons Kuhn, a former ShareNet consultant, noted that there was little aversion to the system at local level: "On the ground, people are very open to information exchange - it was they who demanded it in the first place. The main barriers to usage among sales staff are quite simply that they do not feel they have enough time to respond to requests from across the globe." For him, behavior change occurred simultaneously with culture change during ShareNet's implementation: first experiences made many users believers in the KMS and in a knowledge-intensive culture which in turn reinforced the new behavior. Curiosity and interest usually drove the registration.

Up to that point, only the U.S. turned out to be a difficult environment for ShareNet's implementation. Early on, a qualified IT task force was made up of communication, education, and marketing specialists, headed by Donald Tsusaki. Since U.S. employees were too widespread to use the standard local company workshop briefcases, Kuhn and Tsusaki initiated web-based trainings and tried to convince key contributors/users to set an example by posting best practices. Once Tsusaki left, the situation deteriorated: top executives began to question ShareNet's organizational integration and the missing link to economic benefits. It was not sufficiently communicated that ShareNet was no replacement for existing IS, e.g. Siebel's Customer Relationship Management (CRM) application, but rather a logical add-on. Even though some resistance vanished when contributors/users recognized the possibility to link and access Siebel objects from ShareNet, the U.S. Sales Value Creation Process mapped better to the CRM tool. In addition to the "not invented here" syndrome, the difficult business situation did not create sufficient commitment to the KMS implementation project.

The entire implementation process was centrally-driven and monitored by BTP/BTC, e.g. rollout targets, resources, workshops. Country-specific metrics (rollout scorecards) for feedback and monitoring implementation progress were tracked and discussed with the local ShareNet managers on a monthly basis. 33 ShareNet managers sent in a roadmap for their local rollout which were checked and supported by the ShareNet project team. ShareNet managers regularly received a wrap up of the latest news around ShareNet from the global editor, e.g. global rollout status, systems developments, etc. The back office's technical hotline ensured further help.

The core team organized the ShareNet manager implementation review conference at Sun City, South Africa in February 2000. Some 50 participants attended the workshop: BTP/BTC employees, ShareNet managers, and external KM experts. Goals were to reinforce community spirit, to exchange experiences with the international rollout, and to define future implementation ideas, e.g. motivation of users, expansion to other user groups, and quality assurance. ShareNet's key project stages are depicted in figure 8. Döring felt a substantial commitment to change: "ICN ShareNet is more than a database; it is a new spirit, a new way to cooperate worldwide across country- and organizational boundaries. Knowledge reuse is the key to success, e.g. innovation, time to market, etc. With ICN ShareNet we take advantage of our strengths: local innovations and creativity and global leverage of sales power". Approximately 4,200 ShareNet users had registered and posted more then 2,100 public knowledge objects and 490 urgent requests; news and discussion groups enjoyed significant traffic.

Local rollout success stages were defined along four dimensions: first, the number of workshops (with/without assistance from BTP/BTC), participants,

Figure 8: How ShareNet was Developed

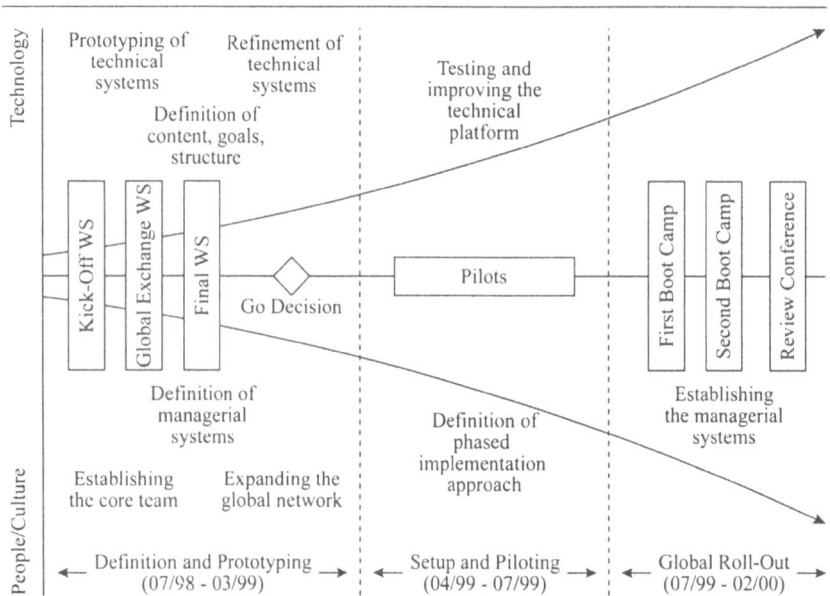

and feedback received; second, the quality of ShareNet manager information-flow to BTP/BTC; third, timeliness of rollout; fourth and last, quantity of ShareNet contributions. There were only few countries without any known roll-out activities, e.g. Hong Kong, Ireland, and Spain, many countries with limited rollout activities, e.g. Canada, France, South Africa, many countries with some substantial rollout activities, e.g. China, Denmark, and United Kingdom, and some countries with best-performed rollout activities, e.g. Australia, Malaysia, and Portugal.

To emphasize the project closing's importance, Koch participated via video-conference on the conference's last day. The participants consolidated their key learnings. Everybody acknowledged that ShareNet needed political attention and ongoing top management support, i.e. Siemens ICN's group executive manage-ment and local ICN heads. Otherwise, time resources and prioritization for ShareNet rollout activities would consequently be too low. An adjustment of goals, incentives, and rewards was required for all members of the ShareNet organization and individual contributors/users. ShareNet managers needed suffi-cient time for support; i.e. 25-50% of their working time; other tasks must be reduced.

All participants agreed that the real infrastructure of a successful knowledge network was a culture based on trust between people. During a formal hand-over ceremony at the end of the implementation review conference, the ShareNet project team transferred the KMS' ownership to the ShareNet operating team, headed by Dr. Michael Wagner. Through their new representatives, contribu-tors/users should finally assume ownership and responsibility for ShareNet's maintenance and evolution. The new team comprised six ShareNet consultants, six IT specialists, two global editors, and one controller. Almost half of the new team members came from other companies since project sponsors did not want to continue with "old Siemens ICN resources", but rather used the project to attract creative and innovative people. They presented their agenda and built a joint contract for change, i.e. all ShareNet managers signed a symbolic docu-ment promising to support ShareNet with all effort. To ensure a smooth transi-tion, BTP/BTC provided ongoing support for a few months in addition to new assignments.

3.5   Operation, Expansion, and Further Development

The fourth key evolution stage - "operation, expansion, and further develop-ment" - lasted from mid February 2000 to the end of November 2001. Objec-tives were to continuously expand ShareNet throughout Siemens ICN and to further refine and develop the technical platform. After the global rollout, the ShareNet operating team noticed that not all registered contributors/users used the KMS for the purpose intended. Since innovation was key to improvement,

Siemens ICN commissioned an external research unit, i.e. a group of master students at the Stuttgart Institute of Management and Technology (SIMT). An email survey was conducted to analyze ShareNet's acceptance and usage. To identify significant differences between user types and to have the smallest possible standard deviation, the sample of 2,200 registered users was stratified between contributors and users who had never made any postings. 2,000 and 200 questionnaires were sent out, respectively.

The research showed that both user types regarded the KMS as an effective tool to save time. A significant difference was found in perceived impact on work, skills, and communication. For heavy users, better access to information and a wealth of new ideas mattered most; low users emphasized better information and contacts. Consequently, information (heavy users: 24%, low users: 20%) and contacts (heavy users: 12%, low users: 5%) constituted the prime motivators for participation, a quality assurance and reward system (heavy users: 4%, low users: 7%) was of a lesser concern. Both user categories perceived time constraints as the most important barrier to usage but low users also dreaded the postings' poor structure. Everybody agreed that ShareNet managers were vital to promote the KM initiative as role models and to conduct user trainings in local companies (Mann, Chopra, Hinojosa, Koma, & Crivat, 2000, pp. 6-41).

Even though it was not included in the marketing study, the ShareNet operating team tried to uncover Siemens ICN's organizational cultures. Knowledge exchange did not come naturally as it implied giving up individual power for the sake of the whole organization. There were old boys' networks, risk adverse decision making, and a strong engineering "do-it-all yourself" culture that made it difficult to get accustomed to new rules of competition (Gerndt, 2000, p. 10). Top engineers had adopted a "hero mentality", showing respect only for individual design achievements (Davenport et al., 1998, p. 52). Innovations no longer originated in centralized R&D; rather they were derived from customers' needs.

Strong hierarchies counteracted an atmosphere of openness, mutual respect, and absence of ambiguity since they placed value on individual achievements at the expense of teamwork. It was possible to achieve good business results with an even sparse exchange of information. Traditionally, Siemens ICN passively waited for orders from monopolistic, government owned telephone companies instead of aggressively developing the market with active sales and marketing. Employees lacked initiative, too: they were expected to fill exactly defined jobs and decision-making was highly centralized. The ShareNet operating team recognized that people were slow to change their justifications of behavior; first results from culture change after a few years showed that the processes needed a decade to become self-sustaining.

Albeit bonus-on-top had been successful beyond expectations, it was unclear whether ShareNet itself was benefiting. Users commented: "Receiving some [...]

award naturally serves as an incentive to sharing our knowledge with colleagues worldwide, but it is not the most important aspect. Getting direct recognition for how much our daily job is appreciated is the most important thing. That's what counts and motivates us." The new team decided to focus incentives and rewards more on the users themselves to get a critical mass of content into the system, to make users active contributors, and to create awareness.

Consequently, the ShareNet quality assurance and reward system went live on March 1, 2000. The main idea was to recognize both knowledge givers and takers. Due to the nature of local markets, some countries were rather net consumers of reusable knowledge whereas other countries with innovative and competitive markets rather were net contributors. There were no monetary incentives since they encountered ambiguity in local companies; a share system, comparable to frequent flyer miles, faced less obstacles. ShareNet shares could be collected, accumulated, and finally turned into knowledge-related rewards. The share system was a flexible incentive scheme that could be adjusted according to needs for motivation and guidance: e.g. objects published and forum responses yielded between three and 20 shares, dependent on a pre-assigned value. One share was equivalent in value to approximately one euro.

ShareNet's technical systems automatically distributed the shares for contributions and reuse feedback on knowledge objects. The formal quality reviews, already conducted by ShareNet managers, and the new reward system, conducted by the entire ShareNet Community, comprised the KMS' two quality assurance steps. The share system's first version was competitive: the top 50 contributors who had collected the most shares by the end of May 2000 and their partners were invited to a ShareNet user conference in New York in October 2000; 600 shares were deducted from the "role models'" accounts. Conference goals were to reinforce community spirit among strong contributors/users, to inform about the implementation's status and success, and to define ideas for further development and expansion. Similar to the boot camps, a friendly and relaxed climate with city tours, sports, and dinner events were key change management measures. After videotaped greetings from Siemens ICN's group executive management, the participants broke into work sessions while their partners went sightseeing.

Depending on personal preferences and background, discussion and support groups formed around a range of topics: mobile ShareNet, intelligent agents, people-to-people section, usability and redesign, CoPs, and change management. Even though lively discussions evolved around ShareNet's integration into existing systems and structures, i.e. after action reviews, employee target agreements, job profiles, and Siemens Leadership Framework (SLF), decisions were neither taken nor implemented by the central function HR. Up to that point, only the 40 sales representatives who participated in ShareNet's key project stages were promoted for KM efforts. Difficult communication and reporting lines were additional hindrances. Siemens' decentralized matrix structure required direct reports from local companies to Siemens' managing board, not to Siemens ICN's group executive management.

Comparing February 2000 to May 2000, the competitive share system yielded remarkable results: there was more awareness for ShareNet (35% new users), more activity (50% additional active contributors), and increasing content quantity (plus 90% knowledge objects posted) and quality (plus 50% reuse feedback per knowledge object). All shares retained their value in the new, non-competitive cafeteria-style reward system that went live on June 1, 2000. The ShareNet operating team still found it difficult to convince overloaded sales representatives to exchange knowledge without any short-term benefits. Goals of the shift to a non-competitive system for a "grown-up" ShareNet were to enhance content quality, to foster the reuse of existing knowledge, and to enable knowledge development. More importance was placed on feedback. Knowledge takers could use free text and a five-star rating scheme to judge the quality of contributions: for every object feedback received, the number of stars times five shares was awarded, urgent request responses yielded the number of stars times two.

Shortly after, an incentive catalog complemented the KMS' quality assurance and reward system and allowed the exchange of shares into knowledge-related rewards: e.g. technical literature (400 shares), COMDEX 2001 participation (1,100 shares), or a Fujitsu-Siemens notebook (2,200 shares). The "ShareNet Special Weeks", i.e. doubled shares for promising knowledge objects, aroused a lot of interest in July 2001. Even though many knowledge objects were posted and several new users registered, the ShareNet operating team criticized special events: an artificial and expensive hype was created that rapidly ebbed off. Employees still rationalized their actions in terms of extrinsic motivators.

In August 2002, the start-up company The Agilience Group was chosen to leverage ShareNet to other business segments and external customers. Its CEO, Dr. Christian Kurtzke was the former head of the central function CC. The intellectual property rights for the technical systems and rollout concept were exchanged for minority equity participation. The cooperation with the central function IT deteriorated when the start-up company developed a completely revised, Microsoft SQL-Server-based version of the IS. This database did not conform to Siemens' corporate IT-standards.

The ShareNet operating team continued with "networking people" at the second ShareNet manager conference in Istanbul in December 2000. In parallel running discussion and support groups, some 60 participants revised the quality assurance steps, defined ShareNet manager targets with corresponding incentives, and discussed the inclusion of other communities into the KMS. Share-

Net's quality assurance and reward system and ShareNet manager targets encountered high interest since they were already part of the conference participants' daily work. There was common agreement to abolish the formal quality reviews in favor of the five-star rating scheme more apt to an informal network of contributors/users. Due to the fact that the incentive system bonus-on-top had expired, a scheme with a more distinct focus on ShareNet was considered for the ShareNet managers: incentives must represent the overall goals of the ShareNet business plan, ensure commitment to local rollouts, and be sufficiently flexible to differentiate between local peculiarities.

In a short survey conducted during the conference, the majority of ShareNet managers acknowledged that their amount of time spent on ShareNet was insufficient. Even though local key executives clearly saw a need for the KM initiative and supported the ShareNet managers' work, almost nobody devoted more than 30% of working time. To overcome the hindrance, four ShareNet manager targets were formulated and linked to incentives and rewards for fiscal 2001. The basic requirement was general user support, e.g. user trainings, presentations, monthly reports. Complementary was the establishment of a constant knowledge input, i.e. 1.5 knowledge objects per registered user per year, plus/minus 30% flexibility according to local peculiarities (knowledge givers vs. knowledge takers). Further required were the documentation of two success stories per 100 registered users per year and high performance knowledge exchange, i.e. an average of ten shares per registered user per month. Some 20 ShareNet managers received 50-120% of an additional fixed monthly salary as a bonus dependent on how well they handled their responsibilities.

Since ShareNet had aroused much interest within Siemens, a rollout within the service community, the R&D community, and Siemens ICM was decided. Taking into account that a former Siemens ICN business unit had become Siemens ICM Networks (N), the KMS' expansion to other business units was a logical consequence. The ShareNet operating team recognized that the first implementation round's centrally-driven global rollout slowly changed to a grassroots approach: an increasing number of users proactively approached the team and the ShareNet managers for registration and support. Neither a phased implementation approach nor the replication of the ShareNet organization with distinct tasks and roles were used for the Siemens ICM rollout. Socialization from the former Siemens ICN employees - setting examples for knowledge-orientation - was deemed sufficient for the KMS' rollout.

A general lack of resources and inconsistent change communications - including a KM strategy for Siemens ICN - had negative impact on the service rollout in December 2000. The central function IT needed more employees for timely development, implementation, and documentation. ShareNet consultants missed financial resources to travel and spread ShareNet's idea globally. The main challenge was to repeat the successful global rollout approach and to ac-commodate desired modifications. The ShareNet operating team realized that not many were needed: on the one hand, service processes closely resembled the Sales Value Creation Process; on the other hand, the service community desired no user involvement. Potential contributors/users received a few hours of infor-mal training based on local company workshop briefcases and screenshots. Ser-vice top management mainly paid lip service and limited commitment to the project; only direct line management experienced disconfirming facts and saw the link between economic benefits and knowledge sharing. Considering Share-Net as "nice-to-have" vs. real business need hindered all other efforts.

Felix Baumann, the ShareNet consultant responsible for the service and R&D rollouts, feared that ShareNet provided less value-add to the service com-munity. There were few contributions and some proprietary tools (e.g. error catalog, problem escalation routines), fiercely guarded by their owners. Share-Net mainly served as user interface plus quality assurance and reward system for Virtual Technical Assistance Center (VITAC). The symbiosis was advantageous for both parties: the new team liked the additional visibility gained and the ser-vice community benefited from the KMS' people-to-people section, usability, and reliability. The difficult business situation allowed only for gradual im-provements: a limited number of new projects led to less knowledge objects posted which finally diminished contributor/user motivation. In conclusion, ShareNet's extension satisfied all demands but was no shining success.

The development of a multi-community system started in October 2000 when von Pierer declared ShareNet's technical systems and phased implementation approach a Siemens-wide KMS best practice. Several means should ensure user involvement: first, a working prototype was provided to the ICN/ICM commu-nity and discussed in a designated ShareNet forum; second, workgroups from the corporate central function corporate information and operations (CIO), i.e. "Siemens ShareNet Task Force", later "Siemens Knows", took part in the expan-sion's steering and planning; third and last, a joint ShareNet development con-sortium was formed with SBS to ensure tight integration with the corporate document management system OpenText Livelink.

3.6   Shifting to a Multi-Community Concept

The fifth and last key evolution stage - "shifting to a multi-community concept" - began in December 2001. Objectives were to sharpen the focus on topics leading to more efficiency, to foster the development and progress of smaller CoPs, and to delegate maintenance responsibilities to new user groups. Siemens ShareNet V1.x marked the introduction of a company-wide, multi-community platform shown in figure 9. The ShareNet operating team had gathered many requests for CoPs focusing on specific topics of interest. Those were seen as a good indicator for an institutionalization of the concepts and meanings inflicted by the culture change.

The conceptual change necessitated a personal workspace (WS) with personal data, email alerts, bookmarks, and links to all CoPs for which contributors/users had registered. Community homepages provided an overview of community-specific content for each user, e.g. new threads since last login. Designated functional modules (M), i.e. knowledge libraries, discussion forums, chat, and news, could be flexibly adapted to each CoP's businesses processes to win over contributors/users. The joint development consortium designed the interface/bridge license and user management to ensure information exchange between ShareNet and Livelink Communities, i.e. linking and accessing objects. Former islands of information, each ShareNet Community used instances of the same site-wide context (e.g. personal workspace, user and group administration, incentive systems), while each Livelink Community employed a separate site-wide context with permission rights and user and group administration. The former ShareNet became one CoP amongst others in the multi-community system but retained by far the largest number of contributors/users.

Even though the central function IT had sufficient resources, organizational restructurings and a difficult coordination of Red Hat led to quickly changing project plans with a delay of several months and had negative impact on soft-

Figure 9: Application Overview Siemens ShareNet V1.x

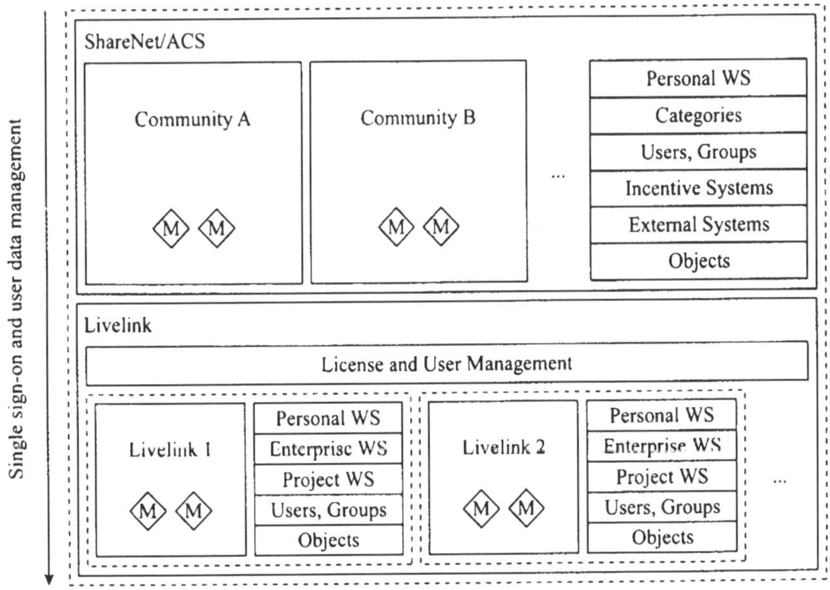

ware quality. The working prototype for user involvement and feedback from the ICN/ICM community encountered only minor traffic and aroused little interest. During Siemens ShareNet V1.x's development, the ShareNet consultants were distracted by an organizational restructuring hindering further involvement. The ShareNet operating team became part of the department Competence and Knowledge Management (CKM), part of Döring's new central function Group Strategy (GS). When the new technical platform went live, some contributors/users complained about the new layout (adapted to Siemens' corporate identity guidelines), many bugs, and weak performance. The majority of bugs were resolved quickly while performance tuning required more time.

Due to unclear specifications, the ShareNet operating team felt that the wheel was reinvented several times: former functionality was missing in Siemens ShareNet V1.x. Community support, i.e. ShareNet consultants and the global editor, was badly prepared and encountered many obstacles over the first weeks. High user demand could not be met with a shortage of resources: the central function IT needed additional human resources for timely development, implementation, and documentation; ShareNet consultants lacked money to travel and to train contributors/users globally. Top management could no longer provide the usual level of support due to other pending problems, i.e. the collapsing telecommunications sector. Siemens ICN's Profit and Cash Turnaround (PACT) program was initiated to cut costs, to consolidate the group division's worldwide manufacturing infrastructure, and to optimize the business portfolio. In fiscal 2002, PACT involved a total headcount reduction of some 20,500 positions (Siemens, 2002, p. 52). The ShareNet operating team was reduced to one ShareNet manager, i.e. Andreas Manuth, three consultants, the global editor, and few full-time IT support people. The new technical platform's implementation collided with those concerns.

To accommodate especially the needs of the R&D community, the ShareNet operating team created a separate knowledge library, still maintaining it as an integral part of the ICN/ICM community. Extensive discussions between community support and the potential contributors/users led to the development of R&D-specific knowledge objects and a corresponding capturing wizard. Since no further user involvement was desired, only brief trainings were conducted at headquarters. Baumann explained a general lack of traffic with a narrow focus, proprietary R&D applications, and security concerns. Up to that point, the sub-community had not experienced sufficient motivation to change and accomplished the shift from "box selling" to a service focus and solutions approach. A virtual R&D conference set a more positive example. Contributors/users could post presentations with links to discussion threads and knowledge objects. Similar to traditional conferences, presentations were organized by time sequence and were available for a window of time. After a slow start on the first day, lots of comments were posted the following days and active discussions evolved among the virtual participants (MacCormack, 2002, p. 11).

Generally, the ShareNet operating team agreed that the KM initiative had succeeded in embedding knowledge-orientation both into the employees' behavior and into the majority of Siemens ICN's organizational cultures: most employees acknowledged the need to identify and leverage Siemens ICN's knowledge globally in order to remain competitive and innovative. A majority shared knowledge freely without ever making personal contact; rather, they were bound together in a global corporate network, worked within the same industry, and had a common code of conduct, e.g. no more than a handful of inappropriately behaving contributors/users were banned from the ICN/ICM community. Team members were unsure about PACT's impact on culture: a lack of resources and top management support made it difficult to sustain culture change's momentum. On the one hand, employees were less inclined to contribute knowledge while they were trying to achieve business targets and were threatened by layoffs. On the other hand, people felt survival anxiety or guilt and started to question isolated working routines. A free rider mentality remained with some contributors/users benefiting without providing input. Figure 10 shows the monthly publishing of knowledge objects worldwide.

In September 2002, the ShareNet operating team communicated a conversion

Figure 10: ShareNet Knowledge Objects Published Worldwide

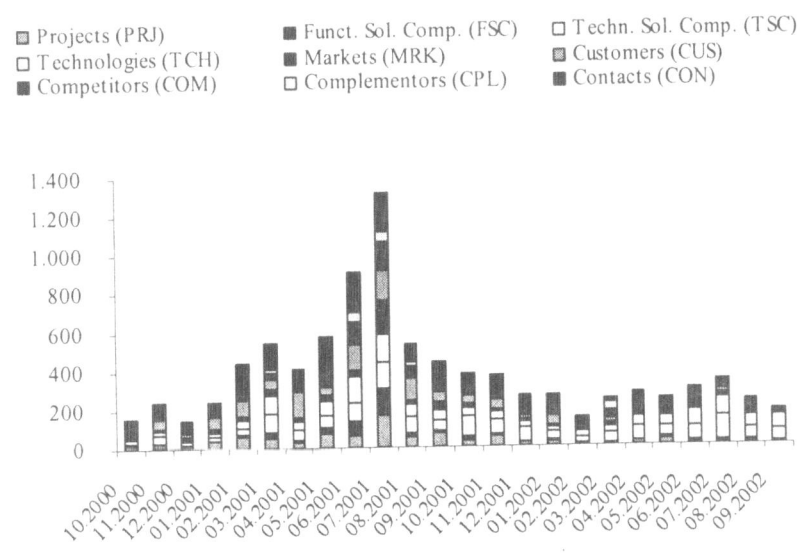

of the incentive system which had generated rather high costs. Two main reasons were given: first, implementation success was established; second, both the current business situation and the business outlook were gloomy. Contributors/users could still keep and accumulate shares, but the incentive catalog was discontinued. For compensation, visibility and recognition of "knowledge champions", invitations to high level events, and integration with business processes, e.g. employee target agreements, were planned. There was no consensus within the ShareNet operating team whether the intrinsic motivation of knowledge exchange had already become apparent and made ShareNet's usage self-perpetuating.

On the one hand, some team members were confident that the power of the ShareNet Community was not founded on incentives only. Contributors/users would keep their motivation on a high level since knowledge sharing was needed more than ever with globally distributed expertise and experiences. Thomas Ganswindt, Siemens ICN's new group president, exclaimed: "global networking and sharing knowledge is key to the success of ICN, even more since we will no longer have all the necessary knowledge in all local companies. The same counts for headquarters. And, if people really contribute to the success of ICN, its has to be beneficial to them." On the other hand, some team members argued that a discontinuation of extrinsic motivators would lead to significant drops in contributions and usage or even to a deadlock situation. Existing contributors/users might become passive and it would be difficult to attract others. With the case study ending in September 2002, the consequences of discontinuing extrinsic motivators cannot yet be determined. Moreover, the general business situation and outlook for Siemens ICN seemed to have additional negative impact on the KMS' usage. Further research is required to establish or reject causal relations and interferences.

4. Case Discussion: Change Paradigms Revisited

The fourth chapter unveils indications for the change paradigms' conceptual variables/factors and their causal interrelations. It discusses the results and their implications. Data examination, i.e. pattern-matching and time-series analysis (Yin, 1994, pp. 106-118), confirmed both theoretical frameworks' goodness of fit with the case study. Depending on the underlying perspectives of culture, each highlights a sequence of critical success factors and prior explanations of success and failure for KMS implementation projects. Following the theoretical foundation's structure, their explanatory power and shortcomings are discussed.

4.1   A Linear, Staged Perspective to Explain Success and Failure

4.1.1   Revealing Critical Success Factors for Unfreezing

As the above account shows, ShareNet's implementation was a text-book example for combined KM and change initiatives. While this chapter deals with specific change interventions, chapter five will make a convincing argument that those factors actually accomplished culture change. The application of time-series analysis (Yin, 1994, p. 113-118) to the Lewin-Schein change paradigm confirms earlier findings from innovation, organizational behavior, and IS implementation literature (e.g. Finlay & Forghani, 1998, p. 58; Ginzberg, 1981b, pp. 47-55; Hahn & Subramani, 2000, p. 309; Krovi, 1993, p. 334; Stein & Zwass, 1995, p. 106; Storey & Barnett, 2000, p. 154): top management support, commitment, user involvement, and user training remain critical success factors in the new setting of KMS. While those factors matched well with Schein's (1999, pp. 124-126) and Zand & Sorensen's (1975, p. 535) predictions for fostering psychological safety, they were not restricted to "unfreezing" but ran across most implementation stages. However, indications weakened in later key evolution stages.

Since KMS use is generally not mandatory (Lucas, 1981, p. 8), I postulate that disconfirmation and business purpose linkage factors can not only enhance motivation to change, but even trigger the initiation of KM projects (comp. Alavi & Leidner, 1999, p. 22; Davenport et al., 1998; Wilson, 2000, p. 9). Both factors were only used for the project's start, congruent with the theory. In the context of ShareNet, most of stage one's six factors were significantly positive and showed the predicted, different pattern over time. Employing the single case study as an early basis for causal inferences, Ginzberg's (1981b, p. 48) proposition of "recurrent themes" is undermined.

Top management support ("TMS") makes clear that KM is critical to the company's competitiveness and innovativeness, allocates funding and resources for an adequate (technology) infrastructure, and communicates the need for a long-term change management initiative (De Long & Seemann, 2000, p. 43; Keen et al., 1982, p. 130; King et al., 2002, p. 93; Schultz et al., 1987, p. 36; Tyran & George, 1993, p. 7). The case study provides indications for both of Jarvenpaa and Ives' (1991, p. 206) categories of managerial support: whereas "executive participation" dominated the first two key project stages, "executive involvement" prevailed afterwards, but not during the "shifting to a multi-community concept" stage. The ShareNet committee was clearly an instrument for "executive participation". It provided project supervision, allocated proper resources, debated major change requests, championed the KMS at top management level, and set examples for knowledge-oriented behavior. Koch's decision to continue the project at the end of the "definition and prototyping" stage and his personal request for local ShareNet manager nominations are further indicators for IS-related activities and behaviors.

I propose that top management's active participation in the implementation of KMS can contribute competitive advantage and trigger substantive "executive involvement" at lower hierarchical levels. While Jarvenpaa and Ives (1991, p. 217) established only a causal relation between managers' participation and a personal favorable view of IT, i.e. executive involvement, I deem spill-overs to colleagues possible as well. The influence is either moderated by a true belief in knowledge-orientation or by short-term opportunism. Key executives in four pilot and 18 major rollout countries began to see a need for the KM initiative, supported the ShareNet managers' work, and even identified projects for later capturing and reuse. Culture change gained momentum during the "global rollout" and "operation, expansion, and further development" stages. Koch participated (virtually) at the ShareNet manager implementation review conference, and von Pierer declared ShareNet's technical systems and phased implementation approach a Siemens-wide KMS best practice.

Nonetheless, the incentive system bonus-on-top put most emphasis on "executive involvement". While yielding impressive financial results from international knowledge exchange and significant bonuses for local ICN heads, it was unclear whether the KMS itself benefited. Case study data indicates top management support's significance for culture change and the difficulties of substitution with other means of psychological safety. For that reason, the December 2000 service rollout was (also) impacted by a lack of senior management backing. Executives guarded proprietary IS (e.g. error catalog, problem escalation routines) and mainly paid lip service to the KMS; only direct line management showed some degree of involvement. In result, the inclusion of the service community was no clear cut success. During the "shifting to a multi-community concept" stage, the gloomy business situation and outlook had similar impact on a larger scale. Management could no longer provide the usual support since it struggled with business targets and a headcount reduction of 20,500 positions (Siemens, 2002, p. 52). Up to that point, it was unclear whether culture change had completely been "refrozen" and no longer needed top management support (as predicted by Lewin-Schein).

Individual and organizational commitment ("COM") creates a climate and a contract for change. All affected stakeholders must understand goals and expectations for the planned IS and be willing to alter behavior and business procedures accordingly, i.e. "commitment to change". Additionally, managers and users have to take all actions necessary to make sure that the KMS is a good one, i.e. "commitment to the project" (Ginzberg, 1981b, pp. 54-55; Jin & Franz, 1986, p. 69; Keen, 1981, p. 26; Schultz et al., 1987, p. 36). Limited indications for the factors can only be found in the three key project stages. In congruence with the theory, their relevance diminished as soon as the IS was institutionalized and embedded into the organizational context. Case study data reveals that commitment factors are no true interventions, but rather the result of successful "unfreezing", i.e. motivation to change. They result from a "felt need" or deliberate actions but are no direct change management measures.

The first sharing of knowledge among sales representatives from the U.S. and Malaysia - early win-showcases - created initial "commitment to change". As Kuhn noted, Siemens ICN's front lines experienced the increasing complexity and knowledge intensity of the telecommunications sector and favored the KM initiative: "On the ground, people are very open to information exchange - it was they who demanded it in the first place." Headquarters showed less "commitment to change" since they were not as much exposed to disconfirmation factors and did not see the link between knowledge-orientation and economic benefits. On the opposite, they were concerned with losing sales opportunities for internal services and did not appreciate value creation in local companies. The U.S. rollout suffered from similar problems: the "not invented here" syndrome and the difficult business situation did not trigger sufficient motivation to change.

The change agents placed similar importance on "commitment to the project". Key local company managers (i.e. local ICN heads, local company heads) were met by BTP/BTC and ShareNet committee members to ensure buy-in for the KM initiative. At the same time, many of the 40 sales representatives involved during the "definition and prototyping" stage volunteered to become committed ShareNet managers. Proactively searching and offering knowledge had already become second nature to them at the KM initiative's start. During the "global rollout" stage, ShareNet managers cooperated widely on a regional basis, e.g. jointly conducted rollout workshops. A final indication for "commitment to the project" was the symbolic contract for change presented at the implementation review conference: all ShareNet managers and operating team members promised to support the KMS with all effort.

User involvement ("UIN") mandates an active participation of all affected stakeholders. Academics still debate the factor's area of impact: on the one hand, it fosters a sense of ownership and increases the assessment of system requirements' quality (Tyran & George, 1993, p. 7); on the other hand, it contributes to forming realistic expectations about the IS (Ginzberg, 1981a, pp. 475-476). Studying ShareNet's rollout, participative development ran across all KMS implementation stages (Ginzberg, 1981b, p. 48). There are indications for two of Nutt's (1986, pp. 246-248) variations of user involvement. "Delegated participation" was selected for the key project stages to avoid lengthy coordination with too many affected stakeholders. "Complete participation" with a restricted role of task forces dominated the key evolution stages. Since ShareNet had some 4,200 registered users by the end of the "global rollout" stage - and spread across four business units and 30 countries - a full delegation of all maintenance and evolution efforts was too complex. I propose that user involvement (in order to create a sense of ownership) is critical to KMS implementation projects, especially to those aiming for the creation of knowledge networks (Alavi & Leidner, 2001, p. 114).

From the outset, 40 sales representatives from headquarters and 15 local companies augmented the ShareNet project team. They were stakeholder advocates for regional markets in all development stages (deployment, extension, upgrade, and customization) and specified complete KMS solutions, i.e. "delegated participation". Key activities were mapping the solutions-selling process with the required knowledge for each step, defining a data model and review process, testing the Bitlab and ArsDigita working prototypes, and proposing a consistent organizational structure. To keep up speed of implementation by avoiding lengthy coordination with other IS owners, ShareNet's integration with other knowledge sources and systems was rejected. The ten regional workshops and the three central workshops during the "definition and prototyping" stage were clear measures for "delegated participation". Nominating one part-time ShareNet manager per country expanded the considerable user base already involved. When the international rollout began, the user champions relayed change requests and other suggestions for improvement to the ShareNet project team - first informally, later formally at the implementation review conference.

The transfer of the KMS' ownership to the ShareNet operating team marked both the beginning of the "operation, expansion, and further development" stage and the shift from "delegated participation" to "complete participation". The delegation of all implementation efforts to stakeholder representatives gave way to full user involvement. However, only the framing of solutions, i.e. change requests, was intended; the definition of implementation details remained the ShareNet operating team's duty. Through the new team, users should finally assume ownership and responsibility for all maintenance and evolution efforts. The case study reveals some indications for this successful variation of user involvement. First, the SIMT study on ShareNet usage and user satisfaction resulted in several change requests and valuable feedback. Second, numerous user requests for CoPs focusing on specific topics of interest triggered the development of a company-wide, multi-community platform. Nonetheless, a new working prototype and a corresponding discussion forum encountered only minor traffic and aroused little interest. While users were inclined to contribute general ideas for improvement, they were reluctant to participate hands-on.

To a minor extent, the ShareNet operating team continued with "delegated participation". In October 2000, the top 50 contributors were invited to New York. While the ShareNet operating team reinforced community spirit and reviewed implementation status and successes, another objective was to define ideas for the KMS' expansion and further development. A better integration with business processes, e.g. employee and executive target agreements, change management measures, and CoPs were crucial discussion points. Two months later, the Istanbul ShareNet manager conference carried on with "delegated participation". Some 60 participants debated the quality assurance and reward system, defined ShareNet manager targets and incentive schemes, and considered the inclusion of other CoPs. While "complete participation" mostly resulted in general ideas for later KMS versions, the user champion conferences were more detailed and effective. Two counterexamples add to user involvement's positive impact: both the service and the R&D community declined most participative development; as a result, the inclusion of the user group was less successful than the main rollout.

User training ("UTR") teaches the KMS' scope and handling, its relation to the firm, and the importance of teamwork at all organizational levels (Brelade & Harman, 2000, p. 28; Krovi, 1993, p. 334; Seeley, 2000, p. 28). The change agents began with informal user trainings, later developed a formal learning plan with the external consultancy Change Factory, and concluded minor rollouts at the end of the "operation, expansion, and further development" stage once again with informal trainings. Up to the mid of the second key project stage, BTP/BTC and BCG employees conducted some basic schooling for the core team's sales representatives and the pilot participants. Main objectives were to develop a concrete appreciation for the KM initiative, to ensure local company preparation, and to identify projects, solutions, and practices for global knowledge leverage. Meinert's first experiences and feedback from the regional and pilot workshops became the origins of the training program for the international roll-out, i.e. local company workshop briefcases.

When the external consultancy Change Factory joined ship, user trainings were formalized with learning plans. Those highlighted: learning topics, i.e. "creating necessary know-how for using ShareNet" and "capturing knowledge with ShareNet", delivery methods, e.g. local company workshops, training videos, and pocket references, responsibilities for ShareNet consultants and ShareNet managers, timing, and feedback mechanisms, i.e. discussion forums. Due to the size of the sales and marketing community, the ShareNet project team decided on a "snowball" training system: during the "global rollout" stage, boot camps enabled ShareNet managers to take over the responsibility for the KMS' implementation in local companies. All training material clarified the KMS' benefits for daily work and the link between knowledge-orientation and economic benefits. Incorporating disconfirmation and business purpose linkage factors enhanced the workshops' credibility and impact.

Indications for user training factors weakened at the end of the "operation, expansion, and further development" stage. For the service rollout, Baumann provided only a few hours of informal trainings based on the workshop concept and screenshots. During the multi-community rollout, a shortage of (financial) resources prevented ShareNet consultants from traveling and conducting trainings. The case description indicates user trainings' importance to combined KM and change initiatives. All SIMT survey participants agreed that ShareNet managers were vital to conduct user trainings adapted to local companies' needs. To convince the user champions to spend even more time on general user support, i.e. user trainings, presentations, and monthly reports, four ShareNet manager targets were formulated and linked to incentives and rewards for fiscal 2001. Due to the strict requirements, only 20 ShareNet managers handled their (KMS) responsibilities well enough to receive a bonus of 50-120% of an additional fixed monthly salary. However, the multi-community platform's user-friendly GUI, as well as sociability and networking with ShareNet "peers" were able to compensate for some lack of formal, top-down trainings (Earl, 2001, p. 225).

Disconfirmation ("DIS") expands the four "traditional" critical success factors for IS implementation projects - analyzed above - with a culture change-based perspective. Due to the human factors involved, KMS rollouts require additional sources of motivation. Disconfirming data are often symptomatic. Instead of revealing the source of problems, they make employees uncomfortable by pointing out defunct business processes, e.g. decreasing revenues, growing customer complaints, and increasing attrition (Lewin, 1947, p. 211; Schein, 1992, pp. 298-299; Spector, 1989, p. 30; Zack, 1999, p. 211). The case study shows indications for all methods Beer (1988, pp. 1-2) recommends for diffusing dissatisfaction, i.e. "top-down creation of competitive awareness", "bottom-up communication of employee concerns", " joint diagnosis of business problems", and "setting high standards and expectations". In accordance with the theory, disconfirmation factors were only used prior to the "global rollout" stage.

As Kuhn already noted, most sales and marketing knowledge resided in local companies; they were the first to recognize and communicate the need for a KM initiative. The "bottom-up communication of concerns and perceptions" was taken up by BTP/BTC who considered a KMS for the first time in 1998. To make sure that ShareNet provided value-add to the sales and marketing community, sales representatives from headquarters and local companies were invited for a "joint diagnosis of business problems". They supported a network of people with similar difficulties.

With the vision statement, the change agents switched to "setting high standards and expectations" for the sales and marketing community: "ICN ShareNet is the global knowledge sharing network. We leverage our local innovations globally. We are a community committed to increase value for our customers and ICN by creating and re-applying leading-edge solutions." At the end of the "definition and prototyping" stage, Koch's decision to continue the project further strengthened the call for changes in the employees' mindset. Again, he emphasized Siemens ICN's shift from "box selling" to a service focus and solutions approach and the need to be among the first to capitalize on existing competencies and experiences.

Of all methods for diffusing dissatisfaction, change agents used "top-down creation of competitive awareness" most widely. For the period of ShareNet's rollout in four pilot countries, the core team informed managers about knowledge-orientation's benefits and educated employees about the different business situation. When the formalized local company workshop briefcases were brought to use, a case study about an almost lost Malaysian sales project fostered dissatisfaction with the prevailing status quo and illustrated Siemens ICN's transformation in the telecommunications sector. The workshop participants should start to reflect isolated working routines and discover that only the global leverage of knowledge ensured long-term success. Relations between disconfirmation factors and KMS implementation success are strengthened with a comparison of local company, headquarters, and R&D rollouts. The latter showed higher implementation resistance than Siemens ICN's front lines: they were more remote from customers, were less impacted by the telecommunications sector's value chain deconstruction, and in consequence showed reduced motivation to change.

Business purpose linkage ("BPL") establishes a connection between KM and change initiatives and important objectives and ideals, e.g. economic benefits or competitiveness. In symbiosis with disconfirmation, it forces organization members to accept the need for (culture) change. A combination of both factors is suggested: today's knowledge workers/specialists no longer need a two-stage education (disconfirmation preceding business purpose); a compelling business case for knowledge-orientation proves sufficient (Drucker, 1988, p. 47). Projects usually get easier funding when some relationship becomes clear (Alavi & Leidner, 1999, p. 22; Davenport et al., 1998, p. 50; Lucier & Torsilieri, 1997, p. 15; Storey & Barnett, 2000, p. 154; Wilson, 2000, p. 9). Employees begin to experience survival anxiety or guilt since disconfirmation factors can no longer be ignored, even if they are threatening (Schein, 1992, pp. 299-300; 1999, pp. 121-124). As prescribed by Lewin-Schein, only the first three key project stages reveal indications for business purpose linkage factors. Most heavy use was made during the "definition and prototyping" and "setup and piloting" stages, showing complementariness with methods for diffusing dissatisfaction.

The vision statement served a dual purpose: it was employed for "setting high standards and expectations" and emphasized ShareNet's overall economic objectives - increasing revenues and value for customers. Change agents continually communicated the intended benefits to all affected stakeholders. Cost reductions and shorter project delivery times should be realized through reuse of technical and functional solutions, as well as by avoiding expensive mistakes made in the past. Quality ought to improve as reusable modules were repetitively sold and enhanced. In result, lower costs, shorter delivery times, and improved quality would increase bids' chances for success and lead to higher turnover.

When the participants of the kick-off workshop mapped the Sales Value Creation Process, knowledge-orientation's impact on competitiveness and innovativeness became clear. Knowledge leverage between local project teams should enhance the competitive positioning since they focused on the same market. As by-products, knowledge sharing between peer countries and market stages were automatically obtained, virtually gratis (Gibbert, Kugler et al., 2002, p. 51). Since more value could be created than after a sales contract was signed, ShareNet was targeted on the business development, pre-acquisition, and bid preparation phases.

As soon as the KMS' connection to Siemens ICN objectives and ideals had become clear, the ShareNet project team decided on two main knowledge categories. Codified knowledge was structured knowledge about everything needed to create a solution. Personalized knowledge fostered the creation of knowledge networks and provided quick help, i.e. less tangible benefits. During the second key project stage, a mission statement reaffirmed the economic benefits anticipated by Koch: "ICN ShareNet intends to network all local sales efforts to facilitate global learning, local reuse of global best practices, and the creation of global solution competencies. ICN ShareNet shall realize considerable and measurable business impact through time and cost savings and through the creation of new sales opportunities." Whereas the missions belonged to passive change communications, the two-sectioned local company workshops allowed for a dynamic discovery of the KMS' benefits for daily work. I postulate that active stakeholder involvement in unearthing the economic benefits of KM and change initiatives is a powerful driver for change. It complements a "joint diagnosis of business problems" and user involvement factors, i.e. shows a direction for overcoming business challenges.

The incentive system bonus-on-top was targeted on local executives. Besides nurturing "executive involvement", it linked knowledge-orientation with economic benefits: local ICN heads should be rewarded for inter-country business generated through substantial international knowledge exchange. For the first time at top management level, Siemens ICN placed more value on teamwork than on individual achievements. Reaching out to peers for knowledge sharing across functional and organizational barriers instead of playing political games was desired (Seeley, 2000, p. 25). With the additional motivators, the local company rollouts proceeded smoothly and in contrast to the headquarters and U.S. rollouts. Negative business purpose linkage factors dominated the latter: business units feared losing sales opportunities for internal services and questioned the local companies' value creation. The same held true for the U.S. where executives questioned ShareNet's organizational integration and the link to business objectives. Furthermore, their Sales Value Creation Process was claimed to map better to Siebel's CRM application than to the KMS.

4.1.2   Revealing Critical Success Factors for Cognitive Restructuring

For "cognitive restructuring", Lewin-Schein's interventions provided less IS-specific guidance. I postulate that trial-and-error factors have minor significance for KMS implementation projects. Since they occurred earlier than theory predicted and often in arrangement with rapid prototyping and user involvement, a grouping of these factors is encouraged. Example setting factors, e.g. pilot studies, success stories, and user champions were more widely used throughout all implementation stages and show considerable overlap with Sathe's (1985; 1993) socialization process. This second "group" factor qualifies as a significant enabler for combined KM and change initiatives aiming for the creation of knowledge networks (Alavi & Leidner, 2001, p. 114).

Trial-and-error learning ("TAE") happens by scanning the work environment for possible options. Learners may choose between means, but not about the final goals which have already been laid out in vision and mission statements (Schein, 1992, pp. 301-302; 1999, pp. 128-129). Considering IS implementation a deliberate, planned "process of preparing an organization for a new system and introducing the system in such a way as to assure its successful use" (Tyran & George, 1993, p. 6) defeats the very nature of trial-and-error learning. It is less applicable to the new setting of KMS than it is for culture change: rapid prototyping or symbolic means were the only occurrences. The first two key project stages' description indeed reveals that prototyping was effective for building commitment, better communication, and developing stakeholder appreciation (Krovi, 1993, p. 334; Teng et al., 1996, p. 282). There are only minimal indications for trial-and-error factors in the "global rollout" stage. The KMS' progressing organizational integration made an experimental path to "cognitive restructuring" obsolete.

At the kick-off workshop, it was true brainstorming when the 40 sales representatives from headquarters and 15 local companies mapped the Sales Value Creation Process. With the facilitation of BTP/BTC and BCG employees, knowledge leverage's impact was jointly discovered. Trial-and-error learning was the next logical step to a "joint diagnosis of business problems." The testing of the Bitlab and ArsDigita working prototypes in the "definition and prototyping" and the "setup and piloting" stages was a further clear measure for experimentation. Since the former suffered from performance problems and low usability, the ShareNet project team decided to switch technology partners. With the latter, fewer obstacles emerged and all feedback forms/change requests were resolved before the international rollout started. Since the core team feared that integration with other knowledge sources and systems would slow down speed of implementation, such proposals were rejected outright.

The workshop participants were never reluctant to overthrow ideas, (change management) interventions, and technologies which had proven unfeasible. Early on, one of the managerial systems' main objectives - the transformation of information into best practices and "wisdom" within "knowledge cells" - was given up. Most affected stakeholders considered it a too formal way to cooperate with unclear benefits. To maintain a friendly and relaxed climate for change, trial-and-error learning was also used in a symbolic way: ShareNet managers had to build rafts without tools at the Feldafing boot camps. They learned that only cooperation led to success - even without prior personal contact and to some extent reliant on digital conversations and discussions (Thomas et al., 2001, p. 872). However, this factor specifically confirms the difficulties Srinivasan and Davis (1987, p. 65) uncovered by applying the Lewin-Schein change paradigm, suffering from too much generality.

Example setting ("ESE") is a second path to chose and implement particular interventions. Individuals, organizational units, and pilot studies can serve as role models for the entire company: they foster credibility at management level and promote an understanding of the KM and change initiative at employee level (Beer, 1988, p. 3; Beer et al., 1990, p. 165; Krovi, 1993, p. 328; Orlikowski, 1992, p. 369; Spector, 1989, p. 32). Case study data shows earlier and more continuous indications for example setting factors than predicted by theory. Similar to trial-and-error learning, rapid prototyping in connection with user involvement altered the predicted, different pattern over time. Example setting and user involvement factors therefore classify as the only two "recurrent themes" running across all implementation stages (Ginzberg, 1981b, p. 48). Even though, the ShareNet project team made most use of examples and role models during the "global rollout" and "operation, expansion, and further development" stages.

During the first two key project stages - and the last key evolution stage - example setting factors were restricted to impersonal means. Technological immaturity did not allow for human role models demonstrating the contribution and sharing of knowledge, making use of KMS (King et al., 2002, p. 96). As an alternative, early win-showcases (projects, solutions, and practices for knowledge leverage) were used to create local company demand and first commitment to change. All content and corresponding discussion forums were hosted on an intranet site for global access. When pilot studies were introduced to a limited four countries (Laudon & Laudon, 2002, pp. 319-320), the core team again aimed for positive spill-overs. BTP/BTC coaches helped to grew employee buy-in, personal networks, and trust among Siemens ICN's front lines. Exemplary sales projects, tips, and tricks were identified for later knowledge capturing and reuse. During the R&D rollout, final and indirect indications for example setting factors showed. While the virtual R&D conference had a weak start, on the following day researchers and developers recognized the full potential of Share-Net's people-to-people section and successfully spread the word among their colleagues.

During the KMS' international rollout and expansion to other user groups, e.g. the Siemens ICM and the service communities, there were several occurrences of (personal) example setting factors. The consistent organizational structure with dedicated ShareNet managers for each country was an important driver for change. Most user champions - many of them sales representatives formerly involved with the core team - had already internalized the benefits of knowledge-orientation and proactively recruited new users. The ShareNet managers' status as role models was confirmed by the SIMT study on KMS acceptance and usage: they were "vital in promoting ShareNet and its workshops" (Mann et al., 2000, p. 33). While user champions served as "professional" multiplicators, i.e. devoting 20-50% of their working time, regular users set informal, but no less effective examples. The core team recognized and rewarded some role models, e.g. the top 50 contributors with the New York ShareNet user conference. Formal commendations surely reinforced community spirit but were not automatically claimed as due by supportive users. For the Siemens ICM rollout, the former Siemens ICN employees' exemplary and unsolicited behavior sufficed.

Contrasting experiences were made with the U.S. rollout: convincing users to post best practices proved to be a difficult task for ShareNet consultants and managers. Considering the exploratory case study as an early basis for causal inferences, isolating the moderating influences from the "not invented here" syndrome, the difficult business situation, and the guarding of proprietary IS (Siebel CRM tool) is impossible. To some extent, the ShareNet project and operating teams continued the use of impersonal examples. Success stories describing successful cases of collaboration - required for the bonus-on-top promotion scheme - illustrated the change process and fostered managerial commitment. In addition, ShareNet's coupling with the service community's VITAC application enhanced visibility with potential users. In conclusion, the case description reveals that personal example setting factors had stronger clout than impersonal ones but lacked global reach. I propose a blend for large scale KMS implementation projects to overcome particular deficits.

4.1.3   Revealing Critical Success Factors for Refreezing

The main "refreezing" activities, i.e. the KMS' organizational integration, the determination of behavioral und cultural shifts, and the dissemination of confirming data, were all found at the research site. The Lewin-Schein change paradigm now again provided good IS-specific direction for change agents. As predicted by theory, first indications for organizational integration and behavioral and cultural diagnosis factors show in the "global rollout" stage and continue for the research period. I propose that both indicators must be positive before a new quasi-stationary equilibrium can be stabilized with confirmation factors (Krovi, 1993, p. 328; Zand & Sorensen, 1975, p. 534). Accordingly, indications for the latter factor are only found during key evolution stages.

Organizational integration ("OIN") describes the process of embedding and institutionalizing IS into the organizational context, i.e. technology's fit with strategy and structure (Grover & Davenport, 2001, pp.12-13). Users assume ownership and responsibility for ongoing maintenance and evolution (Jin & Franz, 1986, p. 71; Keen, 1981, p. 26). When the KMS' international rollout began in August 1999, BTP/BTC coaches and ShareNet committee members visited 18 selected countries for promotion and support. In the absence of obstacles, local implementations required two or three months of ShareNet manager/project work to build a stable user base. The entire implementation process was centrally driven and monitored by the ShareNet project team. All local companies were taken up on the submitted rollout roadmaps. When deviations from agreed on, country-specific metrics were detected, problem discussions and gentle pressure started. In reminiscence, only few environments proved difficult for a broad international rollout, e.g. the U.S.

On conclusion of the first three key project stages, the implementation review conference saw further organizational integration factors, e.g. a formal hand-over ceremony. The ShareNet project team was replaced by a regular line organization with capabilities for consulting and teaching to provide continuing user assistance - right in line with theoretical prescriptions (Keen et al., 1982, p. 141; Krovi, 1993, p. 334). With this decision, Siemens ICN's group executive management signaled that ShareNet was no ordinary headquarters' initiative demanding precious resources (Rothnie, 2001, p. 188), but rather a source of sustainable competitive advantage. The "operation, expansion, and further development" and "shifting to a multi-community concept" stages witnessed several smaller rollouts: the Siemens ICM, service, and R&D communities expanded the ShareNet Community from some 4,200 to 18,000 registered users. Whereas the first implementation round relied on a centrally-driven rollout approach, the later expansions resembled a grassroots initiative. High user demand and socialization from peers made extensive user involvement and training unnecessary; the KMS was ever more regarded as a mature and Siemens-wide best practice.

The ShareNet operating team's increasing responsiveness to end users and other IS owners provide supplementary indications for organizational integration factors. KMS implementation projects depend as much on horizontal integration, i.e. coupling to business processes and applications, as on vertical integration, i.e. user acceptance. For a better embedding into the structural context, Siemens ShareNet V1.x - a company-wide, multi-community platform - was introduced. The new team decided a further delegation of maintenance and evolution responsibilities: for the first time, smaller CoPs could adapt functional modules, organizational roles, and specific content to their business processes. An early goal for the ShareNet Community had become reality. For a better embedding into the technological context, a joint development consortium was formed with the owners of other knowledge sources and systems. It included workgroups from the central function CIO as well as from the group division SBS. Main objective was a tight integration with Siemens ICN's global technology infrastructure, especially with the corporate document management system OpenText Livelink.

Behavioral and cultural diagnosis ("BCD") is employed by change agents to decide either on the project's conclusion or on regresses to preceding stages. Measures and standards are devised to evaluate the results of the combined KM and change initiative, i.e. technology's fit with people/culture (Grover & Davenport, 2001, pp.12-13). User satisfaction - a widely used proxy for the dependent variable - and general end user feedback make for proper behavioral and cultural diagnosis factors. Some academics encourage client self-analysis based on objective evaluation indices (Jin & Franz, 1986, p. 71; Kolb & Frohman, 1970, p. 61; Zand & Sorensen, 1975, p. 542). Similar to organizational integration factors, case study data shows first indications in the "global rollout" stage which continue for the research period. There is significant overlap with Sathe's (1985;

1993) theoretical framework: whereas Lewin-Schein recommend cultural diagnosis only during "refreezing", Sathe proposes constant attention to "justifications of behavior" to adjust change communications and motivators. Consequently, I propose a synthesis of the two factors.

The ShareNet project team found first evidence for the successful internalization of knowledge-orientation into the employees' behavior and Siemens ICN's organizational cultures with the user champions, i.e. ShareNet managers. Most of them volunteered for the semi-formal jobs when they had recognized the benefits of proactively searching and offering knowledge. During the "global rollout" stage, activities and cooperation prospered. On their own initiative, the social network of ShareNet managers conducted joint rollout workshops, e.g. in the Andean region and several other places in Europe. In addition to ShareNet consultants' personal contact with user champions, formal rollout scorecards were used to measure local progress. While the (mainly) quantitative metrics were appropriate to cluster regional projects and to diagnose behavior change, they were less helpful to detect culture change. The core team approved of the local sales and marketing employees' openness to information exchange. In their opinion, behavior change occurred simultaneously with culture change, showed after a few years, but needed a decade to become self-sustaining. Curiosity, interest, and first experiences made many KM believers which in turn reinforced the new behavior.

Resistance at headquarters was taken seriously. Inactivity and lack of implementation support, postponing decisions, and all kinds of mobbing and politics led to less importance placed on the business units. BTP/BTC coaches noticed similar challenges on a smaller scale with the U.S. rollout: on the one hand, employees showed the "not invented here" syndrome; on the other hand, management criticized ShareNet's missing connection to economic benefits and the insufficient degree of organizational integration. The SIMT survey for analyzing ShareNet's acceptance and usage - mentioned several times above - was another formal instance of behavioral and cultural diagnosis factors. Positive evidence for culture change accomplished was that information and contacts were singled out as prime motivators, incentives and rewards were less essential. Time constraints were seen as the most important barrier to KMS usage: overloaded sales representatives did not have "time to respond to requests from across the globe."

Users and the ShareNet operating team experienced the impact from a collapsing telecommunications sector for the first time in the "operation, expansion, and further development" stage and in connection with the service rollout. A limited number of new projects led to less objects contributed to the knowledge library which in turn diminished users' motivation to explore. Before the company-wide, multi-community platform was introduced, the new team tried to size up the current situation. Positive feelings dominated: the successful, bottom-up creation of knowledge networks was reflected by numerous requests for IT-enabled CoPs. A common code of conduct comprised several aspects of a knowledge-intensive culture: the majority of employees acknowledged the need for global knowledge leverage, exchanged content without ever making personal contact, and policed the network for low quality postings. Some team members cautioned that a discontinuation of the incentive catalog would lead to severe drops in contributions or even a deadlock situation.

Confirmation ("CON") concludes the (culture) change process. These new ways of thinking and working had to become personally internalized and part of knowledge-intensive cultures. Confirming data, e.g. positive feedback from change agents to affected stakeholders, are used to bring back the organization to stability (Levasseur, 2001, p. 73; Schein, 1992, p. 303; 1999, p. 129; Srinivasan & Davis, 1987, p. 65; Zand & Sorensen, 1975, p. 542). The case description unveils that confirmation factors lag behind organizational integration and behavioral and cultural diagnosis factors. Both had to yield positive responses before change agents started sparse and often symbolic "refreezing" activities in the key evolution stages.

First results from behavior and culture change showed on the conclusion of the "global rollout" stage: some 4,200 users had registered for ShareNet and posted more than 2,100 public knowledge objects and 490 urgent requests - a critical mass was reached. At the ShareNet manager implementation review conference, Döring approved of the progress made. His confirmatory statement emphasized that "ICN ShareNet [was] more than a database; it [was] a new spirit to cooperate worldwide across country- and organizational boundaries." The praise of the ShareNet managers' work implied no reduction of efforts, but rather more stable responsibilities and tasks. Project work was over. Soon after, he added to confirmation at user champion level: the 40 sales representatives who were involved with the core team were promoted for their KM efforts.

Confirmation factors also spread at employee level. During the New York ShareNet user conference, the new team presented the implementation project's general status and successes. The end users served a dual purpose: they multiplied the change agent's feedback, i.e. satisfaction with the goals achieved, and set a personal example for knowledge-orientation. In the "shifting to a multi-community concept" stage, confirmation factors and top management support factors overlapped. Von Pierer declared ShareNet's technical platform and phased rollout approach a Siemens-wide KMS best practice. He backed up the importance Siemens' managing board placed on the systematic exploitation of internal expertise. Ganswindt also urged the ShareNet Community to keep up the good work: "global networking and sharing knowledge is key to the success of ICN, even more since we will no longer have all the necessary knowledge in all local companies."

Case study data suggests attention to other categories of confirming data besides managerial communications. ShareNet's technical platform offered dedicated feedback channels. Free text comments and a five-star rating scheme could be used to judge the quality of contributions (comp. Schultz et al., 1987, pp. 36-40). While peer messages were somewhat symbolic, their continuity and reach helped to create informal networks. More than would ever be possible with measures like additional revenues and cost savings, the benefits of a knowledge-intensive culture became personally clear. ShareNet showed KMS' potential for the electronic dissemination of confirming data.

4.1.4   Findings Related to a Sequential Implementation Perspective

My exploratory design allowed for a combination of discovery and testing (Cavaye, 1996, pp. 275-276; Darke et al., 1998, p. 236): time-series analysis (Yin, 1994, pp. 113-118) confirmed the applicability of Lewin-Schein's theoretical framework while further causal relations and interferences emerged. Case study data reveals indications for the isolated conceptual variables/factors, listed in table 4. With the exception of user involvement and factors from the change paradigm's second stage, all show the predicted, different pattern over time. In

Table 4: Revealing Success Factors for Linear, Staged Change

	DIS	BPL	TMS	COM	UIN	UTR	ESE	TAE	OIN	BCD	CON
First Key Project Stage Definition and Prototyping	√	√	√	√	√	√	√	√			
Second Key Project Stage Setup and Piloting	√	√	√	√	√	√	√	√			
Third Key Project Stage Global Rollout		√	√	√	√	√	√		√	√	
Fourth Key Evolution Stage Operation, Expansion, and Further Development		√		√	√	√			√	√	√
Fifth Key Evolution Stage Shifting to a Multi-Community Concept				√		√			√	√	√

Factor abbreviations: DIS: disconfirmation, BPL: business purpose linkage, TMS: top management support, COM: commitment, UIN: user involvement, UTR: user training, ESE: example setting, TAE: trial-and-error, OIN: organizational integration, BCD: behavioral and cultural diagnosis, CON: confirmation the "unfreezing" stage, disconfirmation and business purpose linkage factors built a foundation for the "traditional" critical success factors top management support, commitment, user involvement, and user training (matching with psychological safety factors). The "cognitive restructuring" stage provided fewer explanations for IS implementations: trial-and-error factors had limited significance, while (personal and impersonal) example setting factors showed overlap with socialization factors from the other change paradigm. Integration is proposed. Finally, in the "refreezing" stage, organizational integration and behavioral and cultural diagnosis factors paved the ground for concluding confirmation factors.

4.2   A Circular, Continuous Perspective to Explain Success and Failure

4.2.1   Unveiling Critical Success Factors for Behavior Change

The application of pattern-matching (Yin, 1994, pp. 106-110) to the Sathe change paradigm confirms the predicted self-perpetuating processes that shape organizational cultures and their manifestations (Sathe, 1985, pp. 385-386; 1993, pp. 337-339). With the exception of the first process (behavior), the theoretical framework deals more with change driver categories than with particular interventions. Following this line of argumentation, a higher aggregation level consequently turns up "recurrent themes" rather than sequential issues. The Lewin-Schein change paradigm provides more IS-specific guidance for prescriptive analysis. However, indications for all isolated factors are present and for the most part positive. They offer a complementary perspective for understanding success and failure of KMS implementation projects.

Extrinsic and intrinsic motivators ("EIM") are most effective to change people's behaviors, i.e. to foster cooperation, teamwork, and knowledge sharing across functional and organizational barriers (Gold et al., 2001, p. 189; Seeley, 2000, p. 25; Stein & Zwass, 1995, p. 108; Stewart et al., 2000, p. 47). These interventions shape knowledge-intensive cultures, either simultaneously or later on. According to the majority of (former) BTP/BTC members, behavior change occurred simultaneously with culture change: first experiences made many users believers in the KMS and in a knowledge-intensive culture; this in turn reinforced the new behavior. According to one ShareNet consultant, the KMS was intended as a tool for culture change; the smooth implementation served vice versa as an argument for successful change.

Since the change agents used both sources of motivation, literature prescriptions - arguing for long-term, team-based, and intrinsic motivators - were somewhat contradicted (O'Dell & Grayson, 1998, pp. 168-170; Sathe, 1985, pp. 386-387). Extrinsic motivation is commonly associated with compliance while intrin-

sic motivation pertains to commitment (Beer, 1988, p. 3). Case study data corrobates a link between behavior change and commitment to change (Beer et al.,
1990, p. 165), but allows for no differentiation. Indications for extrinsic and
intrinsic motivation factors are found across all implementation stages but the
first. In accordance with a "snowball" implementation approach, extrinsic motivators were first used at user champion level, later at employee level.

Not considering the three main incentive schemes, extrinsic motivation and
top management support factors overlap. While Koch and Meinert's personal
requests for ShareNet manager nominations had positive impact, the forced
selection of user champions resulted in lacks of competence and commitment or
too strong a focus on technology. Most of the sales representatives who were
involved with the KMS' key project stages were promoted for KM efforts. The
ShareNet line organization and user champions were further motivated when von
Pierer publicly praised ShareNet's technical platform and culturally-sensitive
rollout approach. Taking into account all implementation stages, these "symbolic" extrinsic motivators had limited clout.

I postulate that the short-term extrinsic incentive schemes "bonus-on-top"
(for local ICN heads), quality assurance and reward system with incentive catalog, and ShareNet manager targets were main change enablers. While all systems
targeted individuals, they were set up in a way that only teamwork allowed for
reaping the benefits: local ICN executives had to work together to generate inter-
country business, employees had to cooperate as knowledge givers and takers,
and user champions were required to motivate end users. The ShareNet operating and project teams placed more weight on team-based extrinsic motivators
than on intrinsic ones. At user level, the non-competitive share system was key
to acquire a critical mass of content, to make users active contributors, and to
create awareness. The KMS needed integration with daily work without increasing the employees' workload (Vorbeck & Finke, 2001, p. 42).

ShareNet's technical systems distributed shares for postings and reuse feedback that could be redeemed for incentives. Feedback from knowledge takers -
either free text or a five-star rating - was an additional extrinsic motivator and
emphasized the creation of social networks (Alavi & Leidner, 2001, p. 114). In
the "shifting to a multi-community concept" stage, top managers named two
reasons for the share system's conversion: first, implementation success was
established; second, the collapsing telecommunications sector made cost cutting
mandatory for Siemens ICN. Alternative plans were a better integration with
business processes, employee target agreements, and Siemens Leadership
Framework (SLF), or the recognition of "knowledge champions". Up to that
point, decisions were neither taken nor implemented by the central function HR.

While extrinsic motivation factors resembled short-term deliberate interventions, intrinsic motivation factors were casually interwoven with other measures.

In the long term, employees ought to recognize that performance improvements through knowledge leverage were sufficient incentive (Probst et al., 1999, p. 308). Experiencing community spirit and problem solutions build intrinsic motivation. The case description unearths mutual moderating influences between socialization and intrinsic motivation factors. During the "setup and piloting" stage, working prototypes and visits from BTP/BTC and ShareNet committee members informed local key executives about knowledge-orientation's benefits, i.e. created personal awareness and commitment. The local company workshop briefcases were further indications for intrinsic motivation factors: they demonstrated the value-add of global knowledge exchange at organizational and individual level; theory was combined with concrete examples relevant for local sales representatives. Participants were asked to post real urgent requests at the trainings' start. The core team members answered either personally (with pseudonyms), or used their personal networks.

Besides personal interventions - through contacts and user trainings - ShareNet's technical platform itself was intrinsically motivating. The self-explanatory GUI and the capturing wizard reduced barriers of entry and made many end users KM advocates - right in line with literature prescriptions (comp. Goodman & Darr, 1998, p. 425; Jarvenpaa & Staples, 2000, p. 131). Only the multicommunity platform's introduction incurred some criticism: end users complained about the new layout, many bugs, and weak performance. The negative influences had a temporarily negative impact on intrinsic motivation. The difficult economic environment added to this influence: a limited number of new projects led to fewer contributions which finally diminished user interest. To answer Alavi & Leidner's (2001, p. 128) research question concerning effective incentives for knowledge sharing, case study data reveals sparse indications for intrinsic motivation factors. Siemens ICN's emphasis on extrinsic motivation factors for behavior change slowed down sustainable culture change.

4.2.2   Unveiling Critical Success Factors for Behavior Justifications

Behavior rationalization assessments ("BRA") are conducted by change agents to detect challenges for culture change. Diagnosis focuses on prime motivations for behavior change - compliance vs. commitment - to decide on incentives and rewards, as well as replacements. Employees should not rationalize their actions in terms of extrinsic motivators but adopt a new pattern of values and beliefs, e.g. fairness, organizational ownership, and trust (Harper, 2001, p. 14; Jarvenpaa & Staples, 2001, p. 165; Sathe, 1993, pp. 337-338). KMS users must believe that knowledge leverage is "usual, correct, and socially expected workplace behavior (Constant et al., 1994, p. 404). There are significant linkages with the linear, staged change paradigm (Lewin, 1947; Schein, 1992, 1999): while Sathe proposes continuous attention to "justifications of behavior", Lewin-Schein prescribes it only during "refreezing". The higher aggregation level of Sathe's (1985; 1993) factor made it a "recurrent theme" for ShareNet (Ginzberg, 1981b, p. 48). Consequently, I propose the factors' synthesis.

For the most part, the case description indicates informal behavior rationalization assessments. The ShareNet organization relied on personal experiences and appraisals; only two formal email surveys were ever conducted (in March 2000 and in October 2002). Even early in the "definition and prototyping" and the "setup and piloting" stages, the ShareNet project team considered the choice of interventions carefully: team members were aware that extrinsic motivation could only inflict short-term behavior change and should not become the prime driver for knowledge exchange. To accomplish the managerial systems' fourth goal - adopting a culture that rewarded the proactive seeking and offering of knowledge - employees had to internalize the KM initiative's desired benefits over and above their intrinsic motivation. They had to trust each other and Siemens ICN. First indications for anticipated behavior rationalizations were found with the 40 sales representatives who were earlier involved with brainstorming workshops: knowledge-orientation was soon embedded with their identity and relationships.

Later in the "operation, expansion, and further development" stage, the SIMT survey for analyzing ShareNet's impact on work, skills, and communication was another instance of behavior rationalization assessment factors. The ShareNet operating team saw positive evidence for culture change when information and contacts were named prime motivators, incentives and rewards less important. User statements confirmed the study's results: "Receiving some [...] award naturally serves as an incentive to sharing our knowledge with colleagues worldwide, but it is not the most important aspect." Case study data also shows some contradictions. Lots of contributions and registrations during the "ShareNet Special Weeks" - in connection with the quiz "Win a BMW (brand new mobile workstation)" - revealed that many users still justified their actions in terms of extrinsic motivators. Manuth criticized the special event afterwards: an artificial and expensive hype was created that rapidly ebbed off; there was no sustainable increase in the contributions' quality and quantity.

While the ShareNet operating team recognized the interrelationship, no alternative measures were taken. Only the number of shares awarded for particular contributions was adapted downwards. In addition to questionnaires, the ShareNet operating team made other attempts to size up Siemens ICN's organizational cultures. At the beginning of the combined KM and change initiative several obstacles were discovered: there were strong hierarchies, i.e. knowledge was equated with power, old boys' networks, risk adverse decision making, a "do-it-all yourself" engineering culture, and lacks of entrepreneurial initiative. Nevertheless, the shift from a top-down implementation approach to a bottom-up initiative - where users approached ShareNet managers and consultants for registration and support - signaled culture change at employee level.

At the end of the "shifting to a multi-community concept" stage, extensive discussions about incentives and rewards were further clear indications for behavior rationalization assessment factors. Generally, all ShareNet operating team members, sponsors, and user champions agreed that the KMS implementation project had triggered behavior change and initiated culture change. Most Siemens ICN employees showed higher responsiveness to international cooperation and requests for help; it was the only way to remain competitive and innovative, i.e. to foster responsiveness to a turbulent environment. Only a minority had a free-rider mentality and benefited from the system without contributing input.

There was no agreement on whether the knowledge-intensive culture had reached a self-sustaining level (without substantive extrinsic motivators): would users keep their motivation on a high level since they had internalized the benefits of knowledge-orientation, or would a downward spiral start in the electronic knowledge base (Manago & Auriol, 1996, p. 28)? In accordance with the theory, some change agents considered extrinsic motivators the best-manageable tool to steer the number of contributions (Osterloh & Frey, 2000, p. 540; 2001, p. 102). In their words, the share system promised the "biggest bang for the buck": spending the same amount of money on change management, technology, or training would have smaller impact.

4.2.3   Unveiling Critical Success Factors for Cultural Communications

Change Communications ("CCO") comprise a mix of explicit and implicit interventions to emphasize the necessity of knowledge exchange. Change agents must communicate the interrelationship between KM and change process, as well as goals intended (O'Dell & Grayson, 1998, p. 173; Seeley, 2000, pp. 27-28). There are two main requirements: first, communication has to be credible, i.e. backing up words with actual deeds (Jin & Franz, 1986, p. 72; Keen, 1981, p. 30; von Krogh, 1998, pp. 144-145); second, it ought to be persuasive. For the latter prerequisite, Sathe (1985, pp. 393-394; 1993, pp. 338-339) alternatively recommends role model identification or trial-and-error learning - both factors from Schein's (1992; 1999) "cognitive restructuring" stage. Taking up other authors' argumentation (Bhatt, 2001, p. 72; Dewett & Jones, 2001, p. 8; Orlikowski, 1992, p. 386; Thomas et al., 2001, p. 872; Yazici, 2002, p. 550), I deem KMS themselves an important change driver: digital conversations and discussions - across time and space - can promote the diffusion of cultural expectations, norms, and values.

Of all factors, case study data reveals continuous and numerous indications for communication interventions. Nevertheless, the difficult business situation during later key evolution stages also had negative impact on this factor. Top management mainly relied on well-planned explicit forms, i.e. vision, mission, and abundant statements/requests, to bundle resources and commitment to the project. Together with the ShareNet project team, they began early in the "definition and prototyping" stage to communicate the KMS' main goals (cost savings and new sales opportunities) to all affected stakeholders; before long, disconfirmation and economic objectives were widely experienced. A few months later, the same change agents began to meet key local company managers in four pilot and 18 major rollout countries to increase the number of multiplicators. The external consultancy Change Factory began in parallel with the development of a workshop concept and a communications campaign. Training videos, pocket references, and promotion items were measures to create user level buy-in. In agreement with the APQC and MAKE research programs, I consider the local company workshop briefcases the most effective communication medium for the "global rollout" stage.

Success stories served a dual purpose: they were indications for example setting and change communication factors. Their wide and repetitious broadcast made the promotion campaign more persuasive. Kuhn and Tsusaki used the second path to enhance persuasiveness for the U.S. rollout, i.e. web-based trainings and "try it, you will like it" messages. The broad international rollout - and all subsequent expansions - relied not only on top-down communications but left room for adequate feedback mechanisms, e.g. change requests, conferences, and rollout scorecards. ShareNet consultants and the global editor discussed local implementation progress continuously with user champions and informed about new technical developments. The ShareNet user conference, as well as the two ShareNet manager conferences (at Sun City and Istanbul), were additional forums to cultivate community spirit, to exchange experiences, and to discuss the KMS' expansion to other communities. Even when the difficult economic environment mandated a conversion of the share system, clear communications about the underlying reasons were backed-up by top management. Döring and his counterpart from Siemens ICM sent an (electronic) letter to inform all registered users.

The technical platform facilitated culture change through additional communication channels: it changed Siemens ICN's communication flow from a broadcast-oriented "enabling" approach, i.e. headquarters to local companies, to a meshed network approach required for knowledge exchange. Especially the KMS' people-to-people section with urgent requests, discussion forums, news, and chats facilitated informal interactions within the ShareNet Community. Richness and openness were mandatory requirements. Similar to the shift from formal user trainings to informal hand-on experiences, explicit change communication factors were slowly substituted by implicit ones: user champions and committed contributors took over some responsibility for promoting ShareNet.

However, explicit forms could now rely on electronic media as well: email spams emphasized "networking people" and triggered a large number of new registrations; email surveys allowed for a quick assessment of user satisfaction, and web-based trainings reached widespread users.

4.2.4   Unveiling Critical Success Factors for Socialization and Removal

All HR interventions, i.e. hiring, socialization, and replacement, were found at the research site. Case study data barely shows indications for hiring and re-placement factors, and only during the three key project stages. Even though theory mandates a careful handling of both factors (to develop a common cognitive and behavioral ground), I consider the sparse occurrences rather a result of limited significance for IS and KMS implementation projects. Once again, the two factors confirm difficulties in applying organizational behavior change paradigms to the new setting of KM initiatives. In contrast, case study data shows plenty of evidence for socialization factors.

Hiring ("HIR") is one of several HR interventions to alter the "breed" of employees. Creative and innovative people - showing good "fit in" with a knowledge-intensive culture - are brought on board to reinforce the change process (Davenport et al., 1998, p. 52; Davenport & Grover, 2001, p. 4; Sathe, 1985, pp. 394-395; 1993, p. 339; Zack, 1999, p.141). While the ShareNet line organization was staffed with some new hires, culture change was merely fostered by regular attrition. My analysis builds on a broad understanding of hiring. Bringing in temporary external resources, i.e. management consultancies, technology specialists, and university researchers, as well as augmenting the project team with Siemens ICN-internal hires, are all considered particular instances of hiring factors.

Soon during the "definition and prototyping" stage, BTP/BTC and BCG employees (temporary hires) recognized the need for user involvement. In consequence, 40 sales representatives from headquarters and 15 local companies were regularly involved with specifying KMS solutions, supporting peer groups, and setting examples for the change process. Koch and Meinert's personal requests for ShareNet manager nominations further expanded the ShareNet organization. The core team met all ShareNet managers for the first time at a one-week Feldafing boot camp during the "global rollout" stage. The user champions received in-depth formal training in order to take over the responsibility for ShareNet's introduction and utilization in their local companies. This step-wise, internal hiring reflected the KMS' "snowball" implementation approach: a core team was assembled first, followed by the selection of user champions, who finally drove projects for the sales and marketing, Siemens ICM, service, and R&D communities.

The one and only hiring of external people occurred when the ShareNet operating team, i.e. the regular line organization, was staffed. Some 50% of the 15-person team joined from other companies since project sponsors did not want to continue with "old Siemens ICN resources", but rather used the project to attract creative and innovative people. Nobody had worked in the KM field before. Quite often the leaving BTP/BTC members and their successors jointly visited local companies to establish first contact and trust. Even though the transition went smoothly, the new team focused on a long-lasting effort rather than investing enormous resources (working hours, travel, and local support) for quick success. During the "setup and piloting" and the "global rollout" stages, the external consultancies Change Factory and Woodmark Technologies were involved. The former helped with the development of user trainings, user guides, user conferences, boot camps, and ShareNet manager conferences. The latter supported the central function IT with project management, requirements definition, and debugging.

Last symbolic hiring occurred at the end of the "operation, expansion, and further development" stage: top management decided to split responsibilities for the KMS' future development and growth. Specialists from the start-up company The Agilience Group were chosen to sell ShareNet to other business segments and external customers; all intellectual property rights for the technical systems and rollout concept were exchanged for minority equity participation. The new team formed several workgroups to continue with the KMS' expansion: representatives from the central function CIO were involved with steering and planning; representatives from the group division SBS ensured tight integration with corporate document management standards.

Replacement ("REP") is the contrasting HR intervention. Sometimes it remains the only option when people resist a new pattern of values and beliefs, or do not even change their behavior. Since no employment contracts were terminated in relation to ShareNet, literature prescriptions - considering replacements common to major change efforts - were somewhat contradicted (Beer, 1988, p. 4; Beer et al., 1990, p. 163; Sathe, 1985, pp. 394-395). In agreement with the ShareNet project team, I argue that incentives for desired behavior are more appropriate for informal, voluntary KMS and set a more positive tone. In addition, most organizations are short of formal knowledge exchange goals, the basis for evaluating pending layoffs. The majority has no powerful project teams to enforce such drastic measures. The case description shows only one indication for replacement factors during the first key evolution stage; they were no "recurrent theme" for KMS implementation projects.

No Siemens ICN employee was ever laid off due to a resistance to change. In very few cases, ShareNet managers not living up to their obligations were set free from the ShareNet organization. Main reasons were either a lack of motivation or an overemphasis of technical issues at the cost of people/cultural issues. Even though, everybody was able to take over other responsibilities within the group division, and the ShareNet project team tried to influence the successors' nomination. While replacements were already difficult at user champion level, a user base of 18,000 people prohibited their use at employee level. Most inappropriate behavior was sanctioned informally by peer groups. Sometimes end users engaged in illegal behavior (e.g. constantly giving reuse feedback to a small number of others) in order to gain more shares. Over several years, the global editors banned no more than a handful of users formally from the ICN/ICM community; for those severe cases the drastic measures were absolutely mandatory for community maintenance.

During the "shifting to a multi-community concept" stage, PACT's headcount reduction of some 20,500 positions was the only layoff wave during ShareNet's development and implementation. The ShareNet operating team was not spared and reduced to Manuth, three consultants, the global editor, and few full-time IT support people. Declining contribution rates and personal discussions soon confirmed the change agents and sponsors' reluctance to make use of replacement factors: employees threatened by layoffs were less prone to share valuable knowledge; the notion of "trust" took severe and long-term damage.

Socialization ("SOC") determines the sharing of knowledge, corporate routines, and cultural rituals. Tenured employees act as mentors to introduce newcomers to a knowledge-intensive culture. All organization members should commit to two individual responsibilities: to acquire personal knowledge and skills and to help those in need as their own expertise grows. Knowledge repositories have potential for mentoring since they speed up formerly slow, personal exchanges, i.e. chats and storytelling (Davenport et al., 1998, p. 45; Quinn et al., 1996, p. 73; von Krogh, 1998, p. 144). Indications for socialization factors show across all implementation stages. I propose that socialization is not only critical to groups and societies, but also to KMS initiatives trying to build supportive environments for KM processes (Davenport & Prusak, 2000, pp. 149-150; Earl, 2001, p. 225).

At the kick-off workshop, the ShareNet project team made the first attempt to form a close-knit group with 40 sales representatives: the concentration on sales and marketing ensured a community of people with similar problems and experiences, a common language, and comparable business backgrounds. First cross-regional knowledge leverages and an increasing number of participants at the ten regional and two German brainstorming workshops signaled initial success with "expanding the global network". The case description reveals long-lasting impact from early socialization: the majority of these employees cooperated continually during ShareNet's implementation, and even became committed ShareNet managers. During the "global rollout" stage, two boot camps for user champions are further clear measures for socialization factors. Team-building events, e.g. building a raft without tools to cross the Lake Starnberg, and a friendly and relaxed climate complemented in-depth formal trainings. Again, it was an explicit goal to build-up committed social networks, first for a small group, later throughout the sales and marketing community.

Further socialization occurred with key executives at headquarters and local companies almost in parallel. Visits from BTP/BTC and ShareNet committee members - first in pilot countries, later in major rollout countries - informed about knowledge-orientations' benefits and fostered commitment to the KMS implementation project. With several user champions and top managers on board, ShareNet's broad international rollout started large scale socialization. ShareNet managers' general user support and local company workshops build a network of some 4,200 registered users slowly, but successfully. Similar to example setting factors, personal socialization had more clout than technology-mediated socialization, but lacked global reach. The U.S. rollout strengthens Allen's (1977, pp. 234-248) proposition: knowledge exchange occurs in proportion to a level of personal contact. In consequence, web-based trainings were less successful than formal, but personal workshops. Other rollouts were similarly impacted when a lack of financial resources made travel impossible for ShareNet consultants.

The centrally-driven rollout approach changed to grassroots socialization over time: more and more users helped their peers with registration and problems, exchanged knowledge freely and openly, and created a common code of conduct. A main objective from the KMS' mission statement and the managerial systems had become true: ShareNet was now a self-organizing growing system. To some extent, the ShareNet project and operating teams continued with the socialization of user champions and other multiplicators. Two ShareNet manager conferences (at Sun City and Istanbul) and the New York user conference for the top 50 contributors were additional means to reinforce community spirit and exchange experiences with the broad international rollout. Safaris, city tours, sports, and dinner events were key change management measures; they maintained a relaxed and trustful atmosphere among participants.

4.2.5   Findings Related to a Cyclical Implementation Perspective

My exploratory design allowed for a combination of discovery and testing (Cavaye, 1996, pp. 275-276; Darke et al., 1998, p. 236): pattern-matching (Yin, 1994, pp. 106-110) confirmed the applicability of Sathe's theoretical framework while further causal relations and interferences emerged. Case study data reveals indications for the isolated conceptual variables/factors, listed in table 5. With the exception of hiring and replacement factors - providing less IS-specific guidance - all show the predicted, recurrent pattern (Ginzberg, 1981b, p. 48).

For changing the "behavior" process, extrinsic and intrinsic motivation factors for knowledge givers and takers were widely used. However, the emphasis on extrinsic motivators might have slowed down sustainable culture change since they denied people to seize the inherent worth of knowledge-orientation. These interrelationships - or "justifications of behavior" - were recognized and acknowledged during regular behavior rationalization assessments. Personal experiences and appraisals, as well as two formal email surveys, were used to size up the culture change accomplished. "Cultural communications" were mainly supported with explicit change communication factors, the provision of additional (electronic) communication channels, and several conferences for end users and user champions. In addition to exchanging rollout experiences and brainstorming ideas for the KMS' further expansion, the meetings provided forums for the "socialization" of ShareNet supporters. BTP/BTC succeeded with a two-stage approach: committed social networks were first created on a small scale, later they spread throughout the entire sales and marketing community. ShareNet became a self-organizing growing system through grassroots socialization. The case description makes the factor critical to the creation of knowledge networks (Alavi & Leidner, 2001, p. 114).

Table 5: Revealing Success Factors for Circular, Continuous Change

	EIM	BRA	CCO	HIR	SOC	REP
First Key Project Stage Definition and Prototyping		√	√	√	√	
Second Key Project Stage Setup and Piloting	√	√	√	√	√	
Third Key Project Stage Global Rollout	√	√	√	√	√	
Fourth Key Evolution Stage Operation, Expansion, and Further Development	√	√	√		√	√
Fifth Key Evolution Stage Shifting to a Multi-Community Concept	√	√	√		√	

Factor abbreviations: EIM: extrinsic and intrinsic motivation, BRA: behavior rationalization assessment, CCO: change communication, HIR: hiring, SOC: socialization, REP: replacement

5. Conclusions and Implications for Further Research

5.1 Motivators Fitting Knowledge Management Systems

"What types of incentives are effective in inculcating organizational members with valuable knowledge to contribute and share their knowledge" (Alavi & Leidner, 2001, p. 127)? When managers were asked to name concerns about KM, the ability to induce people and business units to exchange knowledge always shows up at the top: Alavi & Leidner's (1999, pp. 21-22) study reports that organizational incentives and rewards are considered effective change interventions; KPMG Management Consulting's research report (1998, p. 4) and Teleos' international KM survey (Chase, 1997, pp. 46-47) rank them among the nine biggest KM drawbacks; King et al.'s (2002, pp. 93-95) top ten KM issues include motivating individuals for contributing to KMS; finally, an Ernst & Young study (Ruggles, 1998, pp. 81-82) revealed that only 19% of the respondents believed they did well with the facilitation of knowledge growth through organizational cultures and incentives. The findings demonstrate that extrinsic and intrinsic motivators are interdependent with behavior and culture change (Sethia & von Glinow, 1985, p. 401). While the problem is well understood, managers still lack guidance for taking it on. First managerial contributions are derived from my exploratory research findings.

Incentive and reward systems have to be adapted to different KM schools: for a codification approach, people ought to be motivated to write down their knowledge and provide it to a knowledge repository (Davenport & Klahr, 1998, p. 208); for a personalization approach, i.e. the mapping of internal expertise, people should be rewarded for direct help and knowledge offered to colleagues (Hansen et al., 1999, p. 113); for a "knowledge community" approach, sociability and networking are important (Earl, 2001, p. 225; Holtshouse, 1998, pp. 278-279). Since ShareNet aimed for the creation of knowledge networks, as well as for the coding and sharing of best practices, drawing inferences and conclusions from the case study findings must be restricted to those two applications (Walsham & Waema, 1994, p. 151).

While the KM literature mainly focuses on motivators for users, i.e. the level of knowledge givers and takers, Siemens ICN change agents employed two main extrinsic incentive schemes for multiplicators/user champions. First, the one-time promotion scheme bonus-on-top (restricted to fiscal 2000) was to reward local ICN heads for international knowledge exchange. 5% revenue from collaboration with other local companies was required for a bonus of approximately 10% of a fixed annual salary (Gibbert, Kugler et al., 2002, p. 273). Taking into account the "snowball" implementation approach for a large user base and that the ShareNet Community was not entirely driven by information and knowledge (like management consultancies), kick-starting the change process with massive short-term bonuses proved successful, but expensive. Bonus-on-top rather helped to overcome early buy-in challenges, to build initial top management support, and to communicate the KMS intended benefits top-down; it had neither long-lasting impact on system usage, nor on culture change. Putting more top-down pressure on local key executives and/or an inclusion into their standard evaluations (e.g. SLF) are less expensive. However, difficult reporting lines forbade those alternatives.

Second, ShareNet manager targets (restricted to fiscal 2001) suffered from similar problems. Since regional sales organizations reported directly to Siemens' managing board, the change agents had no influence on the user champions' daily work and personnel development systems (comp. O'Dell & Grayson, 1998, pp. 168-170). For substitution, general targets including user trainings, presentations, monthly reports, a certain level of end user contributions, and the documentation of success stories were formulated. ShareNet managers could secure a bonus of 50-120% of a fixed monthly salary when performing well. Common user support prospered in many cases. Consequently, a first (hypothetical) managerial guideline can be derived for KMS implementation projects:

⇨ Targeting multiplicators with non-trivial short-term, extrinsic motivation factors speeds up the change process; if change agents have direct influence on communication lines, reports, and job descriptions, the inclusion of knowledge exchange goals into employee target agreements is a cheaper measure with comparable impact. Embedding knowledge exchange into personnel processes links both of Sathe's (1985; 1993) broad approaches to culture change.

As argued in chapter four, literature prescriptions - proposing long-term, team-based, and intrinsic motivators for end users (comp. Davenport et al., 1998, p. 54; O'Dell & Grayson, 1998, pp. 168-170; Sathe, 1985, pp. 386-387) - are at first sight contradicted by my findings. The Siemens ICN change process relied heavily on a share system, comparable to frequent flyer miles. ShareNet shares could be collected, accumulated, and turned into knowledge-related rewards from a catalog. According to my interview partners the incentive scheme was established for multiple reasons: to get a critical mass of content and contributors into the system, to create awareness for the KM initiative, to succeed in the "battle" for capturing time against other important daily issues, and to signal top management expectations. The ShareNet consultants were convinced that contributors needed an immediate positive response to their actions. Making a connection between long-term motivators and personal exemplary behavior was more difficult and had reduced impact.

In addition, the number of shares awarded could consistently be adjusted according to employees' needs for motivation and guidance. BTP/BTC members regarded the share system as the best tool available to influence the number of contributions; compared to other change interventions, it promised the "biggest bang for the buck". This line of argumentation is supported by academic research claiming that extrinsic motivators are more prone to modification and steering than intrinsic motivators (Osterloh & Frey, 2000, p. 540; 2001, p. 102). Case study data shows no evidence for commonly predicted crowding-out effects or undermining, i.e. negative impact on teamwork, commitment, and organizational learning. Teamwork was never endangered since incentive and reward systems required cooperation for payback, commitment was maintained by strong linkages with business processes and economic benefits, and organizational learning was evidenced by steady increases in contributions and shares awarded, i.e. usage rates. The KMS demonstrates that carefully devised extrinsic motivation factors can steer clear of crowding-out effects, especially when both knowledge givers and takers feel similarly rewarded (Goodman & Darr, 1998, p. 420).

As Marwell, Oliver, and Prahl's (1988, p. 532) computer simulation discovered, "collective action happens when a critical mass of interested and resourceful individuals can coordinate their efforts. There is generally no need for all the aggrieved population to be mobilized and no need for all the members of a population to be mutually reachable." Academics propose that the user base's size may have a positive network effect: if the set of connections is too small, it might offer insufficient resources for worthwhile participation (Hahn & Subramani, 2000, p. 306), e.g. the greater the number of objects in the KMS' knowledge library, the higher the chances to find a desired contact or solution. Without positive first reinforcements, a critical mass will not form and the community will remain in a "rut" or suboptimal equilibrium. Once a stable user base is obtained, self-sustaining social fusion results (Macy, 1990, pp. 814-823). Manuth observed these network dynamics during the application's rollout and maintenance: "When more knowledge was shared, knowledge hoarding became less beneficial." End users gave up their reluctance to provide personal knowledge and skills since they turned into a declining source of influence and power.

Even though the share system helped to overcome the "start-up" problem, the overemphasis of extrinsic motivators had negative impact on building a knowledge-intensive culture. This effect has been identified by academic research (Sathe, 1985, pp. 386-387; Schein, 1992, p. 299) but is also evidenced by behavioral and cultural diagnosis factors, as well as by behavior rationalization assessment factors: up to the end of fiscal 2002, the majority of ShareNet users still depended on incentives; only a minority exchanged knowledge based on their own experiences and dependency on international cooperation. When more shares were awarded, e.g. during the "ShareNet Special Weeks", contributions and feedback peaked. Even though most ShareNet consultants acknowledged the dangerous attachment to extrinsic interventions, the problem emerged late during key evolution stages. I postulate that other actions, e.g. communication campaigns and integration with business processes, would have been more apt after a certain number of employees accepted KM. A good point for considering such alternatives - also suggested by the vice president knowledge management platforms and the ShareNet manager - was the end of the "global rollout" stage with 4,200 registered users. ShareNet's start-up registrations are shown in figure 11.

While change processes can be fueled by a blend of reward systems, i.e. motivation through financial incentives (theory E) and motivation through commitment (theory O), the latter should be emphasized for "refreezing". This sequencing of interventions is also recommended by Beer and Nohria (2000, pp. 138-139): "sequenced change is far easier if you begin [...] with "theory E"". When knowledge networks or CoPs have actually formed, experiencing community spirit, help from peers, and performance improvements through knowledge leverage build intrinsic motivation. Organizational citizenship and norms of generalized reciprocity emerge from contacts and experiences: people are sensitive to

Figure 11: ShareNet Start-Up Registrations

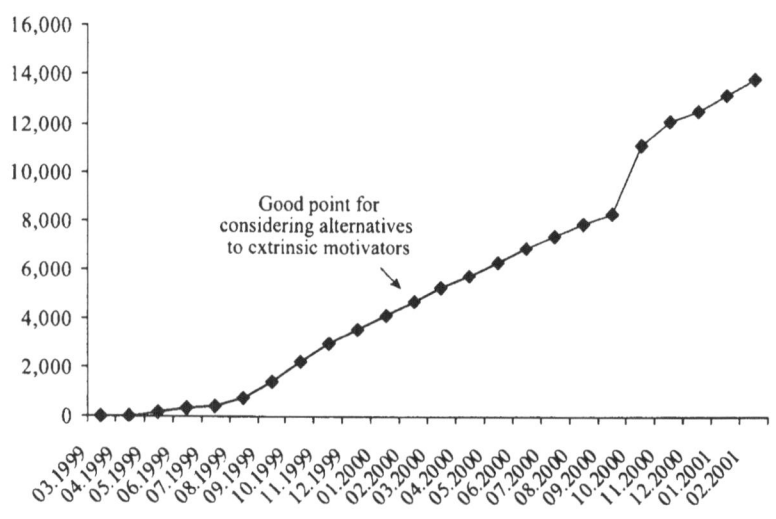

help seekers' needs and to adjust their suggestions accordingly. Earning personal respect, as well as the organizational motivations of "it's part of my job to help" and "it's only fair to help" are validated sources of intrinsic motivation (Constant et al., 1996, pp. 121-127). This interdependence was recognized by ShareNet consultants: employees exchanged knowledge impersonally but openly; they formed a corporate network with a common code of conduct.

Horizontal socialization can to some extent substitute top-down extrinsic HR interventions: first experiences created support for the KMS and the redefinition of business processes. I agree with Kuhn's assessment that any change first needs technical systems and later an appropriate psychological landscape. Whereas rewards and incentives can build first enthusiasm for knowledge leverage, a KMS must be self-rewarding to the user in the long term, i.e. offering knowledge needed or expert recognition (Brelade & Harman, 2000, p. 27). ShareNet demonstrated that technological attributes and conditions cannot only reduce the psychological costs of sharing, but even create intrinsic motivation (comp. Goodman & Darr, 1998, p. 426; Jarvenpaa & Staples, 2000, p. 131): during participative development and prototyping the core team feels valued for its work (Harper, 2001, p. 14); afterwards, smooth handling reduces barriers of entry. In result, a second (hypothetical) managerial guideline is proposed:

⇨ For starting combined KM and change initiatives, short-term extrinsic motivators - for knowledge givers and takers - can quickly assemble a critical mass of end users and contributions; in the long term, change agents should rather invest in long-term intrinsic motivators and user-friendly interfaces.

When true culture change is feasible and intended, organizational behavior and sociology studies resolve the former contradictions between extrinsic and intrinsic motivation factors (e.g. Beer & Nohria, 2000; Marwell et al., 1988): both are needed at different points in time. As a consequent academic contribution, I hypothesize that KM researchers should incorporate findings from the field of sociology in the design of extrinsic incentives and rewards, especially the theory of "critical mass" developed by Oliver, Marwell, and their associates (Marwell et al., 1988; Oliver & Marwell, 1988; Oliver, Marwell, & Teixeira, 1985). Similar attention should be paid to the sequencing of motivation factors.

5.2   Knowledge Management Systems as Change Drivers

"Must culture change occur before knowledge management initiatives can be successfully undertaken or can knowledge management initiatives facilitate culture change" (Alavi & Leidner, 2001, p. 126)? Since case study data provides plenty of evidence for the latter proposition, a hypothetical implementation framework for combined KM and change initiatives is presented in the succeeding section. Here, KMS' aptness for driving change is explored in a broader context - abstracting from the factor analysis. Since ShareNet's implementation success was established by the measures presented in chapter one, and all change interventions were analyzed in detail in chapter four, I am rather concerned about the dynamic interplay of technology and "people issues".

The IS implementation and organizational behavior literature postulates that a conflict between IS and culture can foster employee resistance to such a degree that implementation projects result in less than the desired organizational change, or even fail. This link is an important factor that warrants management recognition and control (Cooper, 1994, p. 19). For successful rollouts, most academics propose to change affected cultural aspects, i.e. the prevailing patterns of beliefs and values, either prior to or concurrent with the rollout. Profound cultural renovations are needed to change employees' attitudes and behaviors so that they willingly and proactively exchange knowledge (Alavi & Leidner, 1999, p. 21; Bhatt, 2001, p. 73; Brelade & Harman, 2000, pp. 28-29; Davenport et al., 1998, pp. 52-53; De Long & Seemann, 2000, p. 38). Share-Net's distribution of expenses, i.e. only 25% of total project costs for the technical systems and the majority for the socialization and training of user champions, communication campaigns, and training material, supports the above academic propositions. Their majority cautions against an overemphasis of technology at the cost of change management and human aspects (Coombs et al., 1992, p. 69).

All my interview partners agreed with ShareNet's success in fostering a knowledge-intensive culture; there were only difficulties to estimate the level of accomplishments and PACT's impact. Criteria commonly cited included: multiple requests for CoPs, the KMS' integration into work routines, the acceptance of knowledge leverage as key to competitiveness and innovativeness, an emerging community spirit, and an increased readiness for international cooperation and help. Besides some earlier work from the central function CC - restricted to select sales teams - there were no other Siemens ICN change initiatives. My observations are in line with the above assessments: indeed, culture change went hand-in-hand with the KMS implementation project. The degrees of culture change accomplished - sorted by groups of affected stakeholders - are compiled in table 6. As one ShareNet consultant put it: "ShareNet was intended as a tool for culture change; the smooth implementation served vice versa as an argument for successful change."

I hypothesize that knowledge dynamics, triggered by KMS, and change dynamics, started with intervention factors, are mutually reinforcing. Organizations that are inclined to change adopt KM initiatives quickly, and advancing knowledge enables successful change initiatives (Lucier & Torsilieri, 1997, p. 23). "Information technology may increase the capacity of organizations to learn and, simultaneously, learning capacity may affect the degree to which new technologies are adopted and used effectively. In the most optimistic scenario, these two effects reinforce each other: the capacity to learn is increased steadily through increased technology adoption and use" (Robey et al., 2000, p. 147). IS need not always respond to changes, but can instead be the vehicle through which change is brought to the organization (Ginzberg, 1978, p. 41).

Case study data and interviews confirm these dynamics: local companies had a strong "felt need" for ShareNet since they lacked cross-country knowledge

Table 6: Degrees of Culture Change Accomplished

Affected Stakeholders	Change	Interview Quotes
End users research and development	-	• Sub-community had not accomplished shift from "box-selling" to solutions approach (Interview 02)
End users sales and marketing	+	• Local companies were first to recognize and accept the KM initiative; higher resistance at headquarters (Interviews 01, 02, 03, 04, 06, 07, 08, 09, 10, 11, 13, 14) • Culture change accomplished: first experiences created many believers in a knowledge-intensive culture (Interviews 01, 02, 04, 06, 07, 09, 10, 11, 12) • Most employees exchanged knowledge freely and openly; higher responsiveness to international cooperation (Interviews 01, 03, 10, 11, 13) • Majority of employees still dependent on incentives; only minority is intrinsically motivated (Interviews 01, 02, 04, 05, 08, 09, 10, 12)
End users service	-	• ShareNet provides less value-add since there were only limited contributions and proprietary tools (Interviews 01, 02, 07) • General lack of resources hindered impact and progress towards knowledge-intensive culture (Interview 01, 02)
User champions (ShareNet managers)	++	• 40 sales representatives who had become ShareNet managers were promoted (Interview 03) • Proactively searching and offering knowledge became soon internalized (Interview 09)
Siemens ICN employees	~	• Increasing number of employees proactively asked for CoPs (Interviews 05, 06, 07, 12) • No socialization for new employees and lack of corporate identity (Interviews 02, 09)
Siemens ICN managers	-	• Culture change happened only with local company managers and conference participants (Interviews 02, 04, 06, 07) • Management attention decreased due to replacements and more pressing topics, e.g. PACT (Interviews 02, 05, 08, 09, 10, 11, 14)

exchange, network access, and solutions expertise. The implementation's business impact - evidenced by success stories and a rapidly growing knowledge library - in turn reinforced local change processes. Local rollouts differed greatly from the headquarters' implementation: the majority of employees experienced no true KM need, or was even resistant, since they had plenty of contacts and resources. Less disconfirmation and pressure from customers created no sufficient commitment to change. Several ShareNet consultants remarked that the more managers were convinced of the KMS' business value, the smoother the implementation went. In consequence, a third (hypothetical) managerial guideline is presented:

⇨ For concurrent KM and change initiatives, managers should focus on key impact areas with inclination to change (comp. Sathe, 1985, p. 377); disconfirmation factors (in a broad sense) can be employed to overcome lacks of "felt need" (Keen, 1981, p. 26; Srinivasan & Davis, 1987, p. 65). The factor expands "traditional" critical success factors for IS implementations with a culture change-based perspective.

During all key project and evolution stages, ShareNet's implementation incessantly incorporated culture change objectives. The core team was convinced that all domains of change management must be addressed simultaneously, e.g. strategic change, process change, technological change, and particularly organizational and people change. Team members agreed on an explicit goal for the managerial systems' design: to enable the KMS' further development and growth by adopting a culture that rewarded the proactive seeking and offering of knowledge. Even the four pilot countries were carefully selected according to their inclination to change, i.e. "friendly turf". There, long-lasting behavior change should trigger culture change: intrinsic motivation ought to multiply to headquarters and other local companies. There was no formalized change management strategy besides managerial statements and well-communicated goals. During the key project stages the ShareNet project team mainly relied on a mix of business purpose linkage, user involvement, user training, and top management support factors; combination and sequencing based on personal experiences.

The mission statement demanded responsibility for topics of interest, group maintenance, and enhancements from the ShareNet Community; in the long term the KMS was to become "a self-organizing growing system." Even though the entire implementation process was centrally-driven, the core team members tried to avoid the image of a top-down process, i.e. another headquarters' initiative demanding precious resources (Rothnie, 2001, p. 58). A Siemens ICN vice president remarked that ShareNet was no isolated effort (ivory tower), parachuted into the local companies. Congruent with theoretical recommendations - proposing that self-design and self-governance of CoPs fosters KM processes

(Gold et al., 2001, p. 189; O'Dell & Grayson, 1998, p. 157) - BTP/BTC promoted no centralized technical platform but community spirit, new ways of collaboration, and trust. All team members agreed that culture change happens individually, through socialization and commitment. It was better to foster ongoing dialogue and interaction among employees than to rely on top-down pressure.

At the end of the "global rollout" stage, the transfer of all KMS responsibilities to the ShareNet operating team gave way to full user involvement: organization members were reminded of their duty for the IS' operation and evolution; the new representatives carried out change requests. First indications for the "mentality shift" surfaced in connection with the Siemens ICM and multicommunity expansions: the prior implementation round's centrally-driven international rollout changed to a user-driven bottom-up initiative. Since Siemens ICN had traditionally no strong culture that rewarded the contribution and reuse of knowledge, the ICN/ICM community's exchange culture emerged independently of other organizational cultures (Goodman & Darr, 1998, p. 438). Given that knowledge communities are by nature reliant on networking and sociability, I claim that combined KM and change initiatives are facilitated by employee self-responsibility and CoP self-governance; "backpacking" change interventions on self-perpetuating social processes fuels implementation success.

My explorative case study recognizes the interrelationship between behavior and culture change as a further critical success factor for KMS implementation projects. It is striking that the majority of interviewees saw simultaneous culture and behavior change; a smaller group was convinced that behavior change preceded culture change while three people remained undecided. According to Sathe (1985, p. 363) and Beer et al. (1990, p. 165) concurrent changes are most stable as they are mutually reinforcing and self-sustaining: employees strongly believe in and value new habits which is intrinsically motivating and in turn reinforces new behavior, i.e. using the KMS. Members of the ShareNet organization and end users agreed that hands-on practice increased technology acceptance and culture change which vice versa fostered knowledge-orientation. Somebody cautioned that both processes needed synchronization: "If the corporate culture remains unchanged, behavior changes could lead to frustration."

I consider the two-sectioned local company workshops a central element of the change process. They were set up in a way that avoided undue "justifications of behavior" but encouraged simultaneous behavior and culture change. During the first section - creating necessary know-how for using ShareNet - employees learned about the KMS' intended benefits and experienced its structure and handling. Several members of the ShareNet operating team explained that the KMS' first impression was critical for the change process; new users either became supporters or sceptics. The global editor reminded of the network effects:

"A ShareNet advocate brings us four new users, an opponent takes 30 away." During the second section - capturing knowledge with ShareNet - participants entered and reviewed real-life projects they brought to the workshop. BTP/BTC tried to convince everybody that only the global leverage of knowledge ensured sustainable business results.

Technology itself drove behavior change - not only during development, but throughout operation and evolution - since it was basically "a package of ideas about how people should work differently" (Markus & Benjamin, 1997, p. 58) Capturing wizards and a self-explanatory user interface made many organization members believers in knowledge leverage (comp. Goodman & Darr, 1998, p. 425; Jarvenpaa & Staples, 2000, p. 131). Those findings agree with Schein's (1992, pp. 318-321) earlier mentioned concept of "unfreezing and change through technological seduction". Siemens ICN's KM initiative was a deliberate, managed IS implementation project which succeeded in seducing employees into new behaviors. In turn, the KMS became emblematic of culture change and required redefinitions of individual values, beliefs, and assumptions (Robey & Azevedo, 1994, p. 28): employees had to reach out to peers for knowledge sharing across functional and organizational barriers instead of playing political games (Seeley, 2000, p. 25). "Culture change is slow and is impacted in the long run by many factors, including MIS implementations" (Romm et al., 1991, p. 101).

The additional (informal) communication channel offered by ShareNet moderated culture's effects on employee mindsets in two ways (Dewett & Jones, 2001, pp. 332-333). First, it enhanced the motivational aspects of cultural values supporting competitiveness and innovativeness: a slew of managerial statements, incl. ShareNet's vision and mission, was posted on community homepages; success stories set examples for successful international collaboration; lastly, feedback about the successful adoption of solutions reinforced employees' technical competency and feelings of self-esteem (Goodman & Darr, 1998, p. 421). Second, it increased exposure to colleagues' efforts. A richer information context with multiple contacts and information sources enlarged Siemens ICN's KM potential: the communication flow changed from a broadcast-oriented "enabling" approach, i.e. headquarters to local companies, to a meshed network approach; (urgent) requests could be sent to a larger pool of help. When organization members perceive that their IS use makes them more effective in fulfilling organizational goals, system usage will become self-reinforcing (Huber, 1990, p. 50). As a summary, a fourth (hypothetical) managerial guideline is derived:

⇨ Change interventions - particularly user involvement and user training factors - have the most impact when behavior and culture change are interwoven, i.e. self-reinforcing KMS usage; only truly committed employees recruit and socialize new users.

Further academic research is needed to single out KMS technology features which foster "technological seduction", e.g. user satisfaction and "community spirit" in computer-mediated exchanges.

5.3   Toward a Culture Change-Based Implementation Framework

5.3.1   Combining Conceptualizations of Change

"How can KMS implementation projects establish knowledge-intensive cultures in order to achieve good fit between the KM context elements technology and people/culture?" After all clarifications and delineations in preceding sections, the last paragraph presents a hypothetical implementation framework as a managerial guideline and preliminary answer to the main research question. The nine-factor implementation model, depicted in figure 12, combines critical success factors from Lewin-Schein's linear, staged theoretical framework (Lewin, 1947; Schein, 1992, 1999) and Sathe's (1985; 1993) circular, continuous approach. Since a mix of punctual and permanent change interventions is proposed, my theory synthesis reconciles propositions for a sequential handling of implementation factors (Armenakis & Bedeian, 1999; Keen et al., 1982; Lucas & Plimpton, 1972; Urban, 1974; Zand & Sorensen, 1975) with suggestions for dealing with "recurrent themes" (Eisenhardt, 2000; Ginzberg, 1981b; Hatch, 1993; Nonaka, 1991; Pettigrew, 1990). Though the findings presented here are based on a single explorative case study, they have significant practical implications.

My nine-factor implementation model addresses most criticism on the underlying two process studies. First, culture is no longer considered "frozen" and stable, but rather in constant evolution (comp. Macredie & Sandom, 1999, p.

Figure 12: Nine-Factor Implementation Model

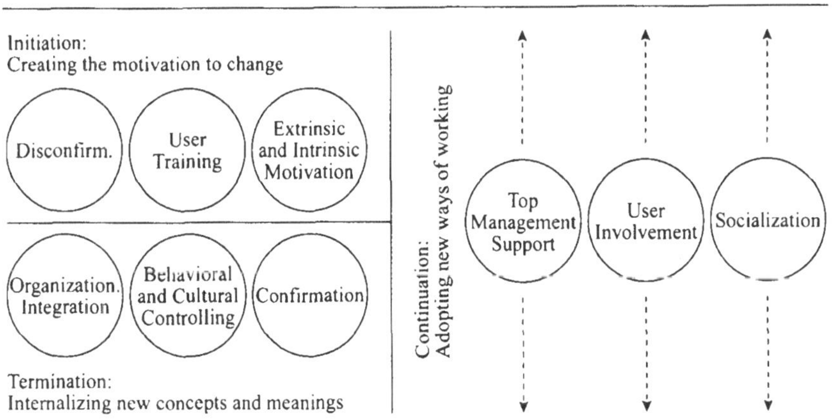

148; Myers, 1994, p. 54; Schein, 1992, p. 21). While Siemens ICN traditionally
valued no exchange of solutions know-how, knowledge-intensive subcultures
emerged in some departments and regional sales organizations - independently
of other organizational cultures (Goodman & Darr, 1998, p. 438). Business
problems or popular executives advanced knowledge-orientation. Second, all IS
and KMS rollouts need specified beginning and ending points to communicate
project statuses and to determine implementation success (Keil, 1995, pp. 438-
439; Keil & Robey, 2001, p. 93); however, change paradigms must allow for
fast adoptions to rapidly changing environmental and organizational conditions
(Orlikowski & Hofman, 1997, pp. 11-12). Third and last, embedded units of
analysis, i.e. headquarters and U.S. rollouts, indeed prove that user groups or
organization members are somewhat recalcitrant and resistant to culture change;
the ShareNet's usage patterns contradict Srinivisan and Davis' (1987, p. 67)
findings.

Despite the fact that those arguments confirm linear, staged change paradigms' goodness of fit with the new context of KMS, change cannot be broken
up into small pieces that are then supposed to be managed. In agreement with
Sathe (1985, p. 385) and Duck (2001, p. 57) I advocate a management of dynamics - not pieces - by connecting and balancing all issues. Consequently, I
follow a dynamic perspective of organizational cultures and reject the idea of
quasi-stationary equilibriums: emergent change in this context is regarded as an
ongoing process, while deliberate change, i.e. a KMS implementation, is viewed
as a constrained project (Carroll & Hatakenaka, 2001, pp. 77-78): "[a]fter all, it
is through structured projects, however imperfect, that anything in companies
actually gets done" (Davenport & Prusak, 2000, p. 144). Though the latter
builds on the same self-perpetuating processes as the former, deliberate change
interventions mark initiation and termination. Particularly when employees lack
commitment to change or to the project, additional social force is needed for
motivation (Ginzberg, 1981b, pp. 54-55; Kolb & Frohman, 1970, pp. 54-56;
Zand & Sorensen, 1975, p. 542). With those measures change agents synchro-
nize KM and change initiatives' timeframes.

Since the case description unveils limited IS-guidance from Lewin-Schein's
"cognitive restructuring" stage - as well as an extension of "traditional" critical
success factors across most implementation stages - the middle stage is omitted
from my theoretical framework. Remaining are the first stage "initiation: creating the motivation to change" (comparable to "unfreezing") and the last stage
"termination: internalizing new concepts and meanings" (comparable to "refreezing"). However, Lewin-Schein's ideas are still valid in the context of KMS
implementation projects and form the basis for my theory synthesis. Given that
the old expressions rather pertain to "frozen" and stable cultures, I changed the
terminology to incorporate a dynamic perspective. To substitute for the stage's

exclusion, a group of "recurrent themes" is added (Ginzberg, 1981b, p. 48): "continuation: adopting new ways of working". Those factors require a continuous handling across all (company-specific) project stages. For consistency and to arrive at true change interventions, I barred or integrated eight from a total of 17 conceptual variables/factors from the nine-factor implementation model.

Four factors are excluded from the Lewin-Schein change paradigm. First, business purpose linkage factors are integrated with disconfirmation factors (in a broad sense). As argued earlier, today's knowledge workers/specialists no longer need a two-stage education (dissatisfaction preceding business objectives). Beer's (1988, pp. 1-2) and O'Dell and Grayson's (1998, p. 171) disconfirmation approaches, especially "top-down creation of competitive awareness" and "joint diagnosis of business problems", already incorporate change processes' business impact. Second, commitment factors result from successful "initiation", they resemble "a partisan, affective attachment to the goals and values of an organization, to one's role in relation to goals and values, and to the organization for its own sake" (Buchanan, 1974, p. 533). While they are critical for successful IS implementations (comp. Ginzberg, 1981b, pp. 54-55) they are outcomes, i.e. dependent variables. Disconfirmation (in a broad sense), extrinsic and intrinsic motivators, as well as top management support (executive participation and executive involvement), fuel commitment to change or to the project.

Third, example setting factors occur either in union or proximity with Sathe's (1985; 1993) socialization factors. Since "imitation of and identification with role models is an acknowledged tool for acculturation (comp. Meyerson, 2001, p. 100; Quinn et al., 1996, p. 73; Spector, 1989, p. 32) - and the case discussion indicates similar effects from impersonal examples, e.g. organizational units and pilot studies - the former change interventions are integrated with the latter. Especially interaction with veteran managers or mentors is a prime means for newcomers to absorb the subtleties of culture (Buchanan, 1974, p. 534). I postulate that the socialization "group factor" is highly relevant to KMS initiatives aiming for the creation of knowledge-oriented contexts (Davenport & Prusak, 2000, pp. 149-150; Earl, 2001, p. 225). Fourth, trial-and-error factors have only (minor) significance for rapid prototyping, user involvement, and symbolic means (Krovi, 1993, p. 334; Teng et al., 1996, p. 282). The deliberate, planned process of most technology-facilitated KM initiatives lacks potential applications. Furthermore, an IS' progressing organizational integration might make an experimental implementation path obsolete.

Following the same line of argumentation, four factors are excluded from the Sathe change paradigm. Particularly hiring and replacement factors look inapposite for large scale KMS implementation projects: with 56,000 potential users, change agents cannot deliberately modify the user base's composition. Devoid of formal knowledge exchange goals, i.e. direct influences on communication lines, reports, and job descriptions, layoff decisions are impossible or bring about severe obstacles. Joshi (1991, p. 238) mandates caution as well: "The decision to terminate users may be beyond the control of implementers. However, to the extent possible, such extreme inequities should be avoided." I consider the factors' sparse occurrences the result of limited significance for voluntary company-wide implementations (Lucas, 1981, p. 8). Since hiring in the context of KM initiatives merely involves bringing in external consultants, Kolb and Frohman's (1970) model of the consulting processes dispenses better advice on the relationship between client and consultant, as well as on the nature of their joint work. During ShareNet's key evolution stages, external people were only hired to staff the regular line organization.

From the less aggressive approach to culture change - getting people to buy into new values and beliefs (processes one, two, and three) - behavior rationalization assessment and change communication factors are barred. Though behavior rationalization assessments are "recurrent themes" for ShareNet's implementation (comp. Harper, 2001, p. 14; Jarvenpaa & Staples, 2001, p. 165), they gain weight prior to project conclusion. Lewin-Schein prescribe passive attention to behavioral and cultural diagnosis factors only during "refreezing", while Sathe (1993, pp. 337-338) favors continuous attention and, if necessary, corrective action. With the integration of both factors into "behavioral and cultural control-

Table 7: Implementation Model Factor Descriptions

Initiation Creating the motivation to change	• Disconfirmation (DIS): diffusing dissatisfaction with the status quo through emotionally-charged business goals • User training (UTR): helping employees to understand change targets and to secure hands-on experience with the KMS • Extrinsic and intrinsic motivation (EIM): combining short-term extrinsic motivators with long-term intrinsic motivators to guide behaviors
Continuation Adopting new ways of working	• Top management support (TMS): emphasizing the KMS' business impact and allocating adequate project resources • User involvement (UIN): mandates active participation in development and evolution to foster identification with and commitment to the project • Socialization (SOC): introducing peers to a knowledge-intensive culture through personal and impersonal example setting
Termination Internalizing new concepts and meanings	• Organizational integration (OIN): embedding project outcomes into line and process organizations • Behavioral and cultural controlling (BCC): assessing behavioral and cultural shifts for taking necessary corrective actions • Confirmation (CON): stopping the change process through disseminating confirmatory data and feedback

ling" I take an intermediate position: during "termination", change agents must judge the KM initiative's progress and implement necessary alternative change interventions.

Finally, change communication factors provide (electronic) outlets for the "traditional" critical success factors top management support, user involvement, and user training. Besides being deliberate change interventions, they contribute to emergent socialization processes - across time and space (Alavi & Leidner, 2001, p. 121; Orlikowski, 1992, p. 368; Thomas et al., 2001, p. 872). The high aggregation level of Sathe's (1985; 1993) factor implies a "change channel" rather than a particular intervention: culture change is essentially communication (Tizard, 2002, p. 65). Table 7 presents a basic overview and description of my theoretical framework's nine factors. Based on theoretical prescriptions and empirical evidence from the case discussion, they are grouped into clusters for delineation in preceding sections.

5.3.2 Initiation

In my first stage - "initiation: creating the motivation to change" - organization members become aware of the need for culture change and new ways of working, i.e. KM processes (Srinivasan & Davis, 1987, p. 65; Zack, 1999, p. 125). They must continuously refine their firm's knowledge-based core capabilities which would otherwise turn into core rigidities or cultural inertia (Denison & Mishra, 1995, p. 213; Leonard, 1998, p. 30; Tushman & O'Reilly, 1996, p. 18). Employees should accept KMS as an effective means to identify and leverage the organization's knowledge in order to remain competitive and innovative (Hackbarth, 1998, p. 590; Meso & Smith, 2000, p. 226; Nonaka, 1991, pp. 96-97; O'Dell & Grayson, 1998, p. 327; von Krogh, 1998, p. 133). This stage starts culture change concurrent with KMS implementation projects. Since it involves deliberate and numerous reorderings, modifications, or even removals of existing beliefs and values, powerful change interventions ought to transform resisters into allies (Sathe, 1985, pp. 381-384). For large user bases and restricted timeframes, solely relying on culture's self-perpetuating processes is clearly insufficient.

⇨ As a fifth managerial guideline, I hypothesize that three intertwined factors kick-start the change process, i.e. create motivation to change along with psychological safety: disconfirmation, user training, as well as extrinsic and intrinsic motivators. Their relevance diminishes during later project stages.

Though my findings agree with Schein's (1992, pp. 298-299; 1999, pp. 124-126) commendations and sequencing for "unfreezing", further (quantitative) academic investigation is needed: multiple regression analysis can clarify the three factors' impact on commitment, making use of Buchanan's (1974, pp. 538-539) combined scale; change statistics might indicate whether the inclusion of additional factors improves discriminating ability (comp. Constant et al., 1996, p. 127; Ginzberg, 1981b, p. 50).

Disconfirmation ("DIS") diffuses dissatisfaction with the status quo through emotionally-charged business goals (comp. Schein, 1992, pp. 298-299; Spector, 1989, p. 30; Zack, 1999, p. 211). In contrast to "traditional" success factors for IS implementation projects, culturally-sensitive KMS rollouts might require stronger impetus and motivation. In the nine-factor implementation framework, disconfirmation is no longer symptomatic but somehow related to business purposes or competitiveness: stakeholders "need to be made aware of [KM's] importance, its whereabouts, its movements, its effects, and its overall state of health in the business" (Holtshouse, 1998, p. 279). Direct and indirect benefit calculations foster support for expensive technology features and change interventions, e.g. cost savings, product/service innovations, and time to market (Alavi & Leidner, 1999, p. 22; Davenport et al., 1998, p. 50; Lucier & Torsilieri, 1997, p. 15; Storey & Barnett, 2000, p. 154; Wilson, 2000, p. 9). My disconfirmation factor matches with Davenport and Prusak's (2000, pp. 156-157) "link to economics or industry value" but aims for emotions and understanding at the affected stakeholder level, too.

Since KMS implementations projects require wide-reaching buy-in, managers and employees have to arrive at shared understandings and common explanations of business and industry challenges. My goodness of fit-analyses, i.e. time-series analysis and pattern-matching, confirm that Beer's (1988, pp. 1-2) four approaches for disseminating business-related information are applicable to the context of KMS implementation projects. Minor rewordings enhance congruence with the synthesized factors: "top-down creation of competitive awareness" furthers problem discussions among employees through information about the competitive environment (O'Dell & Grayson, 1998, p. 171); "bottom-up communication of employee concerns" makes superiors aware of organization members' "felt need" or inclination to change; "joint diagnosis of KM value-add" mandates active stakeholder involvement in unearthing KM's economic benefits (Alavi & Leidner, 1999, p. 15; Beer et al., 1990, pp. 7-8); finally, "setting KM standards and expectations" combines guidelines for behavior change and profit performance (Spector, 1989, pp. 30-31).

User training ("UTR") helps employees to understand change targets and to secure hands-on experience with the KMS. Training explains the KM initiative's organizational scope and instills teamwork at all hierarchical levels: individuals ought to develop new ways of working on the basis of cooperation and knowledge sharing (Brelade & Harman, 2000, p. 28; Krovi, 1993, p. 334; Schultz et al., 1987, p. 40). Before organization members support implementation efforts, "they must understand why the [IS] is being introduced and how the project will affect them during and after implementation" (Zmud & Cox, 1979, p. 39); education and training should be no afterthoughts (comp. LaMarsh, 1995, p. 140; Schein, 1999, pp. 124-126; Seeley, 2000, p. 28). A learning plan outlining learning topics, delivery methods, responsibilities, timing, and feedback mechanisms is mandatory for change agents. Key is sensitivity to resistance issues and main questions affecting the learners. User training factors make use of multiple change interventions, e.g. instructor-led or web-based trainings, videotapes, instruction manuals, quick reference cards. ShareNet's local company workshop briefcases are text-book examples for successful combination.

Noteworthy are the incorporation of disconfirmation factors (to enhance credibility and impact) and the correspondence between user training factors and phased implementation approach. Change agents began with informal user trainings in pilot countries, later developed formal learning plans for 30 major countries, and concluded once again with informal trainings for smaller communities, i.e. service and R&D rollouts. For large user bases "snowball" training systems are the only way to proceed: pilot studies ensure technical reliability and user training quality (comp. Beer et al., 1990, p. 165; Orlikowski, 1992, p. 369); user champion trainings (boot camps) make "missionaries" for the KMS in distinct departments and regions (Curley & Gremillion, 1983, p. 204); after a critical mass is formed, sociability and networking with peers can supplant formal, top-down trainings (Earl, 2001, p. 225). Case studies, early-win showcases, and guidance for solving individual problems are effective measures for "task context training": users do not only learn how to produce certain outputs, but find out how to use this output in the context of their job. When user satisfaction grows, employees begin to share positive experiences (Alavi & Joachimsthaler, 1992, p. 109; Ginzberg, 1978, p. 49).

Extrinsic and intrinsic motivation ("EIM") combines short-term extrinsic motivators with long-term intrinsic motivators to guide behaviors. Though (initially) of greater importance to continuous-change-process paradigms, they are an accepted means for early project stages, i.e. "initiation" (comp. Schein, 1999, p. 124-126). If organizations take KM seriously, they have to adapt their incentive and reward systems. The exploratory case study corroborates mixed motivators' usefulness. Whereas incentives and rewards build first enthusiasm for KM processes, self-rewarding business impact and technology handling are obligatory in the long term (Beer & Nohria, 2000, pp. 134-141; Brelade & Harman, 2000, p. 27): employees "gain personal development in return for sharing their own knowledge; which allows work to become more fulfilling, and makes the organization more attractive to work in, with better retentions of staff" (KPMG, 1998, p. 17). Everybody must notice the shift from knowledge hoarding to proactive knowledge sharing (Gold et al., 2001, p. 189; O'Dell & Grayson, 1998, p. 170; Seeley, 2000, p. 25).

For large scale KMS implementation projects, extrinsic and intrinsic motivation factors and user training factors should be tightly coupled (von Krogh, 1998, p. 144): targeting user champions with non-trivial, extrinsic motivators - or with formal knowledge exchange goals - speeds up the change process. Since "snowball" implementations rely on the quick formation of a critical mass, multiplicators and extrinsic motivation for knowledge givers and takers create significant momentum. However, when knowledge networks or CoPs have actually formed, community spirit, performance improvements, and user-friendly technical platforms build intrinsic motivation - compulsory for culture change (Earl, 2001, p. 225; Goodman & Darr, 1998, p. 426; Holtshouse, 1998, pp. 278-279; Jarvenpaa & Staples, 2000, p. 131; Probst et al., 1999, p. 308; Sathe, 1985, pp. 386-387). Organizational behavior and sociology studies resolve the former incongruity between extrinsic and intrinsic motivation factors (Beer & Nohria, 2000; Marwell et al., 1988): a sequence of both is needed. Of further relevance is the integration of knowledge exchange with business and personnel processes; it can easily compensate for monetary rewards (comp. Davenport et al., 1998, p. 54).

5.3.3   Continuation

In my second, but concurrent stage - "continuation: adopting new ways of working" - employees change attitudes along with behaviors and experience the new behaviors' contribution to improved performance (Srinivasan & Davis, 1987, p. 65). Distinct to "cognitive restructuring" all factors require a continuous and dynamic handling across all (company-specific) project stages - beginning with "initiation", ending with "termination" (comp. Ginzberg, 1981b, p. 48). Weick and Quinn (1999, p. 379) conclude: "when change is continuous, the problem is [...] one of redirecting what is already under way." Success depends on leadership, teamwork, and effective communication with potential users (Levasseur, 2001, p. 73). Similar to traditional IS implementation projects, sponsors usually provide some directive or mandate while the project team carries out the application's rollout and maintenance; regional management retains responsibility for local adaptations. Managerial reviews, evaluations, and sequential improvements of proposals are helpful (Zand & Sorensen, 1975, p. 542). Kolb and Frohman (1970, pp. 56-61) suggest to plan combined KM and change initiatives cooperatively to ensure appropriateness, understanding, and commitment.

⇨   As a sixth managerial guideline, I posit that three "recurrent issues" mandate continuous attention during the implementation process: top management support, user involvement, and socialization. The first is a top-down change intervention, the second addresses bottom-up requirements, while the third spreads horizontally and spontaneously - across functional and regional boundaries.

While top management support factors' general relation to IS implementation success is acknowledged, Jarvenpaa and Ives' (1991, p. 206) categories of managerial support call for further academic attention. Methods of construct validity, e.g. factor analysis (Kerlinger & Lee, 1999), can assess the influences of "executive participation" and "executive involvement" in the context of KMS implementation projects. The overlap between executive example setting, e.g. role models and mentoring, and socialization factors should be made clear. Additional quantitative research, e.g. case studies and ethnographies (Myers, 1999; Yin, 1994), ought to explore user involvement and socialization factors' effects on knowledge networks (Alavi & Leidner, 2001, p. 114).

Top management support ("TMS") emphasizes the KMS' business impact and allocates adequate project resources. Generally, organization members are wary of KM initiatives and show resistance unless project sponsors communicate the significance to competitiveness and innovativeness, provide funding for an adequate (technology) infrastructure, and clarify what types of knowledge are most relevant to the firm (Curley & Gremillion, 1983, p. 207; Davenport & Prusak, 2000, p. 165; Keen et al., 1982, p. 130; Schultz et al., 1987, p. 36; Tyran & George, 1993, p. 7). All affected stakeholders must be convinced that KM regularly implies a long-term change management initiative (De Long & Seemann, 2000, p. 43; King et al., 2002, p. 93). Researchers differentiate between "executive participation" as an activity or substantial personal intervention into IS management and "executive involvement" as a technology-friendly psychological state (Jarvenpaa & Ives, 1991, p. 206). Case study data indicates a shift and possible spill-overs from the former to the latter. This influence is alternatively moderated by true beliefs in knowledge-orientation or by short-term opportunism, i.e. line managers paying lip service to executives' ideas, hoping for better organizational visibility.

Top management support factors comprise a wide range of measures: managerial statements, role models, project supervision, resource allocation, revision of change requests, and HR interventions, e.g. hiring and promotion. Fundamental are a clear and compelling vision, mission, and terminology stressing the goals and values of a knowledge-intensive culture. Visionary leadership opens up possibilities for culture change while command-and-control, top-down micromanagement is an inhibitor (Beer et al., 1990, p. 159; Gold et al., 2001, p. 195; Levasseur, 2001, p. 73; Nonaka, 1991, pp. 103-104; Spector, 1989, p. 33). ShareNet's implementation proved that top management support is needed recurrently, even after an IS' organizational integration: PACT's deflection of management attention was not only noticed by community members but destroyed change accomplishments. Knowledge-oriented cultures and top management support are two sides of the same coin (Davenport et al., 1998, pp. 54-

55); as Schein remarks (1992, p. 5): "one could argue that the only thing of real importance that leaders do is to create and manage culture".

User involvement ("UIN") mandates active participation in development and evolution to foster identification with and commitment to the project. Culturally sensitive KMS implementation projects profit from organization members taking responsibility for their own destiny through defining work objectives, specifying how to reach them, and setting ambitious targets (comp. Dover, 2003, p. 244; Schein, 1999, p. 125; Zmud & Cox, 1979, p. 37). Deficits during early project stages, i.e. planning and design, lead to obstacles which can hardly be removed during maintenance and evolution (Keen et al., 1982, pp. 139-140; Levasseur, 2001, p. 72). The case description shows all predicted outcomes of user involvement factors: on the one hand, participative development fosters employee sense of ownership and increases the assessment of system requirements' quality; on the other hand, users form realistic expectations about KM (comp. Ginzberg, 1981a, pp. 475-476; Tyran & George, 1993, p. 7). Furthermore - as above organizational change models of implementation suggest - they are means to create an acceptable and favorable change environment (Alavi & Joachimsthaler, 1992, pp. 107-108).

I deem all of Nutt's (1986, pp. 246-248) variations of user involvement appropriate for KMS implementation projects; however, full delegation of all maintenance and evolution efforts to large user bases is unfeasible. Even though "comprehensive participation" creates considerable commitment to change, coordination problems get in the way of practical relevance. Better is the project team's transformation into a KMS service unit with capabilities for adjusting and carrying out bottom-up change requests, i.e. "complete participation" (Jin & Franz, 1986, p. 71; Keen, 1981, p. 26). User involvement factors are needed continuously, since the gestalt of CoPs emerges through activity - as opposed to task-related formation: "the actual behaviors of communities-of-practice are constantly changing both as newcomers replace old timers and as the demands of practice force the community to revise its relationship to its environment" (Brown & Duguid, 1991, p. 50). Since employees ought to make knowledge-orientation part of their self-concept, identity, and ongoing relationships, they should also have a say in the consistent maintenance of KMS (Alavi & Leidner, 1999, p. 24). Flexible multi-community platforms have potential to build bottom-up knowledge networks.

Socialization ("SOC") introduces peers to a knowledge-intensive culture through personal and impersonal example setting. Newcomers learn about corporate realities, cultural routines, and individual responsibilities for knowledge sharing. Everybody must acquire personal knowledge and skills and help those in need as their own expertise develops (von Krogh, 1998, p. 144). Socialization factors hold huge potential for those types of KM initiatives that try to build

KMS-friendly environments (Davenport & Prusak, 2000, pp. 149-150; Earl, 2001, p. 225): since executives are usually not in a position to explain to each organization member the implementation's rationale (Curley & Gremillion, 1983, p. 207) - and in accordance with CoP self-design and self-governance (Gold et al., 2001, p. 189; O'Dell & Grayson, 1998, p. 157) - horizontal and implicit means to spread the word grow in importance. I hypothesize that individual experiences from neutral intermediaries, i.e. personal examples, and success stories, i.e. impersonal examples, cultivate trust and contribute to the internalization of beliefs and values; they are convincing and memorable (Sathe, 1985, pp. 390-391; 1993, pp. 338-339; Thomas et al., 2001, pp. 869-871).

KMS in general are important change drivers: they accelerate and expand socialization factors' impact across time and space, along with embodying cultural assumptions (Davenport et al., 1998, p. 45; Dewett & Jones, 2001, p. 8; Saffold, 1988, p. 551; Yazici, 2002, p. 550). While "change as a contact sport" is slowly replaced by spontaneous "electronic weak ties", mentoring remains valuable for acculturation (Constant et al., 1996, p. 119; Markus & Benjamin, 1997, p. 59; Quinn et al., 1996, p. 73). However, formal hierarchies and executive role models are somewhat replaced by tenure and visibility among peers: "communities [...] have little hierarchy; the only real status is that of member" (Orr, 1990, p. 33). This confirms with Döring's memories of the KM initiative: the traditional corporate chain of command weakened, but competent opinion leaders and ShareNet managers evolved from CoPs. When a gloomy business situation and outlook hit Siemens ICN, the multiplicators were able to compensate somewhat for lost top management support and diminished budgets.

5.3.4 Termination

In my third and final stage - "termination: internalizing new concepts and meanings" - the implementation project is concluded. Supportive social norms are created, change is made congruent with employee personalities, and new behaviors are maintained and solidified to bring the firm back to normality (Krovi, 1993, p. 328; Weick & Quinn, 1999, p. 366; Zand & Sorensen, 1975, p. 534). Change agents and organization members work together to ensure the KMS' full installation, testing, debugging, usage, measuring, and further enhancements. Termination requires particularly strong top management support and user involvement until new behaviors have reinstated those existing prior to the change process. Employees must internalize a knowledge-intensive culture's beliefs and values and transform them into group norms and routines. Confirming data stops their adaptation processes (Levasseur, 2001, p. 73; Schein, 1992, pp. 302-303; 1999, p. 129). Unlike temporary adjustments in ways of working, "termination" requires lengthy and meticulous work.

⇨ As a seventh and last managerial guideline, I propose that three main activities wrap up the change process: organizational integration, behavioral and cultural controlling, and confirmation.
Though my findings generally agree with Schein's (1992, pp. 302-303; 1999, p. 129) commendations for "refreezing", further academic research is needed on the latter two factors. First, multiple regression analysis can investigate which indicators are better determinants of KMS implementation success: late-stage behavioral and cultural controlling vs. continuous behavior rationalization assessments (comp. Sathe, 1985, p. 388; Sathe, 1993, pp. 337-338). Second, factor analysis (Kerlinger & Lee, 1999) ought to explore potential sequences: must both organizational integration and behavioral and cultural diagnosis factors show positive indications before confirmation factors can successfully terminate change processes?

Organizational integration ("OIN") embeds project outcomes into line and process organizations. It brings technology into fit with the KM context elements strategy and structure (Grover & Davenport, 2001, pp. 12-13). "A transformational organizational system such as [KMS] is never complete; unless it is institutionalized and evolves, it falls into disuse" (Stein & Zwass, 1995, p. 96). Formal policies, systems, and structures are needed to institutionalize the change process; enacting structural changes any earlier has a propensity to backfire (Beer et al., 1990, p. 164). The project team should gradually withdraw and leave ownership and responsibility for the applications' maintenance and evolution with users and capable successors, e.g. a regular line organization. Service units with consulting and training capabilities - similar to the ShareNet operating team - are in a position to provide ongoing user assistance. They stimulate discussions about post-implementation problems, further enhancements, and respond to suggestions from the community (Ginzberg, 1979, p. 88; Jin & Franz, 1986, p. 71; Keen, 1981, p. 26; Keen et al., 1982, p. 141; Krovi, 1993, p. 334).

Via organizational integration factors, top management signals that KM is no management fad, but a source of sustainable competitive advantage (comp. Rothnie, 2001, p. 188). Kotter (1995, p. 67) contends that change begins to stick "when it becomes "the way we do things around here," when it seeps into the bloodstream of the corporate body." Case study data unveils that the success of KMS implementation projects depends as much on horizontal integration, i.e. combination with key knowledge work processes and other applications (Grover & Davenport, 2001, p. 13; King et al., 2002, p. 96; Yazici, 2002, p. 542), as on vertical integration, i.e. user satisfaction. Joint development consortia and workgroups with the central IS function, as well as with owners of other knowledge sources and systems, ensure smooth interfacing with other applications. Technical platforms can facilitate knowledge application through embedding with corporate routines: IS implanted with culture-bound procedures themselves become examples of organizational norms (Alavi & Leidner, 2001, p. 122).

Behavioral and cultural controlling ("BCC") assesses behavioral and cultural shifts for taking necessary corrective actions. It aligns technology with the KM context elements people/culture (Grover & Davenport, 2001, pp. 12-13). "Termination" requires a thorough assessment of change accomplishments with appropriate evaluation measures and standards; to complement the KMS' organizational hand-over, client self-analysis is encouraged (Jin & Franz, 1986, p. 71; Zand & Sorensen, 1975, p. 542). As mentioned above, there are "hard" and "soft" indicators of success. Business targets, i.e. short-term commercial goals, can alternatively be contrasted with cultural adjustments, i.e. the way people perceive and value their ways of working (Dover, 2003, p. 256). For true culture change, employees can no longer adhere to their prevailing pattern of beliefs and values and only opportunistically change their overt behaviors. In those detrimental cases, new behaviors can merely be attributed to incentives and rewards, resulting in compliance in lieu of cultural commitment (Sathe, 1985, pp. 386-388; 1993, pp. 337-338).

Confidence in organizational ownership of knowledge, fairness, and trust are appropriate intrinsic motivators which trigger long-lasting change (Constant et al., 1994, p. 404; Harper, 2001, p. 14; Jarvenpaa & Staples, 2001, p. 165). User satisfaction studies (a widely used proxy for the dependent variable), general feedback, as well as seasoned change agents' personal experiences and appraisals make for proper behavioral and cultural diagnosis factors. Depending on the KM initiative's progress and the success of people/culture change interventions, implementation managers must either decide on project conclusion or on switches to other stages, i.e. "continuation" and "initiation" (comp. Kolb & Frohman, 1970, p. 61; Krovi, 1993, p. 334). If necessary, they choose alternative extrinsic and intrinsic motivation factors, and, in extreme cases, replacements (comp. Beer, 1988, p. 4; Beer et al., 1990, p. 163; Joshi, 1991, p. 238).

Confirmation ("CON") stops the change process through disseminating confirmatory data and feedback and concludes my nine-factor implementation model. Change agents must produce confirming data to end the employees' search and coping processes; once fixed, they will stay like this until dissatisfaction sets in again (Schein, 1992, p. 303; 1999, p. 129). Two measures are particularly important: the first is a mindful attempt to demonstrate how new behaviors and attitudes have helped organizational outcomes, i.e. example setting; the second is relentless communication (Kotter, 1995, p. 67). Sufficient time is needed to converse evidence of successful application, external recognition, managerial praise, positive feedback from change agents to stakeholders, and user satisfaction with the new KMS and business processes (Levasseur, 2001, p. 73; Srinivasan & Davis, 1987, p. 65; Zand & Sorensen, 1975, p. 542). Based on the case discussion, I contend that organizational integration and behavioral and cultural controlling ought to yield first positive responses before confirmation factors are disseminated.

An emerging area like KMS implementation research - potentially affecting the KM context elements strategy, structure, people/culture, and technology - is characterized by many unresolved issues. My research is an initial attempt to identify and organize the most important ones (Grover & Davenport, 2001, pp. 12-14; King et al., 2002, p. 93). The academic and managerial predictions set forth are not derived from a generally accepted theory, but are pieced together from research on culture change, IS implementation, and KMS. A theory can be defined as a set of related propositions that specify relationships among variables (comp. Blalock, 1969, p. 2; Kerlinger, 1986, p. 9). My synthetic framework, with propositions related to one another (at the very least) through common dependent variables (specifying implementation success), passes this definitional test of theory. Additionally, it offers a framework for integrating the recommended change interventions. Of course, the tentative result requires additional substantiation and tests before gaining general acceptance (comp. Huber, 1990, pp. 64-65).

Appendix

Interview Guidelines

⇨ Please explain your involvement with ShareNet during the given timeframe.

⇨ Please define and describe the stages of ShareNet's development and implementation process (e.g. "definition and prototyping", "setup and piloting", "global rollout", "operation, expansion, and further development", and "shifting to a multi-community concept"). When did each stage start and finish, on time or delayed? Which stage encountered major problems/pivotal moments (e.g. contrasting headquarters, local companies)?

⇨ Which resources, technical or non-technical, were committed to the project? Which were missing? How was top management support employed?

⇨ Can you describe ShareNet's technical systems (aiming to facilitate low effort global publishing and searching and to enable communication in a large geographically dispersed company)?

⇨ Was there a change management strategy for ShareNet's implementation and did it change over time? Was change management undertaken before the KM initiative started or should the project actually facilitate culture change? Was attention paid to the context elements people/culture and technology?

⇨ How was the idea of ShareNet introduced to the users? Was there a "felt need" or some threatening facts, related to some important objectives and ideals? How did the development and implementation staff and the users see their roles? Was a joint contract for change built?

⇨ How was the system implemented in the local companies? Was its value established and user expertise built? Were there trainings, coaches, and feedback? What was the impact on work, skills, communication, and influence at all hierarchical levels?

⇨ Can you describe the development of ShareNet's managerial systems? What were the main decision points during the development and implementation? Was the concept continuously refined?

⇨ What were the underlying assumptions or "messages" behind ShareNet's incentive and reward system? Did it imply trust of employees?

⇨ One of the managerial system's stated objectives was to enable ShareNet's further development and growth by supporting a knowledge-intensive culture (i.e. knowledge sharing vs. knowledge hoarding and proactively seeking and offering knowledge). Was this objective accomplished?

⇨ Culture change can precede, follow, or occur simultaneously with behavior change. Permanent change results from the latter: employees strongly believe in and value new ways of working which are intrinsically motivating and this in turn reinforces the behavior. What was the situation at Siemens ICN?

⇨ The amount of resistance to culture change results from three interlinking factors: magnitude of change in culture's content, strength of the prevailing culture, and overall resistance to change. Along those dimensions, can you describe the resistance ShareNet's development and implementation encountered (e.g. contrasting headquarters, local companies)?

⇨ There are two broad approaches to inflict culture change: getting people to buy into new values and beliefs (e.g. via intrinsic motivation, nullification of inappropriate justifications, credible and persuasive cultural communications) vs. hiring, socializing, and removing organization members. What measures did Siemens ICN take?

⇨ Is there evidence of intrinsically motivated behavior? Would the new behavior persist if extrinsic motivations were diminished?

Interview Synopses

Interview with Horst D. Angerer

Company: Siemens AG
Position: Head of Department Knowledge Management ICM N MS TM C6
Location: Rupert-Mayer-Str. 44, 81359 Munich
Date: August 12, 2002 (in person)
Number: 01

Angerer was a member of the service community (technical product support) and a ShareNet user for two years. With regard to ShareNet, he held three distinct roles: first, he was a regular contributor/user posting and searching for contributions; second, he was a ShareNet manager supporting end users in capturing project experiences and service know-how; third and last, he was responsible for ShareNet's and VITAC's positioning and joint development, e.g. strategies and interfaces. The ShareNet operating team offered support and considered feedback sufficiently. Even though the changes in the new team were apparent, there was no transparency regarding service level and support agreements. There was no community-driven development since contributors/users from Siemens ICM service hardly made any comments.

During the key evolution stage "operation, expansion, and further development" (in December 2000) the service rollout began. Angerer felt that ShareNet provided less value-add to the service community since there were only a limited number of contributions. Service had already established proprietary tools and structures to deal with customer problems (e.g. error catalog, problem escalation routines), only meshed network communication among local companies was missing. In comparison with the ShareNet project team the new team was very open for joint solutions. ShareNet was no longer considered the "one and only" KM tool.

ShareNet's discussion forums were used for problems still too complex and diffuse to be reported in standard error catalogs and to locate experts globally. Users/contributors were automatically reminded to check the VITAC database before they made new forum postings. Even though specific service knowledge objects were later captured in VITAC, ShareNet's standard quality assurance and reward system was used. VITAC cases were entered into a designated input form in ShareNet; the content was later transferred manually to VITAC. The symbiosis was advantageous for both parties: the ShareNet operating team liked the additional visibility gained and the service community benefited from ShareNet's people-to-people section, quality assurance and reward system, and usability.

The high user demand for the service rollout was still increasing. Many employees saw ShareNet as an integral part of their business processes/daily work that provided significant value-add. Nevertheless, a general lack of resources hindered impact and faster progress towards a knowledge-intensive culture. Only Angerer held a full-time KM position, supported part-time by two additional employees. Two product-based discussion forums were maintained, two others would be added later. Top management provided no adequate executive support and leadership; only line management saw the importance of knowledge exchange. Considering ShareNet as "nice-to-have" vs. real business need hindered all other efforts. At Siemens ICM, the ShareNet organization with distinct tasks and roles was not replicated since it was better tailored to Siemens ICN. Consequently, no ShareNet managers raised awareness among potential contributors/users and made ShareNet's positioning clear.

The start of the key evolution stage "shifting to a multi-community concept" was in December 2001 and a pivotal moment in ShareNet's history. Siemens ICM employees disliked the division between urgent requests and regular discussion forums. The number of contributions ebbed off for a while. A general lack of communication from the ShareNet operating team made people unsure about the KM initiative's focus, further direction, and responsibilities. There was no codified/formal change management strategy. During the rollout, ShareNet was rather handled as a tool project. Later Angerer tried to convince key contributors/users that ShareNet provided actual value-add to business processes and business targets. The focus switched to the context elements people/culture and more help with the conceptual implementation/adoption was provided. In contrast to the ShareNet operating team, no mere tool was sold without further advice. A recent email campaign for 500 selected users promoted "networking people" and expert cooperation.

Since local companies often lacked solutions expertise and cross-country knowledge exchange, they were the first to recognize and accept the changing international environment. The KMS was regarded and used as a valuable tool especially after positive first experiences were made. ShareNet encountered some resistance at headquarters: business units questioned ShareNet's positioning among other IS, did not believe in the local companies' experience and creativity that were often incompatible with central strategies, faced no strong pressure from customers, and feared to share previously centralized knowledge, a source of influence and power. ShareNet had first impact on work, skills, communication, and influence at all levels: there was higher responsiveness to international cooperation and requests for help; employees recognized that both knowledge givers and takers benefited.

Angerer considered ShareNet's incentive and reward system an important add-on to the employees' basic salary. Adaptations in the number of shares awarded were recognized but not considered important. The motivators did not communicate mistrust of employees; they rather enforced a positive competitive spirit. The share system was implemented to quickly reach a critical mass of content and reuse, and to succeed in the "battle" for capturing time against other important daily issues. In contrast to management consultancies, Siemens ICM was not entirely driven by information and knowledge and consequently placed lower importance on knowledge exchange.

Including knowledge sharing as a goal into employee target agreements had not been accomplished so far. The majority of ShareNet users were still dependent on incentives; only a minority exchanged knowledge on the basis of their own experiences and dependency on international cooperation. If the extrinsic motivation was diminished, or even cancelled, usage rates would drop significantly or the entire system might shut down within six months (deadlock). Due to the nature of local markets, countries that were net consumers of reusable knowledge needed no further motivation. Net contributors, e.g. countries with innovative and competitive markets, however, were more difficult to motivate.

The managerial system's main objective was to create a mindset of proactively seeking and offering knowledge and a knowledge-intensive culture. Among other measures, ShareNet had significant impact on culture change. "Still, more people talked about knowledge-orientation than actually lived the idea. Besides other pressing daily needs, knowledge exchange had only become norm and routine of very small groups." Some intrinsically motivated employees, i.e. less than 1%, had internalized new habits and ways of thinking. Consequent executive support and credible communication, e.g. from Koch, Döring, and Wagner, sped up the otherwise slow process. During ShareNet's implementation, behavior change occurred simultaneously with culture change: first experiences made many users believers in the KMS and in a knowledge-intensive culture which in turn reinforced the desired behavior. So far, no resisters/deviants had been laid off. Without formal knowledge exchange goals, evaluations for pending layoffs were not possible. There was no ShareNet "socialization" for Siemens ICM employees in local companies but staff exchanges/role models were considered for the future.

Interview with Felix Baumann

Company: Siemens AG
Position: ShareNet Consultant ICN GS CKM
Location: Hofmannstr. 51, 81359 Munich
Date: July 30, 2002 (in person)
Number: 02

Baumann described ShareNet's development and implementation along five stages: "definition and prototyping", "setup and piloting", "global rollout", "operation, expansion, and further development", and "shifting to a multi-community concept". In each implementation stage, both technical and people/cultural issues were explicitly taken into account. During the key evolution stage "operation, expansion, and further development" (in June 2000) Baumann became a ShareNet consultant and consequently a member of the ShareNet operating team. With the start of this stage, development and implementation were formally finished; BTP/BTC handed over the responsibilities to the new ShareNet operating team.

Earlier, local companies lacked information: they were not included in distribution lists, old boys' networks, and had only limited network access and bandwidth. They were the first to recognize the need for a KM initiative; their input was taken up by BTP/BTC. By responding directly to those needs ShareNet became an integral part of their business processes/daily work. The KMS encountered higher resistance at headquarters: business units were afraid of sharing previously centralized knowledge, a source of influence and power. Signs of resistance were: inactivity and lack of implementation support, posting "empty" knowledge objects under pressure, and postponing decisions. In general, the more local ICN heads were convinced of ShareNet's value, the smoother the implementation went.

During the key evolution stage "operation, expansion, and further development" (in December 2000) the service rollout began. Baumann felt that ShareNet provided less value-add to the service community since there were only a limited number of contributions. Additionally, the difficult economic situation allowed only for gradual improvements: a limited number of new projects led to less knowledge objects posted which finally diminished contributor/user interest. AS, ON, and WN's shared service function and EN's service had already established proprietary tools (e.g. error catalog, problem escalation routines); they mostly used ShareNet for problems still too complex and diffuse to be reported in standard error catalogs. ShareNet served mainly as a user interface to those systems which had established linkages to the KMS, e.g. VITAC. The symbiosis was advantageous for both parties: the ShareNet operating team liked the additional visibility gained and the service community benefited from ShareNet's usability and reliability. Since VITAC level three employees cooperated closely with R&D, an additional communication channel was established. Both functions began to share knowledge directly.

There was user demand both for the service and the multi-community rollout but a general lack of resources. The central function IT needed several human resources for timely development, implementation, and documentation. ShareNet consultants lacked financial resources to travel and spread ShareNet's idea globally. A simultaneous top-down and bottom-up approach was used for the service rollout. The service executives were difficult to involve and merely paid lip service to the KMS. Potential contributors/users received basic training (no longer than three hours) developed from local company workshop briefcases and screenshots. Baumann believed that ShareNet should become a self-explanatory tool. Among the service employees, WN users were the most active; AS and ON accounted for less traffic. EN service employees did not become ShareNet users since executives were reluctant to embrace KM and were too busy with the business unit's restructuring. There was no codified/formal change management strategy, rather a pragmatic approach based on personal experiences.

The start of the key evolution stage "shifting to a multi-community concept" was in December 2001 and simultaneous with the beginning of the R&D rollout. To accommodate especially the needs of the R&D community, the ShareNet operating team created a separate knowledge library, still maintaining it as an integral part of the ICN/ICM community. Extensive discussions between community support and the potential contributors/users led to the development of R&D-specific knowledge objects and a corresponding capturing wizard. Since no further user involvement was desired, only brief trainings were conducted at headquarters. Baumann explained a general lack of traffic with a narrow focus, proprietary R&D applications, and security concerns. Merely Siemens ICM R&D was eager to contribute documentation and knowledge objects. Up to that point, the sub-community had not accomplished the shift from "box selling" to a service focus and solutions approach. A virtual R&D conference aroused more interest. For that purpose, ShareNet's R&D knowledge library captured knowledge objects which were linked to presentations within OpenText Livelink; discussions were held in designated forums.

The managerial systems' main objective was to create a mindset of proactively seeking and offering knowledge and a knowledge-intensive culture. A few employees internalized new habits and ways of thinking and became big Share-Net advocates. Even though the need for knowledge exchange had become recognized by all Siemens ICN employees not everybody trusted the company. There was a free-rider mentality within the ICN/ICM community; users benefited from the system without contributing input. Up to that point, the impact on work, skills, communication and influence was rather small. Compliments/support from management and including knowledge sharing as a goal into employee target agreements were simple measures for behavior and culture change. Baumann noticed less top management support than before when Koch was Siemens ICN's group president.

Siemens ICN's financial crisis had an ambiguous impact on the on-going change process: a lack of resources and management attention made it difficult to sustain culture change's momentum. On the one hand, employees were less inclined to contribute valuable knowledge when threatened by layoffs; on the other hand, people felt survival anxiety and/or guilt and started to question isolated work routines. Once people truly recognized the need for sharing, no incentive system was needed. During ShareNet's implementation, behavior change occurred simultaneously with culture change: first experiences made many users believers in the KMS and in a knowledge-intensive culture which in turn reinforced the new behavior. "ShareNet was a tool for culture change; the smooth implementation served vice versa as an argument for successful change."

According to Baumann, ShareNet's incentive and reward system communicated trust of employees. It was implemented to quickly reach a critical mass of content and reuse and to succeed in the "battle" for capturing time against other important daily issues. The majority of ShareNet users were still dependent on incentives; only a minority exchanged knowledge on the basis of their own experiences and dependency on international cooperation. A discontinuation of extrinsic incentives and rewards would at least lead to significant drops in usage or even to a deadlock situation: existing contributors/users might become passive and it would be difficult to attract others. Baumann mentioned that the quality assurance and reward system was the only tool available to influence the number of contributions. Generally, creating a pull-effect for knowledge was better than to assert pressure on employees. During ShareNet's development and implementation, no resisters/deviants were laid off. The project team members felt that the resistance would have been too strong; incentives for desired behaviors would set a more positive tune. There was no ShareNet "socialization" for new Siemens ICN employees and a lack of corporate identity.

Interview with Joachim Döring

Company: Siemens AG
Position: President ICN GS
Location: Hofmannstr. 51, 81359 Munich
Date: August 19, 2002 (in person)
Number: 03

Döring described ShareNet's development and implementation along five stages: "definition and prototyping", "setup and piloting", "global rollout", "operation, expansion, and further development", and "shifting to a multi-community concept". In each implementation stage, both technical and people/cultural issues were explicitly taken into account; a codified/formal change management strategy, however, did not exist. Until the end of the "global rollout" stage, Döring was the head of BTP/BTC. Later he headed the central function GS.

The second key project stage, "setup and piloting", lasted from April to mid July 1999. Objectives were to test and improve the technical platform, to ensure local company buy-in and preparation, and to develop a phased implementation approach including training material. A pilot project team, including Jenzowsky, Meinert, and Popp, continuously refined ShareNet capturing wizard questions. After the KMS' reliability and the knowledge library's structure and linkage possibilities were tested, feedback forms/change requests accumulated. All were resolved before the international rollout started. To create positive first experiences at the beginning, Australian workshop participants were often asked to post some pressing problems as urgent requests. The core team members either answered personally or convinced personal contacts.

Seasoned change managers with large personal networks and early user involvement ensured top management support and end user buy-in. Every aspect of the change process was structured around the interplay of the four crucial elements Sales Value Creation Process, ShareNet Content, ShareNet Community, and ShareNet Systems. Döring considered the project's resources sufficient. Siemens ICN's group executive management members Koch and Maher provided plenty of top management support and budget for incentives, travel, and workshops. In 2000, the entire Siemens ICN group executive management and many local ICN heads became supporters of ShareNet. Döring took over the responsibility to put vision and ideas into practice.

Since most sales and marketing knowledge resided in local companies, they were the first to recognize and accept the changing international environment and the need for a KM initiative. Feeling survival anxiety or guilt was a make-or-break factor like for any other change management initiative. ShareNet encountered higher resistance at headquarters: on the one hand, business units were afraid to lose sales opportunities for internal services that could now be posted for free on ShareNet; on the other hand, they feared to share previously centralized knowledge, a source of influence and power. Resistance came in several flavors: inactivity and lack of implementation support, preventing employees from posting safeguarded knowledge, denying the right to use ShareNet, and all kinds of mobbing and politics. The ShareNet project team decided to continue the implementation with central funding and a focus on key impact areas, i.e. the local companies. Since it would prolong the implementation process, the central function CIO was deliberately not involved at an early stage. In the long run, the KMS' business impact ought to win over the resisters.

In the last two years, the telecommunications sector became less turbulent; many new competitors disappeared. Still, the general shift from a "box selling" to a service focus and solutions approach remained valid. ShareNet had significant impact on work, skills, communication, and influence at all levels. It triggered the redefinition of business processes and facilitated even offline/personal knowledge exchange. Traditional corporate hierarchies were weakened, but new competent opinion leaders evolved from CoPs.

During the "operation, expansion, and further development" stage (in October 2000), von Pierer invited 200 journalists to a conference at Siemens' Center of E-Excellence at Munich airport. He declared ShareNet's technical systems and phased implementation approach a Siemens-wide KMS best practice. The KMS had to be adapted to other business segment's underlying processes, similar to the mapping of Siemens ICN's Sales Value Creation Process. Until September 2002, only Siemens Businesses Services and Siemens Medical had embraced ShareNet with many difficulties. Other business segments lacked clear responsibilities and an understanding of the transformation process: there were no taxonomies, no key players, as well as no comprehension of KM's bottom-line impact.

The managerial system's main objective was to create a mindset of proactively seeking and offering knowledge and a knowledge-intensive culture. Döring felt that much had been accomplished in only a few years: "ShareNet is more than a database; it is a new spirit, a new way to cooperate worldwide across country and organizational boundaries. Unlike in school, you are invited to copy from your neighbor. Knowledge reuse is the key to success, e.g. innovation, time to market, etc. With ShareNet we take advantage of our strengths: local innovations and creativity and global leverage of sales power." The majority of employees exchanged knowledge freely and openly without ever making personal contact; rather, they were bound together in a global corporate network, worked within the same industry, and had a common code of conduct. Complex personal interactions were almost impossible to manage. The term "culture change" never appeared in local company workshop briefcases since earlier change initiatives had encountered too much ambiguity.

Before ShareNet was implemented, Siemens ICN had no strong culture that rewarded the open and transparent communication of solutions know-how. According to Döring, there was plenty of time, the possibility to achieve good business results with an even sparse exchange of information, and old boys' networks. The share system was only one among many of the managerial systems' constituting elements and an add-on to the employees' basic salary. It signaled top management expectations clearly and consistently. Even though, if monetary incentives were decreased or even shut-down in the future, usage rates would not drop significantly. If the KM initiative folded entirely, the ShareNet project team and the ShareNet operating team had not accomplished sustainable change. Better linkage with personnel processes was planned, i.e. inclusion into employee target agreements and criteria for promotion. Some 40 sales representatives who participated in ShareNet's key project stages had already been promoted. Döring recognized that people were slow to make adjustments; whereas first results from culture change showed after a few years, the processes needed a decade to become self-sustaining.

Interview with Stefan Jenzowsky

Company: Siemens AG
Position: Business Innovation ICN GS BI
Location: Hofmannstr. 51, 81359 Munich
Date: August 2, 2002 (in person)
Number: 04

Jenzowsky described ShareNet's development and implementation along five stages: "definition and prototyping", "setup and piloting", "global rollout", "operation, expansion, and further development", and "shifting to a multicommunity concept". In each implementation stage, both technical and people/cultural issues were explicitly taken into account. A codified/formal change management strategy hardly existed; only the external consultancy Change Factory developed some workshops and training material. Until the end of the "global rollout" stage, Jenzowsky was part of BTP/BTC and consequently a member of the ShareNet project team. His responsibilities were managerial systems, including the quality assurance and reward system, and ShareNet's marketing concept.

The second key project stage, "setup and piloting", lasted from April to mid July 1999. Objectives were to test and improve the technical platform, to ensure local company buy-in and preparation, and to develop a phased implementation approach including training material. The technical systems were tested for database functionality, GUI and usability, response times, and reliability. Piloting followed three phases. First, buy-in was established on a political level with local company heads/local ICN heads. Here, culture change happened first, later the project actually facilitated culture change. Second, the ShareNet project team members compiled feedback on additional technical functionality required. Lastly, the knowledge library's structure was tested by capturing one sample project per pilot country.

Jenzowsky considered the pilot countries "friendly turf"; political problems were encountered during the "global rollout" stage in other countries. Koch sent a letter to all local companies to create awareness for ShareNet and to request the nomination of one part-time ShareNet manager per country. Those were supported by BTP/BTC coaches. Koch and Döring provided sufficient top management support; the only thing missing were human resources. The sales peoples' early involvement and quick modifications of the working prototype - based on feedback - ensured sufficient support from later contributors/users.

During the key project stage "global rollout" the KMS was implemented in the local companies. All rollout activities were monitored centrally, e.g. rollout targets, resources, workshops. The core team continuously provided ShareNet managers/multiplicators with performance feedback. 33 ShareNet managers sent in a roadmap for their local rollout. The ShareNet project team checked the roadmaps and provided the requested support. On March 1, 2000 the competitive share system went live; the switchover to a non-competitive system occurred on June 1, 2000. Contributions peaked in May 2000, a good indicator for the technical systems' reliability. In the following months, new postings went to a relatively saturated system. ShareNet was quantitatively oriented, only a large number of objects ensured good matches between contributions and searches.

Since most sales and marketing knowledge resided in local companies, they were the first to recognize and accept the changing international environment and the need for a KM initiative. Besides the phased implementation approach - chosen by the ShareNet project team - an increasing number of users proactively approached the ShareNet managers for registration and support. The core team noticed several local KM initiatives and systems. ShareNet encountered higher resistance at headquarters: business units did not believe in the local companies' experience and creativity that were often incompatible with central strategies. Resistance came in several flavors: politics, competition between local companies, language barriers, and SBS' and Siemens ICM's lack of openness. They just wanted to use the tool without sharing any experiences.

One of the managerial system's main objectives was to lay out a path for the transformation of information into best practices and "wisdom" for Siemens ICN, a process meant to happen within "knowledge cells" (CoPs). Jenzowsky admitted that the third goal had not been realized for two reasons: on the one hand, contributors/users resisted "knowledge cells" as a more formal way to collaborate with an unclear pay-off; on the other hand, a lack of resources forced concentration on other goals. The share system with extrinsic, but knowledge-related rewards was monitored constantly. The top 50 contributors who had collected the most shares by the end of May 2000 and their partners were invited to a ShareNet user conference in New York in October 2000; 600 shares were deducted from their accounts. Due to a lack of money, the meeting was not repeated on an annual basis.

During ShareNet's implementation, behavior change preceded culture change: first experiences made many users believers in the KMS and in a knowledge-intensive culture. Significant culture change was accomplished: the need for knowledge exchange was recognized by all Siemens ICN employees and lived under certain circumstances. The difficult business situation made knowledge sharing a lower priority within Siemens ICN. Even though some employees internalized new habits and ways of thinking, change management could not stop. Credible communication, incentives, and socialization of new employees were still required to maintain culture's momentum. A discontinuation of extrinsic incentives and rewards would at least lead to significant drops in usage or even to a deadlock situation: existing contributors/users might become passive and it would be difficult to attract others. Only "mental extremists" might continue to use ShareNet, not the average Siemens ICN employee. Connecting the KMS to formal and informal business processes would not be sufficient. Jenzowsky considered incentives as the "biggest bang for the buck" and the only tool to influence the number of contributions. Spending the same amount of money on change management, technology, or education would have smaller impact.

Before the KM initiative started, Siemens ICN had no strong culture that rewarded the contribution and reuse of knowledge even though many meetings were held. According to Jenzowsky, there were many hierarchies and bureaucracy, lack of innovativeness, risk adverse decision making, conservatism, trustworthiness, and boredom. Since Siemens ICN had a strong engineering culture, it was difficult to get accustomed to new rules of competition. Innovations no longer originated in centralized R&D; rather they were derived from customers' needs.

Generally, creating a pull-effect for knowledge was better than to assert pressure on employees; incentives for desired behaviors set a more positive tune. During ShareNet's development and implementation, some ShareNet managers were replaced. Either there was a lack of performance or the technology focus was too strong. In addition, the ShareNet project team tried to "socialize" ShareNet managers via boot camps, coaching, and regular meetings. Jenzowsky felt that the highly motivated core team with extrovert members was a critical success factor: "Even a strong and decisive team can be sympathetic and befriend many colleagues."

Interview with Dietmar Krauss

Company: Siemens AG
Position: Application Manager Siemens ShareNet ICN IT CKM ST
Location: Hofmannstr. 51, 81359 Munich
Date: August 13, 2002 (in person)
Number: 05

Krauss described ShareNet's development and implementation along five stages: "definition and prototyping", "setup and piloting", "global rollout", "operation, expansion, and further development", and "shifting to a multi-community concept". In each implementation stage, both technical and people/cultural issues were explicitly taken into account. During the key evolution stage "operation, expansion, and further development" (in May 2000) Krauss became a ShareNet application manager and consequently a member of the ShareNet operating team. With the start of this stage, development and implementation were formally finished; BTP/BTC handed over the responsibilities to the new ShareNet operating team.

During the key evolution stage "operation, expansion, and further development" ShareNet aroused much interest. In August 2000, the start-up company The Agilience Group was chosen to leverage ShareNet to other business segments and external customers. Its CEO Kurtzke was the former head of the central function CC. The intellectual property rights for the technical systems and rollout concept were exchanged for minority equity participation. The cooperation with the central function IT deteriorated when the start-up company developed a completely revised, Microsoft Windows NT-based version of the IS. This database did not conform to Siemens' corporate IT-standards.

The development of a multi-community system began in October 2000 when von Pierer declared ShareNet's technical systems and phased implementation approach a Siemens-wide KMS best practice. Several means should ensure participative development: first, a working prototype was provided to the ICN/ICM community and discussed in a designated ShareNet forum; second, workgroups from the corporate central function CIO, i.e. "Siemens ShareNet Task Force", later "Siemens Knows", took part in the expansion's steering and planning; third and last, a joint ShareNet development consortium was formed with SBS to ensure tight integration with the corporate document management system Open-Text Livelink. Even though the central function IT had sufficient resources, quickly changing project plans, organizational restructurings, and a difficult coordination of Red Hat had negative impact on timely development and software quality. Döring and Wagner provided plenty of top management support.

However, after mid 2001 management attention decreased due to more pressing topics, e.g. Siemens ICN's financial crisis and huge layoffs. There were increasing politics surrounding the Siemens-wide implementation and many new people involved.

According to Krauss, ShareNet was developed on the basis of three-tier client/server architecture. The first tier was the user interface/personal workspace accessible via regular HTML browsers. It ran on the client, usually a PC. The second tier did most of the processing: a SUN SparcServer served as the designated application and web server for all local companies and business units. It ran a software toolkit based on open internet standards: open source web server (AOLServer) and open source community system (ACS). The application was flexible for future changes and comprised tried and tested functions for community building and virtual cooperation. ShareNet' dynamic web implementation was based on ADP, a HTML derivate. Web pages were generated by scripts loading meta data (e.g. object structure and graphical layout) and actual data (e.g. customer description) from the relational database management system (Oracle 8i), housed on the same server, i.e. the third tier. The add-on module Squid implemented tight security mechanisms: SSL, user authentication at login, and object-level read/write access control for the knowledge library. Apache ensured load balancing among different servers.

Siemens ShareNet V1.x marked the introduction of a company-wide, multi-community platform. The ShareNet operating team assumed that people desired CoPs which focused on specific topics of interest. Community homepages provided a personalized overview of community-specific content for each user, e.g. new threads since last login. The conceptual change necessitated a personal workspace with personal data, email alerts, bookmarks, and links to all communities in which the contributor/user participated. Designated functional modules could be flexibly adapted to CoP's differing underlying businesses processes and contained their tacit and explicit knowledge, i.e. knowledge libraries, discussion forums, chats, and news.

The joint development consortium designed the interface/bridge license and user management to ensure information exchange between ShareNet and Livelink communities. Former islands of information, each ShareNet Community used instances of the same site-wide context (e.g. personal workspace, user and group administration, incentive systems), while each Livelink Community employed a separate site-wide context with complicated permission rights and user and group administration. The interface/bridge made it possible to link and access Livelink objects from ShareNet. ICN ShareNet V7.x - originally developed for Siemens ICN-internal use and later expanded to Siemens ICM - became the ICN/ICM community within Siemens ShareNet V1.x. All content, the quality assurance and reward system, and previously earned shares were migrated.

There was no codified/formal change management strategy; rather early user involvement and personal networks ensured executive and contributor/user buy-in. This informal approach was gradually modified: the top-down approach at the beginning, e.g. central definition of the concept and the global rollout, slowly changed to a grassroots approach after the first implementation round. An increasing number of users proactively approached the ShareNet operating team and the ShareNet managers for support. One of the managerial system's main objectives was to lay out a path for the transformation of information into best practices and "wisdom" for Siemens ICN, a process meant to happen within "knowledge cells" (CoPs). Krauss admitted that the review process had been canceled in July 2000. Contributors/users resisted knowledge cells as a too formal way to collaborate with an unclear pay-off.

Two months later, an incentive catalog for the new non-competitive cafeteria-style reward system went live. Shares could now be exchanged into knowledge-related rewards, e.g. technical literature, conference participation, or telecommunication equipment. Further discussions with the sales and marketing community led to the implementation of a five-star rating scheme in November 2000. The KMS automatically distributed the shares for contributions and reuse feedback on any knowledge object. The majority of ShareNet users were still dependent on incentives. Rewards suitable for private communities, e.g. rank, expert status, and visibility, were not sufficient for business-related CoPs. The share system was implemented to quickly reach a critical mass of content and reuse and to succeed in the "battle" for knowledge capturing time against other important daily issues. Krauss considered incentives the "biggest bang for the buck" with direct and sustaining impact.

Even though some employees internalized new habits and ways of thinking, Siemens ICN's financial crisis and huge layoffs set in shortly before a self-sustaining movement was created. Lots of achievements were erased. Culture change focused for too long on the sales and marketing community, the service and R&D rollouts started late. The Siemens-wide development of a knowledge-intensive culture required many more years since every group division had their own approach. For highly motivated users, culture change preceded behavior change: some members of the sales and marketing community lacked knowledge exchange and swiftly embraced the new tool. Before the KM initiative was started, Siemens ICN had no strong culture that rewarded the contribution and reuse of knowledge.

A discontinuation of extrinsic incentives and rewards would at least lead to significant drops in usage or even to a deadlock situation: existing contributors/users might become passive and it would be difficult to attract others. Only integration with employee target agreements and strong topic owners could reverse the downward trend. Generally, creating a pull-effect for knowledge was better than to assert pressure on employees. During ShareNet's development and implementation, no resisters/deviants were laid off. The operating team members felt that incentives for desired behaviors set a more positive tune and decided to rely on existing human resources.

Interview with Alfons Kuhn

Company: Siemens AG
Position: ShareNet Consultant ICN GS CKM
Location: Hofmannstr. 51, 81359 Munich
Date: August 9, 2002 (in person)
Number: 06

Kuhn described ShareNet's development and implementation along five stages: "definition and prototyping", "setup and piloting", "global rollout", "operation, expansion, and further development", and "shifting to a multi-community concept". In each implementation stage, both technical and people/cultural issues were explicitly taken into account. Since the beginning of the "operation, expansion, and further development" stage, Kuhn was a ShareNet consultant and consequently a member of the ShareNet operating team. With the start of this stage, development and implementation were formally finished; BTP/BTC handed over the responsibilities to the new ShareNet operating team.

The new team comprised six ShareNet consultants, six IT specialists, two global editors, and one controller. Some 50 participants attended the first ShareNet manager conference: BTP/BTC, ShareNet managers, and external KM experts. During a formal hand-over ceremony, the ShareNet project team handed over full ownership to the ShareNet operating team, headed by Dr. Michael Wagner. The new team presented their agenda and built a joint contract for change, i.e. all ShareNet managers signed a symbolic document promising to support ShareNet with all effort. To ensure a smooth transition, BTP/BTC provided ongoing support for a few months in addition to new assignments.

Objectives of the key evolution stage "operation, expansion, and further development" were to continuously expand ShareNet throughout the Siemens ICN organization, and to further refine and develop the technical platform. Nevertheless, the focus remained on the sales and marketing community, as well as on local companies: on the one hand, higher implementation resistance at headquarters called for more intensive support; on the other hand, local companies had a stronger "felt need" since they lacked resources and personal networks. The ShareNet consultants visited local companies once or twice a year for buy-in presentations and workshops. Soon, a bottom-up network of coaches formed to support the ShareNet managers. In October 2000, all Siemens ICN employees received an email spam outlining ShareNet's philosophy and mission; an overwhelming number of new users registered. Preparation for the R&D rollout began six months in advance of the "shifting to a multi-community concept" stage.

Only the U.S. turned out to be a difficult environment for ShareNet's implementation. Early on, a qualified IT task force was assembled from communication, education, and marketing specialists, headed by Donald Tsusaki. Top executives were reluctant to embrace a KM initiative with an unclear pay-off. Mainly the local CIO and the vice president information management provided top management support. Since U.S. employees were too widespread to use the standard local company workshop briefcases, Kuhn and Tsusaki relied on web-based trainings and tried to convince key contributors/users to post best practices. Once Tsusaki left, the situation deteriorated: top executives began to question ShareNet's organizational integration and the missing link to business processes. There was no sufficient communication stressing the point that ShareNet was no replacement for existing IS, e.g. Siebel's CRM application, but rather a logical and necessary add-on. In addition, there was no such project organization with earmarked budgets as favored by the Americans. Whereas the U.S. still lacked a designated ShareNet manager and executive support there were some 1,000 registered contributors/users in 2002.

During the "shifting to a multi-community concept" stage, the design and usability of the new KMS was widely acclaimed. The ShareNet operating team admitted some difficulties with setting-up CoPs: there were unclear responsibilities and no policies regulating scope and memberships. Potential contributors/users made proposals for new CoPs and pressed the ShareNet operating team to provide support. Until 2002, Kuhn considered the KM initiative's resources sufficient. There was ample budget for incentives (e.g. "ShareNet Special Weeks"), travel, and workshops. The new team's business plan helped to secure funding: all cost savings and 5% of additional revenues generated with the help of ShareNet were formally credited - but not transferred - to their cost center. Success stories became a separate knowledge object in September 2001. Koch and Döring provided plenty of top management support and budget, but the business unit managements' buy-in remained weak.

There was no codified/formal change management strategy; rather an informal approach based on awareness campaigns and local company executive buy-in. User champions promoted the KMS locally with flyers and dedicated web pages. Additionally, there were target agreements and statistics for ShareNet managers. The external promotion of ShareNet at conferences had positive influence on executives, too. Kuhn recognized a better sharing and feedback culture within Siemens ICN. The KMS had significant impact on work, skills, communication, and influence at all levels: it allowed for virtual global collaboration (especially for local companies), retained knowledge when people left, helped to avoid error repetitions and superfluous activities, contributed to employees' education and satisfaction, and fostered CoPs with a focus on ployees' education and satisfaction, and fostered CoPs with a focus on business problems. Due to the nature of local markets, countries that were net consumers of reusable knowledge needed no further motivation. Net contributors, e.g. countries with innovative and competitive markets, were more difficult to motivate. "What's in it for me?" was a frequently asked question especially in U.S. and U.K.

The managerial systems' main objective was to create a mindset of proactively seeking and offering knowledge and a knowledge-intensive culture. Kuhn felt that bottom-up culture change was completed; for further progress an integration with business processes, e.g. employee target agreements, and other knowledge sources and systems, e.g. Siemens Corporate Directory (SCD) and OpenText Livelink, was needed. During ShareNet's implementation, behavior change occurred simultaneously with culture change: first experiences made many users believers in the KMS and knowledge exchange, which in turn reinforced the new behavior. Any change first needed technical systems and later an appropriate psychological landscape.

Before the KM initiative was started, Siemens ICN had no strong culture that rewarded the contribution and reuse of knowledge. According to Kuhn, it was contradictory in some regards: even though decision making was centralized, some departments and local companies were little autonomous fiefdoms. Information was only shared on the same hierarchical layer. Even though Siemens ICN was quite innovative, many innovations were not brought to market due to slow and risk adverse decision making. There were old boys' networks and a lack of customer orientation at headquarters. Since motivators were needed for additional employee efforts, an incentive and reward system was developed as an add-on to basic salaries. The share system with extrinsic, but knowledge-related rewards was monitored constantly. A rapidly increasing number of users and general awareness for the KM initiative forced the ShareNet operating team to decrease the number of shares awarded. A discontinuation of extrinsic incentives and rewards would only lead to minor drops in usage since contributors/users valued ShareNet. Even though it was better to continue with the quality assurance and reward system, the difficult economic environment might force abandonment.

Generally, creating a pull-effect for knowledge was better than to assert pressure on employees. During ShareNet's development and implementation, no resisters/deviants were laid off but it was tried to influence the nomination of ShareNet managers. The ShareNet project team felt that the resistance would have been too strong; incentives for desired behaviors set a more positive tune. There was ShareNet "socialization" for new team members since the ShareNet core team decided not to continue with "old Siemens ICN resources". No more than a handful of contributors/users behaving inappropriately were banned from the ICN/ICM community.

Interview with Andreas Manuth

Company: Siemens AG
Position: ShareNet Manager ICN GS CKM
Location: Hofmannstr. 51, 81359 Munich
Date: July 31, 2002 (in person)
Number: 07

Manuth described ShareNet's development and implementation along five stages: "definition and prototyping", "setup and piloting", "global rollout", "operation, expansion and further development", and "shifting to a multi-community concept". In each implementation stage, both technical and people/cultural issues were explicitly taken into account. During the key evolution stage "operation, expansion, and further development" (in June 2000) Manuth became first a ShareNet consultant, later the ShareNet manager (head of virtual ShareNet team) and consequently a member of the ShareNet operating team. With the start of this stage, development and implementation were formally finished; BTP/BTC handed over the responsibilities to the new ShareNet operating team.

During the stages "setup and piloting" and "global rollout" Manuth considered the external consultancy Change Factory a key success factor. The firm helped with the development of local company workshop briefcases, ShareNet joggers (user guides), boot camps, New York user conference, and ShareNet manager conferences. Another external consultancy - Woodmark Technologies - supported the central function IT with project management, requirements definition, and systems debugging during the "global rollout" stage. Koch and Döring provided plenty of top management support. There was no codified/formal change management strategy; rather an informal approach based on early user involvement and personal networks. It was gradually modified: the top-down approach at the beginning, i.e. centrally-driven global rollout, slowly changed to a grassroots approach after the first implementation round. An increasing number of users proactively approached the ShareNet operating team and the ShareNet managers for registration and support.

Community-driven development changed over time: ShareNet managers became user representatives; the ShareNet operating team was responsible for conceptual work. On the one hand, the new team reacted directly to user requests; on the other hand, it implemented major changes (e.g. multi-community features) on its own behalf. Since most sales and marketing knowledge resided in local companies, they were the first to recognize and accept the changing international environment and the need for a KM initiative. ShareNet encountered higher resistance at headquarters: business units did not believe in the local companies' experience and creativity that were often incompatible with central strategies. In general, the more the local ICN heads were convinced of Share-Net's value, the smoother the implementation went. ShareNet consultants hardly provided users/contributors and ShareNet managers/multiplicators with explicit performance feedback. More often they provided hints for performance improvements. Feedback mechanisms for users ensured participative development with many suggestions for improvement.

The managerial system's main objective was to create a mindset of proactively seeking and offering knowledge and a knowledge-intensive culture. The share system with extrinsic, but knowledge-related rewards was monitored constantly. The top 50 contributors who had collected the most shares by the end of May 2000 and their partners were invited to a ShareNet user conference in New York in October 2000; 600 shares were deducted from their accounts. All shares collected before June 1, 2000 retained their value in the new, non-competitive cafeteria-style reward system. The "ShareNet Special Weeks" in connection with the quiz "Win a BMW (brand new mobile workstation)" aroused a lot of interest in July 2001. Even though many knowledge objects were posted and several new users registered for ShareNet, Manuth criticized special events: an artificial and expensive hype was created that rapidly ebbed off. A sustainable increase in the contributions' quality and quantity was not accomplished by such activities.

The start of the key evolution stage "operation, expansion, and further development" was a pivotal moment for ShareNet's evolution. Some 50% of the ShareNet operating team members were drawn from external companies; nobody had worked in the KM field before. Often, the leaving BTP/BTC members and their successors jointly visited the local companies for first contact and to build trust for the new team. Even though the transition went smoothly, the operating team's different focus made the change notable to outsiders: rather than investing an enormous amount of resources (working hours, travel, and local support) to ensure quick success, the focus switched to pragmatically sustaining a long-lasting effort. In December 2000, a ShareNet manager conference was held in Istanbul, Turkey. Based on a proposal from the ShareNet operating team, qualitative and quantitative target agreements (e.g. local company's number of shares) for ShareNet managers were formulated and implemented. Dependent on target achievement, some ShareNet managers received 50-120% of an additional fixed monthly salary as a bonus.

A general lack of resources and no consistently communicated KM strategy for Siemens ICN had negative impact on the service rollout that started in December 2000. The main challenge was to repeat the successful global rollout approach and to accommodate desired modifications. The ShareNet operating team realized that not many were needed: on the one hand, service processes closely resembled the Sales Value Creation Process; on the other hand, the service community desired no in-depth involvement. Only the name of the technical solution components object was changed to technical solutions and services. Among the service employees, WN users were the most active; AS and ON accounted for less traffic. EN service employees did not become ShareNet users since executives were reluctant to embrace the KM initiative and were busy with restructuring. The situation improved only gradually. Generally, ShareNet's extension satisfied all demands satisfied but was no shining success.

The beginning of the key evolution stage "shifting to a multi-community concept" was in December 2001 and delayed for several months. Even though IT had sufficient resources, organizational restructurings and a difficult coordination of Red Hat led to quickly changing project plans with a delay of several months and had negative impact on software quality. The working prototype for user involvement and feedback from the ICN/ICM community encountered only minor traffic and aroused little interest. Even ShareNet consultants hardly cooperated during the development since they were distracted by an organizational restructuring and considered it a pure programming task. When the new technical platform went live, some contributors/users complained about the new layout (adapted to Siemens' corporate identity guidelines), many bugs, and weak performance. The majority of bugs were resolved quickly while performance tuning required more time.

Due to unclear specifications, the ShareNet operating team felt that the wheel was reinvented several times: former functionality was missing in Siemens ShareNet V1.x. Community support, i.e. ShareNet consultants and the global editor, were badly prepared and encountered many obstacles over the first weeks. High user demand could not be met with a shortage of resources: the central function IT needed additional human resources for timely development, implementation, and documentation; ShareNet consultants lacked money to travel and spread ShareNet's idea globally. Management provided less leadership and support due to other pending problems, i.e. Siemens ICN's PACT program. Goals were to cut costs, to streamline processes, and to significantly reduce the global workforce. The new technical platform's implementation collided with those concerns.

Some employees (5-20%) internalized new habits and ways of thinking which had even become norms and routines of some groups. While those employees considered the share system an add-on, attracting other employees was still dependent on incentives. For extrinsically motivated users, Manuth considered some degree of mistrust helpful. Sometimes they engaged in illegal behavior (e.g. constantly giving reuse feedback to a small number of others) to gain more shares. Such behavior was disfavored. The global editors had to prosecute it on behalf of the community to strengthen trust. A discontinuation of extrinsic incentives and rewards would lead to significant drops in usage. Only highly motivated employees would continue with knowledge exchange and ShareNet contributions would stabilize at a lower level (downward spiral vs. deadlock). For those users, ShareNet already had major impact on communication, knowledge exchange, and skills, i.e. virtual collaboration across hierarchies. When more knowledge was shared, knowledge hoarding became less beneficial.

During ShareNet's implementation, behavior change occurred simultaneously with culture change: first experiences made many users believers in the KMS and in a knowledge-intensive culture which in turn reinforced the new behavior. Whether the new users became strong advocates or opponents depended on their first impression of ShareNet. Workshop participants were often asked to post some pressing problems as urgent requests at the beginning. Many problems were usually resolved prior to the workshops' end. Before the KM initiative was started, Siemens ICN had lots of hierarchies, old boys' networks, and risk adverse decision making. Since there was a strong engineering culture, it was difficult to get accustomed to new rules of competition. Innovations no longer originated in centralized R&D; rather they were derived from customers' needs. The ShareNet operating team recognized that people were slow to make adjustments; whereas first results from culture change showed after a few years, the processes needed a decade to become self-sustaining. So far, there had been no change in management culture.

Generally, creating a pull-effect for knowledge was better than to assert pressure on employees. During ShareNet's development and implementation, only one ShareNet manager was replaced. Working only on technical systems he neglected change management aspects. The operating team members felt that incentives for desired behaviors set a more positive tune. There was no ShareNet "socialization" for new Siemens ICN staff but ShareNet's positive image attracted employees to join.

Interview with Rolf Meinert

Company: Siemens AG
Position: Vice President Change Management ICN GS
Location: Hofmannstr. 51, 81359 Munich
Date: July 22, 2002 (in person)
Number: 08

Meinert described ShareNet's development and implementation along five stages: "definition and prototyping", "setup and piloting", "global rollout", "operation, expansion, and further development", and "shifting to a multi-community concept". In each implementation stage, both technical and people/cultural issues were explicitly taken into account; a codified/formal change management strategy, however, did not exist. Until the end of the "global rollout" stage, Meinert was part of BTP/BTC and consequently a member of the ShareNet project team.

Before the KM initiative officially started, the central function CC was created as part of Siemens' continuous improvement process (top). As a response to several Siemens ICN problems, the objective was to develop new values and visions. Naturally, those had to be adapted to business units' and local companies' needs. The central function CC conducted a series of workshops (Team-Shops) to provide whole sales teams with a better customer focus. Similar to ShareNet, TeamShops were organized around the solutions-selling process. The facilitators gained insights into the knowledge that sales people required and ought to share globally. The discoveries became influences for the later Share-Net concept.

The first key project stage, "definition and prototyping", lasted from July 1998 to the end of March 1999. Objectives were to establish the ShareNet project team, to create conceptual definitions and refinements, to start the prototyping of the technical platform, and to ensure early executive and user buy-in. Koch succeeded Pribilla as Siemens ICN group president and the central function CC was renamed to BTP/BTC, headed by Döring. Meinert remarked that Pribilla had a stronger culture focus than his successor who placed more importance on technical/business issues. BTP/BTC realized early that the KMS' development should be no isolated effort (ivory tower), later parachuted into the local companies. Consequently, the ShareNet project team comprised six employees from BTP/BTC, four external consultants from BCG, and some 40 sales representatives from headquarters and 15 local companies. Team members were selected because they were personally known to the BTP/BTC team, thought positively about the planned KMS, and were representatives for markets in all stages (deployment, extension, upgrade, and customization) and all regions (Europe, Latin and North America, Asia and Australia).

The group president, the head of BTP/BTC, and high ranking sales managers formed the steering committee responsible for project supervision and top management support. A first kick-off workshop was held at Frankfurt airport, Germany. BTP/BTC and BCG presented the KMS' vision, basic concept, and GUI mock-ups for prototyping. The sales people were asked whether the solutions-selling process and the critical questions for the capturing wizard were understood correctly and whether the system provided any value-add for their daily work. After a great need for the IS was established, the core team went ahead with conceptual refinements. To maintain user involvement, i.e. to make sales and marketing people aware that they had a vested interest in the KMS' development, two more German workshops were planned (December 1998 in Garmisch, February 1999 in Munich). During the workshops, the sales people were asked to identify regional solutions which could be leveraged globally (early-win showcases). At the end of the workshops, BCG's task was completed and the consultants withdrew from the project.

The sales peoples' early involvement and quick modifications of the working prototype - based on feedback - ensured sufficient support from later contributors/users. A highly motivated core team without regard for hierarchies and structures was another critical success factor. It had impact both on winning the APQC award for the best global knowledge network and on becoming a Siemens-wide KMS best practice. There was no codified/formal change management strategy; rather early user involvement and personal networks ensured executive and contributor/user buy-in. This approach was never modified.

There was a smooth hand-over to the ShareNet operating team at the Sun City, South Africa ShareNet manager conference (in February 2000). Meinert mentioned that culture change was dependent on business models, leadership, and resources. A first important step was to recognize that most sales and marketing knowledge originated from local companies, not from headquarters. Nevertheless, the KMS encountered higher resistance at headquarters: business units were afraid of sharing previously centralized knowledge, a source of influence and power. According to Meinert, more than half of the local companies' employees supported the KMS and some 20% resisted its implementation; numbers at headquarters were roughly vice versa. In general, the more local ICN heads were convinced of ShareNet's value, the smoother the implementation went. ShareNet consultants provided users/contributors and ShareNet managers/multiplicators with feedback on their performance.

Technical systems accounted for only 25% of total project costs; the majority was spent on the selection and training of prospective ShareNet managers, communication campaigns, and training material. The core team abstained from monetary rewards since they were perceived ambiguously in some national cultures. The share system with extrinsic, but knowledge-related rewards, encountered less ambiguity. There were three types of users: the first group with a global mindset exchanged knowledge on the basis of personal experiences and dependency on international cooperation; the second group favored expert recognition from peers; the third group depended on extrinsic motivators, especially in developing countries. The rewards were often the only chance to travel abroad or to acquire new telecommunication devices. A discontinuation of extrinsic incentives and rewards would lead to significant drops in usage. According to Meinert, ShareNet's reward system communicated trust of employees: "The intention was to keep an open eye to misuse but to avoid extensive regulation". Illegal behavior could not be avoided even with extensive policies and rules; it was better to display trust in contributors/users first.

"Every good idea dies without sufficient support". Even though some employees had internalized new habits and ways of thinking, culture change was a continuous process. It had to be constantly improved; credible communication, incentives and rewards, and socialization of new employees were still required to maintain culture's momentum. ShareNet could significantly shorten the time formerly required for the socialization of new employees. Especially the difficult business situation and outlook made a focus on customer-relevant knowledge mandatory. KM was more dependent on culture than on formal structures and metrics. During ShareNet's implementation, behavior change preceded culture change: first experiences made many users believers in the KMS and in a knowledge-intensive culture. This process was successfully driven by the ShareNet consultants. Before the KM initiative was started, Siemens ICN had no strong culture that rewarded the contribution and reuse of knowledge. Nevertheless, there were many subcultures, mostly driven by popular department heads.

Generally, creating a pull-effect for knowledge was better than to assert pressure on employees. During ShareNet's development and implementation, no resisters/deviants were laid off. The core team members felt that the resistance would have been too strong; incentives for desired behaviors set a more positive tune. Only illegal behavior should have been punished more consequently. For Meinert, change management was a mixture of vision, credible communication, incentives, connection with business processes, and involvement of key players. People did not change quickly but first benefits were realized, e.g. in fiscal 2000 €145.9 million in additional revenues through knowledge exchange.

The second key project stage, "setup and piloting", lasted from April to the end of July 1999. Objectives were to test and improve the technical platform, to ensure local company buy-in and preparation, and to develop a phased implementation approach including training material. The technical systems were tested for database functionality, GUI and usability, response times, and reliability. Due to performance problems that arose even before the "setup and piloting" stage had started, several changes were made to the programming language, database, and GUI. The ShareNet project team switched from Microsoft Access to an Oracle database and from Bitlab to ArsDigita, a leading U.S. web publishing company later acquired by Red Hat. Integration with other knowledge sources and systems was intended, but never realized due to a short timeframe. The ShareNet project team favored speed of implementation over lengthy coordination with other IS owners.

Interview with Dr. Johannes Müller

Company: Siemens AG
Position: ShareNet Global Editor ICN GS CKM
Location: Hofmannstr. 51, 81359 Munich
Date: July 30, 2002 (in person)
Number: 09

Müller described ShareNet's development and implementation along five stages: "definition and prototyping", "setup and piloting", "global rollout", "operation, expansion, and further development", and "shifting to a multi-community concept". In each implementation stage, both technical and people/cultural issues were explicitly taken into account. During the key evolution stage "operation, expansion, and further development" (in June 2000) Müller became a global editor and consequently a member of the ShareNet operating team. With the start of this stage, development and implementation were formally finished; BTP/BTC handed over the responsibilities to the new ShareNet operating team.

The beginning of the key evolution stage "shifting to a multi-community concept" was in December 2001 and delayed for several months. Even though IT had sufficient resources, organizational restructurings and a difficult coordination of Red Hat led to quickly changing project plans with a delay of several months and had negative impact on software quality. A working prototype for user involvement and feedback from the ICN/ICM community encountered only minor traffic and aroused little interest. Even ShareNet consultants hardly cooperated during the development since they were distracted by an organizational restructuring and considered it a pure programming task. When the new technical platform went live, some contributors/users complained about the new layout (adapted to Siemens' corporate identity guidelines), many bugs, and weak performance. The majority of bugs were resolved while performance tuning took more time. Due to unclear specifications, the ShareNet operating team felt that the wheel was reinvented several times: former functionality was missing in Siemens ShareNet V1.x. Community support, i.e. ShareNet consultants and the global editor, was badly prepared and encountered many obstacles over the first weeks.

High user demand could not be met with a shortage of resources: the central function IT needed additional human resources for timely development, implementation, and documentation; ShareNet consultants lacked money to travel and spread ShareNet's idea globally. Müller thought that the start of the "shifting to a multi-community concept" stage would have been a good time to refresh awareness in local companies, to provide some additional training/workshops, and to make knowledge exchange a goal in the employee target agreements. Management provided less leadership and support due to other pending problems, i.e. Siemens ICN's PACT transformation process. Goals were to cut costs, to streamline processes, and to significantly reduce the global workforce. The new technical platform's implementation collided with those concerns. Through attrition the ShareNet operating team shrinked from 18 to eleven people. This change forced concentration on fewer topics. Participation in ShareNet was voluntary since linkage with business processes, i.e. employee target agreements and after action reviews, had not yet been established. Earlier than June 2000, Müller did encounter no other Siemens ICN change initiatives.

Since most sales and marketing knowledge resided in local companies, they were the first to recognize the need for a KM initiative; their input was taken up by BTP/BTC. The ShareNet operating team still considered itself an advocate of the local companies' needs. ShareNet encountered higher resistance at headquarters: business units were afraid to lose sales opportunities for internal services that were now posted for free on ShareNet. The ShareNet project team decided to continue the implementation with central funding and a focus on key impact areas, i.e. the local companies. Many problems arose: lack of time, deficit of top management support and feedback, no inclusion in target agreements, fear of additional work, and language barriers. There was no active resistance but sometimes a lack of commitment. Generally, the more local ICN heads were convinced of ShareNet's value, the smoother the implementation went. ShareNet consultants provided users/contributors and ShareNet managers/multiplicators with performance feedback. User feedback mechanisms ensured community-driven development with many suggestions for improvement.

A central boot camp for ShareNet managers was held at the beginning of the "global rollout" stage. The ShareNet project team intended to build-up high value social networks, first among ShareNet managers, later among members of the sales and marketing community. Proactively searching and offering knowledge became part of their self-concept, identity, and ongoing relationships. However, it was difficult to achieve some identification with a virtual community. For that reason, Müller considered a yearly ShareNet manager conference helpful. Additionally, a positive vision toward change, formal trainings, working prototypes, coaches, and incentives (bonus-on-top) were provided for the broad international rollout. Sometimes even small measures, e.g. happy holiday emails, triggered favorable feedback. So far, ShareNet had established itself as a search engine for Siemens-relevant knowledge. If the desired knowledge was not included in the system, at least an experienced contact could be located quickly (yellow pages). Success stories had huge impact on work and communication at all levels: first, they justified ShareNet's existence; second, they were an important promotion tool for the KMS; third, both knowledge givers and takers gained visibility within the ICN/ICM community; fourth and last, reference projects were communicated openly.

The managerial system's main objective was to create a mindset of proactively seeking and offering knowledge and a knowledge-intensive culture. The share system with extrinsic, but knowledge-related rewards was monitored constantly. The ShareNet operating team made the decision to adapt the incentive system only twice a year; the contributors/users' "income" should not be tangled with arbitrarily. The top 50 contributors who had collected the most shares by the end of May 2000 and their partners were invited to a ShareNet user conference in New York in October 2000; 600 shares were deducted from their accounts. All shares collected before June 1, 2000 retained their value in the new, non-competitive cafeteria-style reward system. The "ShareNet Special Weeks" - in connection with the quiz "Win a BMW (brand new mobile workstation)" - aroused a lot of interest in July 2001. Many knowledge objects were posted and several new users registered.

External communications described the incentive and reward system as an add-on to the employees' intrinsic motivation. Still, the majority of contributors/users were dependent on incentives. Only a minority exchanged knowledge on the basis of own experiences and dependency on international cooperation; they had usually accumulated a significant number of shares without claiming the rewards. A discontinuation of extrinsic incentives and rewards would lead to significant drops in usage. Even though some employees had internalized new habits and ways of thinking, change management could not stop. Credible communication, incentives, and socialization of new employees were still required to maintain culture's momentum. Some local companies still ran their own incentive programs with local resources, but other local company executives forbade the employees to use the KMS. They were to spend their valuable working hours on more important matters.

During ShareNet's implementation, behavior change preceded culture change: first experiences made many users believers in the KMS and in a knowledge-intensive culture. Interest and curiosity usually drove the registration. Whether the new users became strong advocates or opponents depended on their first impression of ShareNet's content and categories: "A ShareNet advocate brings us four new users, an opponent takes 30 away." Before the KM initiative was started, Siemens ICN had no strong culture that rewarded the contribution and reuse of knowledge. Only in the last years did Siemens begin to recognize employees as its greatest asset. Success, after all, was accomplished, e.g. ShareNet became a Siemens-wide KMS best practice. Community feeling (i.e. "networking people") was stronger in the small pioneer community at the beginning and the difficult business situation and outlook was an important detriment to culture change.

Generally, creating a pull-effect for knowledge was better than to assert pressure on employees. During ShareNet's development and implementation, no resisters/deviants were laid off. The project team members felt that the resistance would have been too strong; incentives for desired behaviors set a more positive tune. There was no ShareNet "socialization" for new employees at Siemens ICM and ICN but a linkage with personnel processes was considered for the future.

Interview with Barbara Stahl

Company: Siemens AG
Position: ShareNet Change Management, Consultant ICN GS CKM
Location: Hofmannstr. 51, 81359 Munich
Date: August 26, 2002 (in person)
Number: 10

Stahl described ShareNet's development and implementation along five stages: "definition and prototyping", "setup and piloting", "global rollout", "operation, expansion, and further development", and "shifting to a multi-community concept". In each implementation stage, both technical and people/cultural issues were explicitly taken into account. Since the beginning of the "operation, expansion, and further development" stage Stahl was a ShareNet consultant and consequently a member of the ShareNet operating team. Her responsibilities were managerial systems, including the quality assurance and reward system, and the support of ShareNet managers in local companies. With the start of this stage, development and implementation were formally finished. BTP/BTC handed over the responsibilities to the new ShareNet operating team at the ShareNet manager implementation review conference in Sun City, South Africa.

During the key project stages "setup and piloting" and "global rollout" Stahl saw the external consultancy Change Factory and the localized, phased implementation approach as critical success factors. The start of the key evolution stage "shifting to a multi-community concept" was a pivotal moment for ShareNet's evolution. First, Siemens ICN's business situation and outlook, as well as huge lay-offs, led to less top management support and consequently to a diminished budget for change management. Second, through attrition the ShareNet operating team shrinked from 18 to eleven people. This change forced concentration on fewer topics. Third and last, with all the leaving experts, Siemens ICN needed knowledge exchange more than ever but employees where less inclined to contribute personal knowledge. In result, the KMS became more reliant on ShareNet managers.

Stahl considered the KM initiative's resources sufficient. Up to PACT's start, there was ample budget for incentives (e.g. "ShareNet Special Weeks"), travel, and workshops. From that point on, management provided less leadership and support due to other pending problems; the implementation of the multi-community platform collided with the new concerns. Even though lively discussions evolved around ShareNet's integration into the employees' daily work, i.e.

after action reviews, employee target agreements, job profiles, and SLF, decisions were neither taken nor implemented. The central function HR favored only an inclusion into local ICN head target agreements, comparable to bonus-on-top. Moreover, difficult communication and reporting lines were major hindrances. Siemens' decentralized matrix structure required direct reports from regional sales organizations to Siemens' managing board, not to Siemens ICN's group executive management.

There was no codified/formal change management strategy; rather an informal approach based on early user involvement and personal networks. It was never adopted to accommodate different national cultures and mindsets. Up to that point, culture change had been somewhat neglected and lagged behind the KM initiative. There were only isolated and insufficiently supported culture change efforts. Siemens ICN's group executive management was late to realize the cultural implications of knowledge exchange and open and transparent communication. The increasing focus on financial indicators made it more and more difficult to get commitment from local company key executives.

Since most sales and marketing knowledge resided in local companies, they were the first to recognize and accept the changing international environment and the need for a KM initiative; their input was taken up by BTP/BTC. Generally, the more local ICN heads were convinced of ShareNet's value, the smoother the implementation went. A positive vision (present state vs. desired future state), formal trainings, working prototypes, coaches, and incentives (bonus-on-top) were employed for the international rollout. ShareNet consultants provided users/contributors and ShareNet managers/multiplicators with performance feedback. User feedback mechanisms ensured community-driven development with many suggestions for improvement. The KMS encountered higher resistance at headquarters: business units had already established proprietary tools, dreaded language barriers, and/or were afraid of sharing previously centralized knowledge, a source of influence and power. ShareNet had first impact on work, skills, and communication: there was higher readiness for international cooperation and requests for help; employees recognized that both knowledge givers and takers benefited.

The managerial system's main objective was to create a mindset of proactively seeking and offering knowledge and a knowledge-intensive culture. The share system with extrinsic, but knowledge-related rewards was monitored constantly. The incentive catalog and the number of shares awarded were regularly adapted to maintain attractiveness. Stahl mentioned that the quality assurance and reward system was the only tool available to influence the number of contributions. Increasing intrinsic motivation, e.g. peer recognition according to the employees' national culture, would not yield similar results. ShareNet's quality assurance and reward system did not communicate mistrust of employees; extra efforts had to be supported since they were no integral part of job profiles. Nevertheless, incentives should not become normality. A discontinuation of extrinsic incentives and rewards would lead to significant drops in usage. Even though contributors/users would be disappointed they understood the response to the difficult business situation and outlook. If community support, i.e. ShareNet consultants and the global editor, was not further reduced by layoffs, the KMS was to stay alive.

Half of the contributors/users who used ShareNet for their daily work internalized new habits and ways of thinking. During ShareNet's implementation, behavior change preceded culture change: first experiences made many users believers in the KMS and in a knowledge-intensive culture, especially in local companies. Up to that point, no resister/deviants were laid off. Without formal knowledge exchange goals, evaluations for pending layoffs were not possible. It was difficult to control some 70 ShareNet managers who had volunteered for the assignment (in addition to their daily work). Many younger employees joined the company through continuous attrition. For those, knowledge exchange was more natural than for older employees (generation problem). Stahl believed that ShareNet was a self-explanatory tool with high usability. Adoptions to CoPs' underlying processes and languages - similar to the mapping of the Sales Value Creation Process - ensured executive and user buy-in. This process was driven by CoP initiators and supported by ShareNet consultants.

Before the KM initiative was started, Siemens ICN had no strong culture that rewarded the contribution and reuse of knowledge. According to Stahl, it was possible to achieve good business results with an even sparse exchange of information. Since Siemens ICN had a strong engineering culture, it was difficult to get accustomed to new rules of competition. Innovations no longer originated in centralized R&D; rather they were derived from customer needs. Traditionally, Siemens ICN passively waited for orders from monopolistic, government owned telephone companies instead of aggressively developing the market with active sales and marketing. There were many hierarchies and a lack of personal initiative: employees were expected to fill exactly defined jobs and decision-making was highly centralized.

Interview with Ursula Streit

Company: Siemens AG
Position: Director Knowledge Management ICN EN S SC4
Location: Rupert-Mayer-Str. 44, 81359 Munich
Date: August 23, 2002 (in person)
Number: 11

Streit was a member of the service community (technical product support, formerly customer care integration) and a ShareNet manager for two years. With

regard to ShareNet, she held three distinct roles: first, she was a regular con-
tributor/user posting and searching for contributions; second, she was a Share-
Net manager supporting end users in capturing project experiences and service
know-how; third and last, she was responsible for ShareNet's and Livelink's
positioning and joint development, e.g. strategies and interfaces. There was no
community-driven development; rather the ShareNet organization made centralized decisions and discussed them later with the ShareNet managers.

During the key evolution stage "operation, expansion, and further development" (in December 2000) the service rollout began. Streit used a simultaneous
top-down and bottom-up approach at headquarters. She designed intranet portals
combining ShareNet with other content to attract more users. Up to that point,
the KMS had been too complicated. Since the difficult business situation and
outlook distracted employees from knowledge exchange, EN did not adopt the
lengthy local company workshop briefcases. ShareNet's positive impact on
business processes was discussed regularly during team meetings. Experts were
often asked to answer urgent requests in order to provide positive first experiences for people with a concrete "felt need". Those intrinsically motivated employees automatically became multiplicators. A general lack of business understanding was a hindrance for many ShareNet managers. In local companies they
mainly served as technology facilitators. There had been no lack of resources
yet. Only Streit held a full-time KM position, supported part-time by a virtual
team.

Several line managers were nominated as prime points of contact but PACT
and the KM initiative's unclear pay-off forced concentration on more pressing
topics. EN's top executives still communicated the vision of a knowledge-based
company. The difficult environment had an ambiguous impact on the on-going
culture change; many achievements had already been erased. On the one hand,
the lack of top management support hindered change management efforts. Employees were less inclined to contribute knowledge while they were trying to
achieve business targets and were threatened by layoffs. On the other hand,
people felt survival anxiety and/or guilt and started to question isolated work
routines. Additionally, they were concerned about better organizational visibility. With all the leaving experts, Siemens ICN needed knowledge exchange
more than ever.

Since Siemens ICN employees did not fully appreciate CoPs, a multi-
community version provided little value-add. When the new technical platform
went live, users complained about a changing focus (business processes vs.
technology), many bugs, and weak performance. ShareNet still missed a tight
integration with OpenText Livelink including role-based access. Streit felt that
the wheel was reinvented several times when the central function IT tried to
develop ShareNet functionality already offered by the corporate document man-

agement system. Developing a Livelink-based ShareNet version plus urgent request feature was more beneficial.

There was no codified/formal change management strategy; rather early user involvement and a well-conducted phased implementation approach ensured executive and contributor/user buy-in. The external consultancy Change Factory was a critical success factor during the key development stages "setup and piloting" and "global rollout". The ShareNet operating team's general lack of communication made people unsure about the KM initiative's focus, further direction, and responsibilities. ShareNet manager conferences were discontinued, too. Nevertheless, in the long-term the ShareNet Community should drive ShareNet's evolution through its input and formulation of requirements.

ShareNet had some impact on work, skills, communication, and influence at all levels: urgent requests could be sent to a larger pool of help, employees were more inclined to offer support, and Siemens ICN gained external recognition. Since local companies often lacked solutions expertise and cross-country knowledge exchange, they were the first to recognize and accept the changing international environment. The KMS was regarded and used as a valuable tool after positive first experiences were made. ShareNet encountered higher resistance at headquarters: business units did not believe in the local companies' experience and creativity that were often incompatible with central strategies, and lacked the front-line's customer understanding.

Streit considered the share system an unnecessary add-on to the employees' basic salary. It was implemented to quickly reach a critical mass of content and reuse and to succeed in the "battle" for capturing time against other important daily issues. In contrast to management consultancies, Siemens ICN was not entirely driven by information and knowledge and consequently put a lower importance on knowledge exchange. Adaptations in the number of shares awarded were recognized but not considered important. The five-star rating scheme or balanced scorecards were better indicators to test the KMS' user acceptance. Streit considered some degree of mistrust helpful with regard to the quality assurance and reward system. Sometimes employees engaged in illegal behavior (e.g. constantly giving reuse feedback to a small number of others) to gain more shares. A discontinuation of extrinsic motivation would lead to significant drops in contributions and usage or even to a deadlock situation; ShareNet would probably continue to run for a year. Afterwards, a better linkage with business processes, i.e. inclusion into employee target agreements and after action reviews, was required. If the KM initiative folded entirely, BTP/BTC had not accomplished sustainable change.

The managerial system's main objective was to create a mindset of proactively seeking and offering knowledge and a knowledge-intensive culture. For Streit, change management was a mixture of vision, mission, creating a win-win feeling for employees, and connection with business processes. Among other measures, ShareNet had some impact on culture change. Even though a few employees internalized new habits and ways of thinking and became big Share-Net advocates, Siemens ICN's lack of top management support delayed the change process. During ShareNet's implementation, behavior change occurred simultaneously with culture change: first experiences made many users believers in the KMS and in a knowledge-intensive culture which in turn reinforced the new behavior. "If organizational cultures remain unchanged, behavior changes could lead to frustration." Many younger employees joined the company through continuous attrition. For them, knowledge exchange came more natural than for older Siemens employees (generation problem). The latter's resistance was the result of long-term socialization and a static team environment.

Interview with Donald Tsusaki

Company: Siemens AG
Position: Vice President Knowledge Management Platforms ICN IT KM
Location: Hofmannstr. 51, 81359 Munich
Date: August 20, 2002 (in person)
Number: 12

Tsusaki described ShareNet's development and implementation along five stages: "definition and prototyping", "setup and piloting", "global rollout", "operation, expansion, and further development", and "shifting to a multi-community concept". In each implementation stage, both technical and people/cultural issues were explicitly taken into account; a codified/formal change management strategy, however, did not exist. In October 1999, Tsusaki volunteered as ShareNet manager for the U.S. Eight months later, he took over responsibilities for eknowledge management within the global ebusiness initiative eICN. When a new organizational structure went into effect in March 2001, Tsusaki became vice president for KM platforms.

Up to that point, only the U.S. turned out to be a difficult environment for ShareNet's implementation. Early on, a qualified IT task force was assembled from communication, education, and marketing specialists, headed by Tsusaki. Top executives were reluctant to embrace a KM initiative with an unclear payoff. Since U.S. employees were too widespread to use the standard local company workshop briefcases, Kuhn and Tsusaki initiated web-based trainings and tried to convince key contributors/users to post best practices. Once Tsusaki left, the situation deteriorated: top executives began to question ShareNet's organizational integration and the missing link to business processes. There was no sufficient communication stressing the point that ShareNet was no replacement for existing IS, e.g. Siebel's CRM application, but rather a logical and necessary add-on. Even though some resistance vanished when contributors/users recognized the possibility to link and access Siebel objects from ShareNet, the U.S. Sales Value Creation Process better mapped to the CRM tool. Adding to the "not invented here" syndrome, the difficult business situation made knowledge sharing lower priority.

Siemens ShareNet V1.x marked the introduction of a company-wide, multi-community platform. The ShareNet operating team had gathered many requests for CoPs focusing on specific topics of interest. Community homepages provided a personalized overview of community-specific content for each user, e.g. new threads since last login. The conceptual change necessitated a personal workspace with personal data, email alerts, bookmarks, and links to all CoPs for which contributors/users had registered. Designated functional modules could be flexibly adapted to CoP's differing underlying businesses processes which ensured executive and user buy-in. The modules contained tacit and explicit knowledge, i.e. knowledge libraries, discussion forums, chats, and news.

A joint development consortium designed the interface/bridge license and user management to ensure information exchangeability between ShareNet and Livelink Communities. Former islands of information, each ShareNet Community used instances of the same site-wide context (e.g. personal workspace, user and group administration, incentive systems), while each Livelink Community employed a separate site-wide context with complicated permission rights and user and group administration. The interface/bridge made it possible to link and access Livelink objects from ShareNet. The former ShareNet became one CoP amongst others in the multi-community system. All content, the quality assurance and reward system, and previously earned shares were migrated. Users still dreaded the separate environments: there was a different look and feel, search and retrieval, and user administration. A seamless IS integration with role-based access (single sign-on, common structure for the storing of data, information and knowledge) was needed; portals were only a stopgap solution. "Don't focus on systems stuff; rather take a close look at the work done in business processes." Here, ShareNet's local company focus became a detriment.

Tsusaki considered the phased implementation approach a key make-or-break factor. The KM initiative went hand-in-hand with culture change, each depended on the other. This approach changed gradually when ShareNet consultants lacked financial resources to travel and spread ShareNet's idea globally. Siemens ICN's transformation became more reliant on the ShareNet managers. Since local companies often lacked solutions expertise and cross-country knowledge exchange, they were the first to recognize and accept the changing international environment and the need for a KM initiative. ShareNet encountered higher resistance at headquarters: the business units did not clearly understand value creation in local companies and were reluctant to provide the necessary budget. The ShareNet project team decided to continue the implementation with central funding and a focus on key impact areas, i.e. the local companies. In the long run, the business impact ought to win over resistance at headquarters and ensure buy-in. The corporate central function CIO was deliberately not involved since the core team dreaded lengthy coordination.

The key evolution stage "operation, expansion, and further development" encountered several pivotal moments. Since the ShareNet operating team members blended smoothly, much confusion was created by the split into a community support and a technical platform group. During the development of the multi-community version, personal interaction deteriorated even further. Even though the central function IT had sufficient resources, organizational restructurings and a difficult coordination of Red Hat led to a delay of several months and had negative impact on software quality.

The managerial system's main objective was to create a mindset of proactively seeking and offering knowledge and a knowledge-intensive culture. Especially ShareNet's world-class phased implementation approach had significant influence on culture change. The KMS showed a first positive impact on work, skills, communication, and influence of people who underwent training/transformation. During the last years, there was a positive trend towards open and transparent communication, evidenced by success stories, as well as by external enthusiasm and recognition. ShareNet provided less value-add to the service community. There were already proprietary quasi-KM tools and structures, fiercely guarded by their owners.

Tsusaki considered ShareNet Content's usefulness a stronger motivator than the share system. Extrinsic motivation had its highest impact at the time of the ShareNet manager implementation review conference (in February 2000). Even though the KMS was technically open, a common code of conduct evolved around the acceptance of contributions. Low quality postings were shunned quickly. A discontinuation of extrinsic motivation would lead to significant drops in contributions and usage, or even to a deadlock situation. Then, an intelligent communications campaign outlining the further development of the incentive and reward system was mandatory. Integration with business processes would easily compensate for lost monetary rewards, e.g. employee target agreements and after action reviews.

Interview with Gerhard Vogt

Company: Siemens AG
Position: Project Management ICN AS AN PM5
Location: Hofmannstr. 51, 81359 Munich
Date: August 7, 2002 (in person)
Number: 13

Vogt was a member of the sales and marketing community and a ShareNet user for 1.5 years. His responsibilities were customer project management, an interface function between the business unit and local companies (incl. the sales organization for Germany). With regard to ShareNet, he held three distinct roles: first, he was a regular contributor/user posting and searching for contributions; second, as a discussion forum maintainer he was responsible for the postings' quality and the forum's policy; third and last, he participated in the KMS' further development with change requests. The ShareNet operating team considered his feedback sufficiently and responded with technical modifications. Generally, feedback mechanisms ensured many suggestions for improvement and community-driven development.

During the "operation, expansion, and further development" and "shifting to a multi-community concept" stages Vogt encountered only minor changes. With the multi-community version, forum memberships were kept consistent; only saved search patterns were lost. Two reasons led to a decreasing number of discussion contributions (minus 33-50%): on the one hand, more postings were made urgent requests; on the other hand, Siemens ICN's business situation and outlook created a deadlock situation. Layoffs and a limited number of new projects led to fewer contributions which finally diminished user interest. Nevertheless, there were always new projects and topics warranting discussion. "Dumb" requests had negative impact on the forums' quality. Since the department project management was involved during early project stages, mainly ShareNet discussion forums and urgent requests were used. Usually, new project debates were found first in ShareNet's people-to-people section. The knowledge library was of lower relevance since local companies posted project objects later. Vogt considered ShareNet, OpenText Livelink, and SCD key IS for Siemens ICN.

Since local companies often lacked solutions expertise and cross-country knowledge exchange, they were the first to recognize and accept the changing international environment and the need for a KM initiative. ShareNet encountered some resistance at headquarters: there was no strong top management support; executives feared that the KMS distracted employees from concentrating on business targets; business units were afraid of sharing previously centralized knowledge, a source of influence and power. This fear was irrational since personal contact was still needed for project support. From the business units,

WN users were the most active due to long product histories and large-sized projects. ON accounted for less traffic since its technology was relatively basic. The amount of resistance decreased over time: employees recognized that Share-Net was a valuable tool that would render no jobs obsolete.

Up to that point, Vogt had encountered no formal ShareNet change management strategy. Rather a link on Siemens ICN's intranet home page, peer recommendations, and features in the corporate newspapers Siemens World and IC-Netline attracted new users. Generally, there were high awareness for ShareNet at headquarters and in local companies and responsive ShareNet managers. Vogt assumed that the group executive management saw ShareNet as a tool to enable sales. Headquarters experienced no true "felt need" or some threatening facts which could foster ShareNet's adoption. Most business units had already adopted a service focus and solutions approach, "box selling" was mainly restricted to original equipment manufacturer (OEM) products. AS mainly used ShareNet to broadcast information to local companies and to search for information about implemented solutions. ShareNet had no impact on work, skills, communication, and influence at all levels; it was rather an additional communication channel.

Vogt considered the share system an add-on to the employees' basic salary. Adaptations in the number of shares awarded were recognized but not considered important. ShareNet's quality assurance and reward system communicated no mistrust of employees: the majority of users/contributors concentrated on posting and answering requests that were relevant for daily work. Only few employees tried to collect as many shares as possible and posted the same contributions several times. A discontinuation of extrinsic incentives and rewards would only lead to minor drops in usage since contributors/users valued ShareNet. Nevertheless, spending the whole day on ShareNet was counterproductive and other work remained unfinished.

The managerial system's main objective was to create a mindset of proactively seeking and offering knowledge and a knowledge-intensive culture. Among other measures, ShareNet had significant impact on culture change. During the last years, there was a positive trend towards open and transparent communication. Before the KM initiative was started, Siemens ICN had no strong culture that rewarded the contribution and reuse of knowledge. According to Vogt, information was only shared at the same hierarchical layer, especially in business units with a long history and traditional structures. As a global player, the company was very customer-oriented. Being a conglomerate was a distinct advantage. Even though Siemens ICN was often not the first to market, the quality offered was usually very high. Many younger employees joined the company through continuous attrition. For those, knowledge exchange was more natural than for older Siemens employees (generation problem). During ShareNet's implementation, behavior change occurred simultaneously with culture change: first experiences made many users believers in the KMS and in a knowledge-intensive culture which in turn reinforced the new behavior.

Interview with Marc Widuch

Company: Siemens AG
Position: Vice President Competence and Knowledge Management ICN GS CKM
Location: Hofmannstr. 51, 81359 Munich
Date: August 5, 2002 (in Person)
Number: 14

Widuch described ShareNet's development and implementation along five stages: "definition and prototyping", "setup and piloting", "global rollout", "operation, expansion, and further development", and "shifting to a multi-community concept". In each implementation stage, both technical and people/cultural issues were explicitly taken into account. During the key project stage "operation, expansion, and further development" (in October 2001) Widuch became vice president competence and knowledge management and consequently a member of the ShareNet operating team. His responsibilities were KM, including ShareNet, and competence management. With the start of this stage, development and implementation were formally finished; BTP/BTC handed over the responsibilities to the new ShareNet operating team.

During the "global rollout" stage, the change management approach put emphasis on people/culture. The group executive management's support and a vast amount of financial resources ensured quick contributor/user buy-in but also had some negative effects. Many employees changed their behavior opportunistically, however, adhered to the same justifications of behavior as before. Headquarters and local companies' were upset that some of their projects were neglected while so much money was spent on the KM initiative. With decreasing sales and negative earnings, business units stressed the point again. Moreover, the change management approach targeted mainly front-line employees without control of key resources while top management support was more important during a difficult business situation.

Since most sales and marketing knowledge resided in local companies, they were the first to recognize and accept the changing international environment and the need for a KM initiative. Smaller local companies expected from Share-Net additional resources and more visibility at headquarters. Siemens ICN communicated the shift from "box selling" to a service focus and a pragmatic solutions approach: "Starting from a strong position, we have to change proactively in anticipation of different rules of competition." Headquarters showed higher implementation resistance than local companies: business units were afraid of sharing previously centralized knowledge, a source of influence and power. This fear was irrational since headquarters were still needed for global product management and almost no contributors/users employed ShareNet to join forces against headquarters.

During the "operation, expansion, and further development" stage, Widuch considered Siemens ICN's difficult business situation and outlook as a pivotal moment. For the first time, ShareNet's implementation - focused on local companies - became a detriment: both the ShareNet project team and the ShareNet operating team had problems to understand business processes/economic realities and to adapt the KMS accordingly. A further drawback was the leaving of Dr. Michael Wagner who switched positions to Siemens Medical. Even though, Döring and Widuch provided sufficient top management support in order to ensure ShareNet's continuation. Siemens ICN's group executive management promoted ShareNet accordingly even under difficult circumstances. There was no general lack of resources, rather a lack of focus. Up to that point, no member of the ShareNet operating team had asked for additional investments and he did not decline any.

Widuch considered the share system an add-on to the employees' basic salary. Several changes were intended as a response to the difficult business situation and the need to integrate knowledge sharing into the employees' daily work. On the one hand, monetary incentives should be decreased or even shut-down in the future. On the other hand, rewards ought to be increased, e.g. peer recognition according to the employees' national culture. Better linkage with personnel processes was planned, i.e. inclusion into employee target agreements and executives' SLF. ShareNet's quality assurance and reward system communicated trust of employees. Humans needed incentives for additional effort. A discontinuation of extrinsic incentives and rewards would lead to a 10% drop in usage. If the KM initiative folded entirely, the ShareNet project team and the ShareNet operating team had not accomplished sustainable change. For the first time, culture change's status would become transparent. The budget for incentives and rewards should rather be invested into high potentials and other change management measures.

The managerial system's main objective was to create a mindset of proactively seeking and offering knowledge and a knowledge-intensive culture. Many employees internalized new habits and ways of thinking and became big ShareNet advocates. Whereas the need for local knowledge exchange had been recognized earlier, ShareNet brought a broader global focus. Up to that point, the KMS did not accomplish to take over/supplant local KM initiatives. There was no change in management culture: executive support for the KMS during economic downturns and better organizational integration were still missing. According to Widuch, quality guidelines should be open for other languages besides English. German and English were sufficient for more than 80% of the contributor/user population but a translation tool was even better. Among the business units, Siemens ICM N, EN and WN users were the most active; AS and ON accounted for less traffic.

It was difficult to say whether behavior change preceded culture change or vice versa. The dynamics depended on the different types of employees: first, some employees embraced everything new and became early adopters; second, some employees were somewhat critical but became either advocates or opponents, depending on their first impressions; third and last, some people rejected all changes. Nevertheless, it was the mix of contributors/users that made Share-Net's rollout successful. Before the KMS was implemented, Siemens ICN had no strong culture that rewarded the open and transparent communication of solutions know-how. According to Widuch, information was only shared at the same hierarchical layer, especially financials and information about the actual business situation. There was danger that the employees interpreted rumors differently, contrary to the original intention. Once decisions were made, the firm had high persistence in following through. Results were lacks of flexibility and mobility. Even though there were visions, strategies, and policies, not all decisions were implemented since too much attention was spent on details. Ganswindt challenged risk adverse decision making resulting from punishment of failures and bad communication.

Generally, creating a pull-effect for knowledge was better than to assert pressure on employees; incentives for behavior set a more positive tune. During ShareNet's development and implementation, few ShareNet managers were replaced. The ShareNet project team took almost everybody on board to quickly gain a critical mass of multiplicators. Nevertheless, once knowledge exchange was embedded into personnel processes, both broad approaches to culture change would be linked, i.e. getting people to buy into new values and beliefs and socializing and removing members of the organization.

References

Alavi, M. (1997). *KPMG Peat Marwick U.S.: one giant brain* (No. Case 9-397-108). Boston: Harvard Business School.

Alavi, M., & Joachimsthaler, E. A. (1992). Revisiting DSS implementation research: a meta-analysis of the literature and suggestions for researchers. *MIS Quarterly, 16*(1), 95-116.

Alavi, M., & Leidner, D. (1999). Knowledge management systems: issues, challenges, and benefits. *Communications of the AIS, 1*(7), 1-37.

Alavi, M., & Leidner, D. E. (2001). Knowledge management and knowledge management systems: conceptual foundations and research issues. *MIS Quarterly, 25*(1), 107-136.

Allen, T. J. (1977). *Managing the flow of technology.* Cambridge: MIT Press.

Ambrosio, J. (2000). Knowledge management mistakes. *Computerworld, 34*(27), 44.

Armenakis, A. A., & Bedeian, A. G. (1999). Organizational change: a review of theory and research in the 1990s. *Journal of Management, 25*(3), 293-315.

Barth, S. (2000). KM horror stories. *Knowledge Management, 3*(10), 37-30.

Bazley, P. (2002). The evolution of a project involving an integrated analysis of structured qualitative and quantitative data: from N3 to NVivo. *International Journal of Social Research Methodology, 5*(3), 229-243.

Beer, M. (1988). Leading change (pp. 1-6). Boston: Harvard Business School.

Beer, M., Eisenstat, R. A., & Spector, B. (1990). Why change programs don't produce change. *Harvard Business Review, 68*(6), 158-166.

Beer, M., & Nohria, N. (2000). Cracking the code of change. *Harvard Business Review, 78*(3), 133-141.

Benbasat, I., Goldstein, D. K., & Mead, M. (1987). The case research strategy in studies of information systems. *MIS Quarterly, 11*(3), 369-386.

Bhatt, G. D. (2001). Knowledge management in organizations: examining the interaction between technologies, techniques, and people. *Journal of Knowledge Management, 5*(1), 68-75.

Blalock, H. M. (1969). *Theory construction: from verbal to mathematic formulations.* Englewood Cliffs: Prentice Hall.

Borgman, H. P. (1994). *Navigating the information seas: managers' information search behavior using executive information systems.* Delft: Eburon Academic Publishers.

Brelade, S., & Harman, C. (2000). Using human resources to put knowledge to work: where rewards, recruitment and retention sit on the KM agenda. *Knowledge Management Review, 3*(1), 26-29.

Brown, J. S., & Duguid, P. (1991). Organizational learning and communities of practice: toward a unified view of working, learning, and innovation. *Organization Science, 2*(1), 40-57.

Buchanan, B. (1974). Building organizational commitment: the socialization of managers in work organizations. *Administrative Science Quarterly, 19*(4), 633-546.

Carroll, J. S., & Hatakenaka, S. (2001). Driving organizational change in the midst of crisis. *Sloan Management Review, 42*(3), 70-79.

Cavaye, A. L. M. (1996). Case study research: a multi-faceted research approach for IS. *Information Systems Journal, 6*(3), 227-242.

Chase, R. L. (1997). The knowledge-based organization: an international survey. *Journal of Knowledge Management, 1*(1), 38-49.

References

Conklin, E. J. (1996). *Capturing organizational memory.* Retrieved September 22, 2003, from www.gdss.com/questmap/com.htm

Constant, D., Keisler, S., & Sproull, L. (1994). What's mine is ours, or is it? A study of attitudes about information sharing. *Information Systems Research, 5*(4), 400-421.

Constant, D., Sproull, L., & Kiesler, S. (1996). The kindness of strangers: the usefulness of electronic weak ties for technical advice. *Organization Science, 7*(2), 119-135.

Coombs, R., Knights, D., & Willmott, H. C. (1992). Culture, control and competition; towards a conceptual framework for the study of information technology in organizations. *Organization Studies, 13*(1), 51-72.

Cooper, R. B. (1994). The inertial impact of culture on IT implementation. *Information & Management, 27*(1), 17-31.

Crowley, C., Harré, R., & Tagg, C. (2002). Qualitative research and computing: methodological issues and practices in using QSR NVivo and NUD*IST. *International Journal of Social Research Methodology, 5*(3), 193-197.

Curley, K. F., & Gremillion, L. L. (1983). The role of the champion in DSS implementation. *Information & Management, 6*(4), 203-209.

Damodaran, L., & Olphert, W. (2000). Barriers and facilitators to the use of knowledge management systems. *Behavior & Information Technology, 19*(6), 405-413.

Darke, P., Shanks, G., & Broadbent, M. (1998). Successfully completing case study research: combining rigour, relevance and pragmatism. *Information Systems Journal, 8*(4), 273-289.

Davenport, T. H., De Long, D. W., & Beers, M. C. (1998). Successful knowledge management projects. *Sloan Management Review, 39*(2), 43-57.

Davenport, T. H., & Grover, V. (2001). Special issue: knowledge management. *Journal of Management Information Systems, 18*(1), 3-4.

Davenport, T. H., & Klahr, P. (1998). Managing customer support knowledge. *California Management Review, 40*(3), 195-208.

Davenport, T. H., & Prusak, L. (2000). *Working knowledge: how organizations manage what they know* (2nd ed.). Boston: Harvard Business School Press.

De Long, D. W., & Seemann, P. (2000). Confronting conceptual confusion and conflict in knowledge management. *Organizational Dynamics, 29*(1), 33-44.

Denison, D. R., & Mishra, A. K. (1995). Toward a theory of organizational culture and effectiveness. *Organization Science, 6*(2), 204-223.

Dewett, T., & Jones, G. R. (2001). The role of information technology in the organization: a review, model, and assessment. *Journal of Management, 27*(3), 313-346.

Dover, P. A. (2003). Change agents at work: lessons from Siemens Nixdorf. *Journal of Change Management, 3*(3), 243-257.

Drucker, P. F. (1988). The coming of the new organization. *Harvard Business Review, 66*(1), 45-53.

Duck, J. D. (2001). Managing change: the art of balancing. In *Harvard Business Review on change* (pp. 55-81). Boston: Harvard Business School Press.

Earl, M. J. (2001). Knowledge management strategies: toward a taxonomy. *Journal of Management Information Systems, 18*(1), 215-233.

Eisenhardt, K. M. (1989). Building theories from case study research. *Academy of Management Review, 14*(4), 432-550.

Eisenhardt, K. M. (2000). Paradox, spirals, ambivalence: the new language of change and pluralism. *Academy of Management Review, 25*(4), 703-705.

Fahey, L., & Prusak, L. (1998). The eleven deadliest sins of knowledge management. *California Management Review, 40*(3), 265-276.

Finlay, P. N., & Forghani, M. (1998). A classification of success factors for decision support systems. *Journal of Strategic Information Systems, 7*(1), 53-70.

Fluss, D. (2002). Why knowledge management is a "dirty" word. *Customer Interface, 15*(2), 40-41.

Galliers, R. D. (1999). Towards the integration of e-business, knowledge management and policy considerations within an information systems strategy framework. *Journal of Strategic Information Systems, 8*(3), 229-234.

Gerndt, U. (2000). Serving the community. *KM Magazine, 3*(9), 7-10.

Gibbert, M., Jenzowsky, S., Jonczyk, C., Thiel, M., & Völpel, S. (2002). ShareNet - the next generation knowledge management. In T. H. Davenport & G. J. B. Probst (Eds.), *Knowledge management case book: Siemens best practices* (2nd ed.). Erlangen and New York: Publicis Corporate Publishing and John Wiley & Sons.

Gibbert, M., Kugler, P., & Völpel, S. (2002). Getting real about knowledge sharing: the premium-on-top bonus system. In T. H. Davenport & G. J. B. Probst (Eds.), *Knowledge management case book: Siemens best practices* (2nd ed., pp. 260-278). Erlangen and New York: Publicis Corporate Publishing and John Wiley & Sons.

Ginzberg, M. J. (1978). Redesign of managerial tasks: a requisite for successful decision support systems. *MIS Quarterly, 2*(1), 39-52.

Ginzberg, M. J. (1979). A study of the implementation process. In R. Doktor, R. L. Schultz & D. P. Slevin (Eds.), *The implementation of management science.* New York: North Holland Publishing.

Ginzberg, M. J. (1981a). Early diagnosis of MIS implementation failure: promising results and unanswered questions. *Management Science, 27*(4), 459-478.

Ginzberg, M. J. (1981b). Key recurrent issues in the MIS implementation process. *MIS Quarterly, 5*(2), 47-59.

Gold, A. H., Malhotra, A., & Segars, A. H. (2001). Knowledge management: an organizational capabilities perspective. *Journal of Management Information Systems, 18*(1), 185-214.

Goodhue, D. L., & Thompson, R. R. (1995). Task-technology fit and individual performance. *MIS Quarterly, 19*(2), 213-236.

Goodman, P. S., & Darr, E. D. (1998). Computer-aided systems and communities: mechanisms for organizational learning in distributed environments. *MIS Quarterly, 22*(4), 417-440.

Grant, R. M. (1996). Prospering in dynamically-competitive environments: organizational capability as knowledge integration. *Organization Science, 7*(4), 375-387.

Greenwood, R. (2000). How investments in organizational design impacts the effectiveness of KM. *Knowledge Management Review, 3*(4), 10-11.

Grover, V., & Davenport, T. H. (2001). General perspectives on knowledge management: fostering a research agenda. *Journal of Management Information Systems, 18*(1), 5-21.

Hackbarth, G. (1998). The impact of organizational memory on IT systems. In E. Hoadley & I. Benbasat (Eds.), *Proceedings of the Fourth Americas Conference on Information Systems* (pp. 588-590).

Hahn, J., & Subramani, M. R. (2000). *A framework of knowledge management systems: issues and challenges for theory and practice.* Paper presented at the Twenty-First International Conference on Information Systems, Brisbane.

Hansen, M. T., Nohria, N., & Tierney, T. (1999). What's your strategy for managing knowledge? *Harvard Business Review, 77*(2), 106-116.

Harper, G. R. (2001). Organizational culture and successful information technology implementation. *Engineering Management Journal, 13*(2), 11-15.

Hatch, M. J. (1993). They dynamics of organizational culture. *Academy of Management Review, 18*(4), 657-693.

Heier, H., & Borgman, H. P. (2004). Deutsche Bank: leveraging human capital with the knowledge management system HRbase. *Annals of Cases on Information Technology, 6*(1), 114-127.

Heisig, P., & Vorbeck, J. (2001). Benchmarking survey results. In K. Mertins, P. Heisig & J. Vorbeck (Eds.), *Knowledge management: best practices in Europe* (pp. 97-123). Berlin and Heidelberg: Springer-Verlag.

Hibbard, J., & Carillo, K. M. (1998). Knowledge revolution. *Informationweek, 5*(663), 49-54.

Holtshouse, D. (1998). Knowledge research issues. *California Management Review, 40*(3), 277-280.

Huber, G. P. (1990). A theory of the effects of advanced information technologies on organizational design, intelligence, and decision making. *Academy of Management Review, 15*(1), 47-71.

Huber, G. P. (1991). Organizational learning: the contributing processes and the literatures. *Organization Science, 2*(1), 88-115.

Inkpen, A. C., & Dinur, A. (1998). Knowledge management processes and international joint ventures. *Organization Science, 9*(4), 454-468.

Jarvenpaa, S. L., & Ives, B. (1991). Executive involvement and participation in the management of information technology. *MIS Quarterly, 15*(2), 205-227.

Jarvenpaa, S. L., & Staples, D. S. (2000). The use of collaborative electronic media for information sharing: an exploratory study of determinants. *Journal of Strategic Information Systems, 9*(2-3), 129-154.

Jarvenpaa, S. L., & Staples, D. S. (2001). Exploring perceptions of organizational ownership of information and expertise. *Journal of Management Information Systems, 18*(1), 151-183.

Jin, K. G., & Franz, C. R. (1986). Obstacle coping during systems implementation. *Information & Management, 11*(2), 65-75.

Joshi, K. (1991). A model of users' perspective on change: the case of information systems technology implementation. *MIS Quarterly, 15*(2), 229-242.

Keen, P. G. W. (1981). Information systems and organizational change. *Communications of the ACM, 24*(1), 24-33.

Keen, P. G. W., Bronsema, G. S., & Zuboff, S. (1982). Implementing common systems: one organization's experience. *Systems, Objectives, Solutions, 2*(2), 125-142.

Keil, M. (1995). Pulling the plug: software project management and the problem of project escalation. *MIS Quarterly, 19*(4), 421-447.

Keil, M., & Robey, D. (2001). Blowing the whistle on troubled software projects. *Communications of the ACM, 44*(4), 87-93.

Kerlinger, F. N. (1986). *Foundations of behavioral research*. New York: Holt, Rinehart & Winston.

Kerlinger, F. N., & Lee, H. B. (1999). *Foundations of behavioral research* (4th ed.). Belmont: Wadsworth Publishing.

King, W. R., Marks, P. V., & McCoy, S. (2002). The most important issues in knowledge management: what can KM do for corporate memory, management thinking, and IS responsibility, as well as for overall business performance? *Communications of the ACM, 45*(9), 93-97.

Kolb, D. A., & Frohman, A. L. (1970). An organization development approach to consulting. *Sloan Management Review, 12*(1), 51-65.

Kotter, J. P. (1995). Leading change: why transformation efforts fail. *Harvard Business Review, 73*(2), 59-67.

KPMG. (1998). *Knowledge management: research report*. McLean.

KPMG. (2003). *Insights from KPMG's European knowledge management survey 2002/2003*. Amsterdam.

Krovi, R. (1993). Identifying the causes of resistance to IS implementation: a change theory perspective. *Information & Management, 25*(6), 327-335.

Kydd, C. T., & Jones, L. H. (1989). Corporate productivity and shared information technology. *Information & Management, 17*(5), 277-282.

LaMarsh, J. (1995). *Changing the way we change: gaining control of major operational change.* Reading: Addison Wesley.

Laudon, K. C., & Laudon, J. P. (2002). *Management information systems: managing the digital firm.* Upper Saddle River: Prentice Hall.

Leavitt, H. J. (1965). Applying organizational change in industry: structural, technological and humanistic approaches. In J. G. March (Ed.), *Handbook of organizations* (pp. 1144-1170). Chicago: Rand McNally.

Lee, A. S. (1989). A scientific methodology for MIS case studies. *MIS Quarterly, 13*(1), 32-50.

Leidner, D. (2000). Editorial. *Journal of Strategic Information Systems, 9*(2), 101-105.

Leonard, D. (1998). *Wellsprings of knowledge: building and sustaining the sources of innovation.* Boston: Harvard Business School Press.

Leonard, D., & Sensiper, S. (1997). *American Management Systems, Inc.: the knowledge centers.* Boston: Harvard Business School.

Levasseur, R. E. (2001). People skills: change management tools - Lewin's change model. *Interfaces, 31*(4), 71-73.

Lewin, K. (1947). Group decision and social change. In T. N. Newcomb & E. L. Hartley (Eds.), *Readings in social psychology* (pp. 329-340). Troy: Holt, Rinehart & Winston.

Lucas, H. C. (1981). *Implementation: the key to successful information systems.* New York and Guildford: Columbia University Press.

Lucas, H. C., & Plimpton, R. B. (1972). Technological consulting in a grass roots action oriented organization. *Sloan Management Review, 14*(1), 17-36.

Lucier, C. E., & Torsilieri, J. D. (1997). Why knowledge programs fail: a C.E.O.'s guide to managing learning. *Strategy, Management, Competition, 3*(4), 14-28.

MacCormack, A. (2002). Siemens ShareNet: building a knowledge network (pp. 1-27). Boston: Harvard Business School Press.

Macredie, R. D., & Sandom, C. (1999). IT-enabled change: evaluating an improvisational perspective. *European Journal of Information Systems, 8*(4), 247-259.

Macy, M. W. (1990). Learning theory and the logic of critical mass. *American Sociological Review, 55*(6), 809-826.

Manago, M., & Auriol, E. (1996). Mining for OR. *OR/MS Today, 23*(1), 28-32.

Mann, J., Chopra, A., Hinojosa, J., Koma, B., & Crivat, C. (2000). *Acceptance and use of ICN ShareNet by current users at Siemens ICN.* Stuttgart: Stuttgart Institute of Management and Technology.

Marakas, G. M. (1999). *Decision-support systems in the twenty-first century.* Englewood Cliffs: Prentice Hall.

Markus, M. L. (1989). Case selection in a disconfirmatory case study. In J. I. Cash & P. R. Lawrence (Eds.), *The information systems research challenge: qualitative research methods.* Boston: Harvard Business School Press.

Markus, M. L., & Benjamin, R. I. (1997). The magic bullet theory of IT-enabled transformation. *Sloan Management Review, 38*(2), 55-68.

Marshak, R. J. (1993). Lewin meets Confucius: a review of the OD model of change. *Journal of Applied Behavioral Science, 29*(4), 393-415.

Marwell, G., Oliver, P. E., & Prahl, R. (1988). Social networks and collective action: a theory of the critical mass. III. *American Journal of Sociology, 94*(3), 502-534.

McElroy, M. W. (2000). Using knowledge management to sustain innovation: moving toward second generation knowledge management. *Knowledge Management Review, 3*(4), 34-37.

McLure Wasko, M., & Faraj, S. (2000). "It is what one does": why people participate and help others in electronic communities of practice. *Journal of Strategic Information Systems, 9*(2-3), 155-173.

Mertins, K., Heisig, P., & Vorbeck, J. (2001). *Knowledge management: best practices in Europe.* Berlin and Heidelberg: Springer-Verlag.

Meso, P., & Smith, R. (2000). A resource-based view of organizational knowledge management systems. *Journal of Knowledge Management, 4*(3), 224-234.

Meyerson, D. E. (2001). Radical change, the quiet way. *Harvard Business Review, 79*(9), 92-100.

Miles, M. B., & Huberman, A. M. (1984). *Qualitative data analysis: a sourcebook of new methods.* Newbury Park: Sage Publications.

Myers, M. D. (1994). Dialectical hermeneutics: a theoretical framework for the implementation of information systems. *Information Systems Journal, 5*(1), 51-70.

Myers, M. D. (1997). Qualitative research in information systems. *MIS Quarterly, 21*(2), 241-242.

Myers, M. D. (1999). Investigating information systems with ethnographic research. *Communications of the AIS, 2*(23), 1-19.

Nonaka, I. (1991). The knowledge-creating company. *Harvard Business Review, 69*(6), 96-104.

Nonaka, I., & Takeuchi, H. (1995). *The knowledge-creating company.* New York and Oxford: Oxford University Press.

Nutt, P. C. (1986). Tactics of implementation. *Academy of Management Journal, 29*(2), 230-261.

O'Dell, C., & Grayson, C. J. (1998). If only we knew what we know: identification and transfer of internal best practices. *California Management Review, 40*(3), 154-174.

O'Hara, M. T., Watson, R. T., & Kavan, C. B. (1999). Managing the three levels of change. *Information Systems Management, 16*(5), 63-70.

Oliver, P. E., & Marwell, G. (1988). The paradox of group size in collective action: a theory of critical mass. II. *American Sociological Review, 53*(1), 1-8.

Oliver, P. E., Marwell, G., & Teixeira, R. (1985). A theory of critical mass. I. Interdependence, group heterogeneity, and the production of collective action. *American Journal of Sociology, 91*(3), 522-556.

Orlikowski, W. J. (1992). *Learning from notes: organizational issues in groupware implementation.* Paper presented at the ACM Conference on Computer-Supported Cooperative Work, Toronto.

Orlikowski, W. J., & Barley, S. R. (2001). Technology and institutions: what can research on information technology and research on organizations learn from each other? *MIS Quarterly, 25*(2), 145-165.

Orlikowski, W. J., & Hofman, J. D. (1997). An improvisational model for change management: the case of groupware technologies. *Sloan Management Review, 38*(2), 11-21.

Orr, J. (1990). *Talking about machines: an ethnography of a modern job.* Ithaca: ILR Press.

Osterloh, M., & Frey, B. S. (2000). Motivation, knowledge transfer, and organizational forms. *Organization Science, 11*(5), 538-550.

Osterloh, M., & Frey, B. S. (2001). Knowledge and culture. In H. Simon (Ed.), *Corporate culture and strategy.* Frankfurt am Main: Frankfurter Allgemeine Zeitung.

Pettigrew, A. M. (1979). On studying organizational cultures. *Administrative Science Quarterly, 24*(4), 570-581.

Pettigrew, A. M. (1990). Longitudinal field research on change: theory and practices. *Organization Science, 1*(3), 267-292.

Polanyi, M. (1962). *Personal knowledge: toward a post-critical philosophy.* New York: Harper Torchbooks.

Polanyi, M. (1967). *The tacit dimension.* London: Routledge and Keoan Paul.

Porras, J. I., & Robertson, P. J. (1992). Organizational development: theory, practice, research. In M. D. Dunnette & L. M. Hough (Eds.), *Handbook of organizational psychology* (2nd ed.). Palo Alto: Consulting Psychology Press.

Probst, G. J. B., Raub, S., & Romhardt, K. (1999). *Managing knowledge: building blocks for success.* Chichester: John Wiley & Sons.

QSR International. (2002). *Using NVivo in qualitative research.* Melbourne: QSR International.

Quinn, J. B., Anderson, P., & Finkelstein, S. (1996). Managing professional intellect: making the most of the best. *Harvard Business Review, 74*(2), 71-80.

Robey, D., & Azevedo, A. (1994). Cultural analysis of the organizational consequences of information technology. *Accounting, Management, and Information Technologies, 4*(1), 23-37.

Robey, D., Boudreau, M.-C., & Rose, G. M. (2000). Information technology and organizational learning: a review and assessment of research. *Accounting, Management, and Information Technologies, 10*(2), 125-155.

Romm, T., Pliskin, N., Weber, Y., & Lee, A. S. (1991). Identifying organizational culture clash in MIS implementation: when is it worth the effort? *Information & Management, 21*(2), 99-109.

Rothnie, D. (2001). ShareNet: Siemens Information and Communication Networks. In V. Mellor, E. Barnfield & N. Aitken (Eds.), *Strategies for best practice intranet management* (pp. 186-194). London: Melcrum Publishing.

Ruggles, R. (1998). The state of notion: knowledge management in practice. *California Management Review, 40*(3), 80-89.

Saffold, G. S. (1988). Culture traits, strength, and organizational performance: moving beyond "strong" culture. *Academy of Management Review, 13*(4), 546-558.

Sathe, V. (1985). *Culture and related corporate realities: text, cases, and readings on organizational entry, establishment, and change.* Homewood: Richard D. Irwin.

Sathe, V. (1993). Implications of corporate culture: a manager's guide to action. In L. A. Maniero & C. L. Tromley (Eds.), *Developing managerial skills in organizational behavior: exercises, cases, and readings* (pp. 329-340). Upper Saddle River: Prentice Hall.

Schein, E. H. (1985). *Organizational culture and leadership.* San Francisco: Jossey-Bass.

Schein, E. H. (1992). *Organizational culture and leadership* (2nd ed.). San Francisco: Jossey-Bass.

Schein, E. H. (1999). *The corporate culture survival guide: sense and nonsense about culture change.* San Francisco: Jossey-Bass.

Schultz, R. L., Slevin, D. P., & Pinto, J. K. (1987). Strategy and tactics in a process model of project implementation. *Interfaces, 17*(3), 34-46.

Scott, W. R. (1992). *Organizations: rational, natural and open systems.* Englewood Cliffs: Prentice Hall.

Seeley, C. (2000). Change management: a base for knowledge-sharing. *Knowledge Management Review, 3*(4), 24-29.

Sethia, N. K., & von Glinow, M. A. (1985). Arriving at four cultures by managing the reward system. In R. H. Kilmann, M. J. Saxton & R. Serpa (Eds.), *Gaining control of the corporate culture* (pp. 400-420). San Francisco: Jossey-Bass.

Siemens. (1999). *Annual report 1999.* Berlin and Munich.

Siemens. (2001). *Annual report 2001.* Berlin and Munich.

Siemens. (2002). *Annual report 2002.* Berlin and Munich.

Siemens Information and Communication Networks. (2002). *Facts and figures 2002.* Munich.

Sole, D., & Applegate, L. (2000). *Knowledge sharing practices and technology use norms in dispersed development teams.* Paper presented at the Twenty-First International Conference on Information Systems, Brisbane.

Spector, B. (1989). From bogged down to fired up: inspiring organizational change. *Sloan Management Review, 30*(4), 29-34.

182   References

Spiegler, I. (2000). Knowledge management: a new idea or a recycled concept? *Communications of the AIS, 3*(14), 1-24.

Srinivasan, A., & Davis, J. G. (1987). A reassessment of implementation process models. *Interfaces, 17*(3), 64-71.

Stein, E. W., & Zwass, V. (1995). Actualizing organizational memory with information systems. *Information Systems Research, 6*(2), 85-117.

Stewart, K. A., Baskerville, R., Storey, V. C., Senn, J. A., Raven, A., & Long, C. (2000). Confronting the assumptions underlying the management of knowledge: an agenda for understanding and investigating knowledge management. *Database, 31*(4), 41-53.

Stickland, F. (1998). *Dynamics of change: insights from the natural world into organizational transition*. London: Routledge.

Storey, J., & Barnett, E. (2000). Knowledge management initiatives: learning from failure. *Journal of Knowledge Management, 4*(2), 145-156.

Swan, J. (1999). Introduction. In H. Scarbrough & J. Swan (Eds.), *Case studies in knowledge management*. London: Institute of Personnel and Development.

Teng, J. T. C., Grover, V., & Fiedler, K. D. (1996). Developing strategic perspectives on business process reengineering: from process reconfiguration to organizational change. *Omega, International Journal of Management Science, 24*(3), 271-294.

Thomas, J. C., Kellogg, W. A., & Erickson, T. (2001). The knowledge management puzzle: human and social factors in knowledge management. *IBM Systems Journal, 40*(4), 863-884.

Tizard, J. (2002). Managing change. *New Zeeland Management, 49*(2), 64-65.

Tuomi, I. (1999). *Data is more than knowledge: implications of the reversed knowledge hierarchy for knowledge management and organizational memory*. Paper presented at the Thirty-Second Hawaii International Conference on Systems Sciences, Maui.

Tushman, M. L., & O'Reilly, C. A. (1996). Ambidextrous organizations: managing evolutionary and revolutionary change. *California Management Review, 38*(4), 8-17.

Tyran, C. K., & George, J. F. (1993). The implementation of expert systems: a survey of successful implementations. *Database, 24*(1), 5-15.

Urban, G. L. (1974). Building models for decision makers. *Interfaces, 4*(3), 1-11.

von Krogh, G. (1998). Care in knowledge creation. *California Management Review, 40*(3), 133-153.

Vorbeck, J., & Finke, I. (2001). Motivation and competence for knowledge management. In K. Mertins, P. Heisig & J. Vorbeck (Eds.), *Knowledge management: best practices in Europe* (pp. 37-56). Berlin and Heidelberg: Springer-Verlag.

Walsham, G., & Waema, T. (1994). Information systems strategy and implementation: a case study of a building society. *ACM Transactions on Information Systems, 12*(2), 150-173.

Weeks, J., & Galunic, C. (2001, 29.10.2001). A cultural evolution in business thinking. *Financial Times Mastering People Management Series*, pp. 2-3.

Weick, K. E., & Quinn, R. E. (1999). Organizational change and development. *Annual Reviews of Psychology, 50*(1), 361-386.

Weitzman, E. A., & Miles, M. B. (1995). *Computer programs for qualitative data analysis: a software sourcebook*. Thousand Oaks: Sage Publications.

Wilson, R. (2000). Don't make culture another item on the KM checklist. *Knowledge Management Review, 3*(4), 8-9.

Yazici, H. J. (2002). The role of communication in organizational change: an empirical investigation. *Information & Management, 39*(7), 539-552.

Yin, R. K. (1984). *Case study research: design and methods*. Beverly Hills: Sage Publications.

Yin, R. K. (1993). *Applications of case study research*. Thousand Oaks: Sage Publications.

Yin, R. K. (1994). *Case study research: design and methods* (2nd ed.). Thousand Oaks: Sage Publications.

Zack, M. H. (1999). Developing a knowledge strategy. *California Management Review, 41*(3), 125-145.

Zand, D. E., & Sorensen, R. E. (1975). Theory of change and the effective use of management science. *Administrative Science Quarterly, 20*(4), 532-545.

Zmud, R. W., & Cox, J. F. (1979). The implementation process: a change approach. *MIS Quarterly, 3*(3), 35-43.

Planning and Realising Archiving Projects Efficiently

Markus Korschen
Efficient SAP® R/3®-Data Archiving
How to Handle Large Data Volumes
2002. x, 156 pp. with 15 figs. Hardc. € 49,90   ISBN 3-528-05799-8

Contents: Introduction - Important Archiving Terminology (Concept, Procedure and Necessity of Data Archiving) - Data Archiving and Business Processes in SAP R/3 - Database Analysis - Customizing-Settings for SAP R/3-Data Archiving - Practical Archiving Management - Selection-Criteria for Archive Systems

This book is a practical guide for managing archiving projects with SAP R/3 efficiently. Hereby it is addressing both R/3 consultants, system administrators and key-users. Detailed solutions for optimal archiving strategies as well as the manual for a comprehensive database analysis are provided in this book. But thereby not only the technical side, but also the business side of data archiving is taken into account. Thus the reader will be able to implement an archiving project.

vieweg

Abraham-Lincoln-Straße 46
65189 Wiesbaden
Fax 0611.7878-400
www.vieweg.de

Prices and other details are subject to change without notice. Please order at your bookstore.

Component Pascal and BlackBox

J. Stanley Warford
Computing Fundamentals
The Theory and Practice of Software Design
with BlackBox Component Builder
2002. xx, 611 pp. with 229 figs. Softc. € 34,90   ISBN 3-528-05828-5

Contents: Theory: Languages and Grammars, Complexity Analysis,
Guarded Command Language - Programming Basics: Flow of Control,
Functions, Procedures, Recursion - Graphical User Interfaces: Dialog
Boxes, Window Input/Output - Algorithms: Searching, Sorting, Ran-
dom Numbers - Data Structures: Arrays, Linked Lists, Stacks, Queues,
Binary Trees - Object Orientation: Class Composition, Inheritance,
Polymorphism - Design Patterns: Factory, Iterator, MVC, State - Design
Topics: Abstraction, Frameworks, UML Diagrams, Interfaces

The book introduces the reader to computer programming, i.e. algorithms and data structures. It covers many new programming concepts that have emerged in recent years including object-oriented programming and design patterns. The book emphasizes the practical
aspects of software construction without neglecting their solid theoretical foundation.

Abraham-Lincoln-Straße 46
65189 Wiesbaden
Fax 0611.7878-400
www.vieweg.de

Prices and other details are subject to change
without notice. Please order at your bookstore.